A **SmartMoney** book

How to Raise Kids Without Going Broke

A **SmartMoney** book

How to Raise Kids Without Going Broke

THE COMPLETE FINANCIAL GUIDE FOR PARENTS

**Peter Finch and
Delia Marshall**

AVON BOOKS ◆ NEW YORK

AVON BOOKS, INC.
1350 Avenue of the Americas
New York, New York 10019

Copyright © 1999 by Hearst Communications, Inc.
Front cover illustration by Jean Schnell/nonstock
Interior design by Stanley S. Drate/Folio Graphics Co. Inc.
ISBN: 0-380-80842-0
www.avonbooks.com

First Avon Books Trade Paperback Printing: April 1999

AVON TRADEMARK REG. U.S. PAT. OFF. AND IN OTHER COUNTRIES, MARCA REGISTRADA, HECHO EN U.S.A.

Printed in the U.S.A.

OPM 10 9 8 7 6 5 4 3 2 1

Acknowledgments

This book is the product of many people, not the least of which is the staff of SmartMoney, both current and former. The world is a better place for the blood, sweat and fear that they put into their reporting. If it weren't for the guiding light and unflagging spirit of Nancy Marx Better, this book would not be in your hands today. Jean Sherman Chatzky was a big help in the beginning stages of the book, while Melanie Rehak was indispensable down the stretch. Jersey Gilbert is the brains behind most of the worksheets you'll find here. Much of the college and health-care reporting came from Walecia Konrad, and much of the real estate reporting from Nellie S. Huang. Our coverage of taxes would have been impossible without Bill Bischoff's knowing counsel. And several people accepted such exciting tasks as finding out how big a discount an alarm system will get you on your homeowner's insurance, or how much a container of Flintstone's vitamins costs in four cities, with grace and enthusiasm: Eric R. Tinson, Daisy Chan, Lindsay Holmen, Jena McGregor and Scott Herndon. Finally, any spirit and brilliance in this book is a direct result of being edited by two masters of the craft, Steven Swartz and Stuart Emmrich, president and editor of *SmartMoney* magazine, respectively.

Contents

Chapter **14** *258*

THE BIG PICTURE

Creating a portfolio to meet your family's long- and short-term financial needs • **Worksheet:** The SmartMoney asset allocation plan • Where to invest: stocks, bonds, money market funds demystified • Making the most of your retirement savings

TEN THINGS YOUR MUTUAL FUND WON'T TELL YOU

PART 8

TAXING MATTERS *277*

Chapter **15** *279*

DEMYSTIFYING YOUR TAX RETURN

How to hire an accountant • Family tax breaks • Avoiding the marriage penalty • When to file a return for your kids • Audit-proofing your return • Should your pc be your CPA? • Using the kiddie tax to your advantage • *The Real World:* Employing your kids for fun and profit

TEN THINGS YOUR TAX PREPARER WON'T TELL YOU

PART 9

ESTATE PLANNING BASICS *299*

Chapter **16** *301*

WHERE THERE'S A WILL

Making sure your kids are well taken care of when you're gone • Organizing your assets and calculating your estate's value • Writing a will • Naming trustees, guardians and custodians • Creating a durable power of attorney, a healthcare proxy and a living will • What you need to know about probate • What's not covered by your will • Is a living trust for you? • Giving money to your children while you're alive: UTMAs, UGMAs, and trusts • *The Real World:* Who will take care of the kids?

TEN THINGS YOUR LAWYER WON'T TELL YOU

PART 10

BLENDED FAMILIES   *321*

STEP BY STEP

How "blended families" avoid fighting over money
• Prenuptial agreements • The best way to set up everyone's accounts
in a step family • Figuring out who pays for what, from diapers to
diplomas • Alimony and child support • Establishing who pays
for college • Doing your taxes correctly • Updating your will • *The
Real World:* They were the best of friends . . .

TEN THINGS YOUR DIVORCE LAWYER WON'T TELL YOU

Introduction

It's the moment you've waited for: In your arms is your new baby. And, as you look down, your thoughts race to the future— dropping her off for the first day of school, grilling her prom date, beaming as she's named valedictorian, dropping in for a chat with her at the Oval Office. Then reality hits: This little bundle is going to cost you a small fortune. How are you ever going to pay for it?

We first posed this question three years ago in a special issue of our magazine. Since then, our staff of more than 50 reporters and editors has delved ever more deeply into the special needs of parents with kids of all ages, from healthcare to nannies, from wills to college saving tips.

This book reflects—and expands on—that coverage. To head up the project, we turned to two of our best editors, Peter Finch and Delia Marshall, who, more importantly, bring to the subject more than a dozen years of child rearing experience and five kids between them. Collectively, they've negotiated eight mortgages (in cluding refinancings), gone through eight cars (new, used, and leased) paid for 11 years of preschool and bought seven mutual funds (so far) solely for the kids' college education fund.

At SmartMoney, our aim is to help all types of people take greater control of their financial lives—without having to give up their day jobs to do it. But as a new father myself, I've become all too aware of the special problems that parenting poses, such as how on earth are you supposed to put money away each year for retirement when the need for exer-saucers and battery-powered swings—not to mention braces and summer camp—keep inter- vening?

This book won't make those problems go away, but we hope it will convince you they can be managed in a way that gives you the time and the confidence to take advantage of all the opportunities life offers you and your children.

STEVEN SWARTZ
Editor in Chief and President
SmartMoney Magazine
SmartMoney.com

Part 1

GETTING STARTED

Perhaps the only thing that gives a sleep-deprived parent insomnia is money. How much to spend, how much to save, how much was wasted on that inane toddler music class. The only way out of this late-night quagmire is to get organized. No, this doesn't mean balancing your checking account with a sharpened pencil every month. It doesn't mean saving every single receipt for a year, or writing an inspirational paragraph about your financial goals. It means getting a system in place so you can focus on the more important things in life.

The starting point of this system is knowing what you're worth. In Chapter 1 you can take a quick snapshot of your current financial standing, including your net worth as well as your monthly income and expenses. The next step is making sure your bank is doing its job. Chapter 2 explains how to get a bank to handle your complicated life—either online or not—without gouging your paycheck in the process. We also tell you where to get the best credit cards, so you don't end up paying interest instead of taking the family on a summer vacation.

With just a small investment of time, you'll gain a lot: You'll save money. You'll save time. You'll stop paying late fees. You'll have a good idea of where your money is going. And you'll stop counting sheep.

1

Getting a Grip

Plenty of people think financial planning equals tedious paperwork and heavy-duty soul searching. We don't. The way we figure it, life is too short to calculate to the penny how much you spend on paper towels each month. Or, even worse, to take a pop psychology test designed to tell you what you know already: *You don't have enough money.*

You need a system that runs on automatic. All you need to get going are some general numbers about your net worth and your spending habits. They don't have to be exact. The vagaries of family life make it nearly impossible to set a strict budget in the first place, let alone stick to it.

It should take less than an hour to fill out the following three worksheets. Once you have these numbers—your monthly expenses, your monthly income, your net worth—you can plug them into the various worksheets throughout the book to help you figure out how much house you can afford, what life insurance you need, what kind of mortgage is best for you, and in Chapter 14, an asset-allocation strategy you can use to start investing for your family's future.

One other step to help you get started: our guide for what you need to save (the receipt for those golf clubs, for insurance purposes) and what you can toss (that stack of utility bills). Cut down on the amount of useless paper in your life, and you'll be surprised at how much easier it is to handle your paperwork.

Your Monthly Expenses

Following is a list of just about every possible expense your family might face. Add up all that apply (just estimate when in doubt). What you need to fill in the list: a recent paystub, your checkbook, a recent bank statement (to note those forgotten automatic withdrawals), and a calculator.

We know that other random expenses crop up: The driveway needs to be repaired, your toddler needs to move from a crib to a bed, the dog just broke its leg. But for planning purposes, just count up the regular monthly hits.

401(k) payments	$_____
IRA or Keogh payments	_____
Automatic deposits to investments	_____
Employer-sponsored pension or investment deposits	_____
Union dues	_____
Gas & electric	_____
Oil	_____
Water	_____
Cable	_____
Garbage removal	_____
Telephone	_____
Newspaper delivery	_____
Magazine subscriptions	_____
Bank charges	_____
Mortgage	_____
Rent	_____
Child care	_____
Current tuition	_____
Children's extracurricular activities	_____
Clothing	_____
Grooming	_____
Landscaping	_____
Accountant	_____
Medical expenses	_____
Membership dues	_____
Country club dues and charges	_____
Entertainment (movies, arts, dinner out)	_____
Life insurance	_____
Disability insurance	_____
Health insurance	_____
Car payment	_____
Car insurance	_____

Commuting _____

Dry cleaning _____

Groceries _____

Health club _____

Other _____

TOTAL MONTHLY EXPENSES $_____

Your Monthly Income

Salary $_____

Investment income _____

Interest on checking and savings accounts _____

Any year-end payments, like bonuses, etc. _____

(divided by 12) _____

GROSS MONTHLY INCOME $_____

Less taxes withheld _____

NET MONTHLY INCOME $_____

Your Net Worth

You have a net worth—even if it's negative. It's just a snapshot of your financial position right now. If you're in the red, you're not alone. In fact, many new parents are still scrambling from paycheck to paycheck. The solution? Read on.

ASSETS

Checking account $_____

Savings account _____

Money-market account _____

Certificates of deposit _____

Mutual funds _____

U.S. Treasury bills _____

Stocks _____

Bonds _____

Cash value of life insurance policy _____

Trust funds _____

Company savings accounts _____

Cash value of pension _____

Stock options _____

Equity value of a business _____

401(k) _____

IRA or KEOGH _____

Other investments _____

Money owed you _____

Real estate _____

Cars _____

Furnishings _____

Collectibles _____

Jewelry _____

Other luxury goods _____

TOTAL ASSETS $_____

DEBTS

Mortgage $_____

Personal loans _____

Home equity line of credit _____

Car loans _____

Other installment loans _____

Life insurance loans _____

Loans against investments, such as margin loans _____

Student loans _____

Credit card debts _____

Taxes due _____

Taxes due on investments when you cash them in _____

Taxes due on retirement accounts when you cash them in _____

TOTAL DEBTS $_____

NET WORTH (subtract debts from assets) $_____

The going rate: The cost of being financially oblivious

Your spirit is willing, but your flesh—well, it reaches for the remote. Before you consign this book to the bottom of your nightstand pile, consider how easy it is to waste your hard-earned money on things that sound like a good idea—and are anything but.

	Boise, Idaho	Tulsa, Okla.	Cleveland, Ohio	White Plains, N.Y.
$100,000 in life insurance for your kid (per month)	$ 25.00	$ 10.00	$ 15.00	$ 9.54
Badger bassinette	$ 39.99	$ 39.99	$ 59.98	$ 39.99
Nike sneakers, size 0	$ 45.99	$ 46.00	$ 35.00	$ 23.95
Playskool 1-2-3 Microban high chair	$ 79.99	$ 79.99	$ 79.99	$ 79.99
The Totally Awesome Money Book for Kids (and Their Parents)	$ 10.95	$ 10.95	$ 10.95	$ 10.95
Baby Gap onesie	$ 18.00	$ 18.00	$ 18.00	$ 18.00
Art class for a 2-year-old*	$ 32.00	$ 35.00	$ 35.00	$ 35.00
Do-it-yourself will	$ 2.95	$ 2.95	$ 2.95	$ 2.95
American Express "Credit Aware" service**	$ 71.00	$ 71.00	$ 71.00	$ 71.00
$400,000 in travel insurance	$ 17.00	$ 17.00	$ 17.00	$ 17.00
TOTAL	$342.87	$330.88	$344.87	$308.37

*Up to 12 half-hour classes
**13 months' coverage

What You Should Keep (and Where)

Think you need an attic to store all those old records? Think again. You don't need to squirrel away nearly as much as you think. Those five-year-old Bloomingdale's statements? Ten-year-old utility bills? Chuck 'em. The key here is to cut the clutter. Chances are, you can get copies of almost anything you lose: Even the IRS will give you copies of your old 1040s'(ask for them on Form 4506). For those documents that you do need to keep, however, you should invest in a safe-deposit box at a local bank, a fireproof safe (see Your Money's Worth on page 311) and a filing cabinet (see Your Money's Worth on page 8).

While it may seem easiest to store everything in your safe-deposit box, bear in mind that in many states a safe-deposit box is

---

Your money's worth

G one are the days of a few untidy piles on a bookshelf somewhere. Your baby started generating paperwork the minute he was born, and you'll need a reliable home for all those precious documents. And you'll soon find that a poorly constructed filing cabinet is about as welcome as a paper cut.

Worth it: **Hon 682L Series 2-drawer lateral file** ($239.99 at Staples). Just try to knock this baby over. You can't do it. This file cabinet has a counterweight (basically an iron slab in the rear of the base) and an interlocking system that lets you open only one drawer at a time, which virtually eliminates tipping. Plus, the ball-bearing suspension makes for quiet, easy drawer sliding, and the 36-inch width lets you organize legal- and letter-size files in the same drawer. Its heavy-gauge steel frame can withstand a lifetime of angry slamming (think tax time), and its modest height (just under 29 inches) means it can fit neatly under most desks.

Not worth it: **GMI's 18" Euro-Style File Cabinet** ($59 at OfficeMax). It's cheap, that's for sure. But without a counterweight or interlocking system, this 18-inch-deep vertical file is more prone to tipping (a scary thought, considering that it's 46 inches tall). GMI's cabinet has four drawers, but it still has about 360 fewer square inches of drawer space than the Hon 682L. And that's not even accounting for the fact that the back three or four inches of each drawer are basically unreachable. (The nylon roller cradle system stops the drawer from being pulled out all the way.) Two final straws: The cabinet only accommodates letter-size files, and only two of the drawers lock.

---

sealed upon the death of the renter—delaying the probate process and incurring additional costs. One way around this is to include a trusted friend or family member as one of the renters. Otherwise, check with your bank to see what its procedures are in the event that you die.

Assuming that your bank seals your safe-deposit box upon your death, here's what we recommend that you keep and where to store it.

IN YOUR SAFE-DEPOSIT BOX

Jewels or other valuables
Stock or other securities certificates
Savings bonds

Copy of will, power of attorney, living will
Copy of all important papers that you keep in your safe
Videotape of your house contents for insurance purposes
Receipts of large purchases for insurance purposes

AT YOUR LAWYER'S OFFICE

Will
Power of attorney
Living will
Trust documents

IN A FIREPROOF SAFE AT HOME

Real estate deeds
Titles to cars or other property
Life insurance policies
Copy of your will, power of attorney, living will
List of items in safe-deposit box
List of items at lawyer's office
Life, disability, home and car insurance policies
Phone numbers of all insurance agents, lawyers, executors to wills, brokers, accountants
Passports, birth certificates, marriage certificates, other personal papers
Annual statement of your employee benefits
Phone number of your employee benefits office
List of all bank and investment accounts
Any PIN numbers
Proof of paid-off debts
Proof of money owed to you

IN A FILING CABINET AT HOME

Bank statements (for the past year)
Credit card statements, for tax purposes (for one year)
Old insurance policies (for three years)
Latest loan statements
Medical bills, for tax purposes (for a year)
Instructions or warranties for any appliances or equipment you own
An innocuous file with your safe-deposit key and safe combination

IN A BOX IN THE ATTIC

Canceled checks

Tax documents for every year you file

Bank statements (for seven years)

2

Ground Zero

Before Danielle and John Barkhouse had their son Connor, they "never used to take any time at all to balance the checkbook or look at where the money was going," says Danielle. Now Danielle figures out how much the Raleigh, North Carolina, family spends every month on dining out, groceries, car expenses, household expenses, and the like. Where does she find the time? She doesn't. She banks online, and she's addicted to Quicken—the checkbook-balancing, bill-paying, life-simplifying software program. The Barkhouses couldn't be happier with the arrangement. "With Quicken, I've caught some billing mistakes that I wouldn't have had a clue about otherwise," says Danielle.

At a cost of about $4.00 a month for paying bills online at their local bank, Centura Bank, it's a lot cheaper than the cost of checks, postage, and running around to pay all the bills, Danielle points out. Everything else they leave to Quicken. They've set up the software to include all of their various bank accounts, their car loan, and all other asset or liability accounts. This way, they're able to see exactly what goes where after John's paycheck is added in at the beginning of each month. Furthermore, Quicken keeps impeccable records of everything, which is a great way to avoid those April 14th panics.

The Barkhouses have also discovered some of the more advanced features of the software, like the savings goal feature, which siphons off a certain amount of money from your bank accounts each month to be put toward a particular end. Right now, they're saving up almost effortlessly for a down payment on a house. "We don't even think of the money throughout the month. Once our down payment is complete, then our next savings goal will be for Connor's tuition."

The house payment, along with other regular monthly payments like the car loan, are "memorized" so that they occur each month without any prompting from John or Danielle. Who wants to worry about writing a check when their two-year-old is running amok? And by using the Quicken websites (accessible through the finance program), Danielle was able to calculate how much mortgage the couple will be able to afford, how much of a monthly car payment they could afford when they bought a new car, and how much to put away each month for Connor's college education.

The biggest surprise in all this? Danielle's new love of home finances. "Although my husband thinks it's made me obsessed about finances," she admits sheepishly, "I like to account for every penny. As soon as I come home with receipts, I enter them into Quicken. At 5 P.M. every day, I download our current transactions from the bank." Not bad for a family who never knew the balances of their accounts and wrote checks based on "rough estimates" in order to ensure they'd clear. "Quicken has certainly made us more organized and in control," says Danielle. "And that's something every parent could use a little more of."

Will an AMA simplify your life?

Here's a notion parents are bound to find appealing: Consolidating your bank and brokerage accounts into one. Less mail and less paperwork equals less headache, right? Asset Management Accounts, or AMAs, mimic traditional checking accounts with their check-writing privileges and ATM access, while allowing you to boost the return on your money by not letting it sit idle. Each day, AMAs "sweep" your cash into money funds, at rates about two points higher than bank accounts. That'll give you an extra $200 a year in earnings on a $10,000 balance.

Plus, open your AMA at a discount brokerage firm like Schwab and you'll have hundreds of no-load, no-transaction-fee mutal funds at your disposal. (For more on mutual funds, see Part 7.) Of course, these benefits have their price: Mimimum balance requirements—$5,000 at Schwab—are often higher than you'd find for standard checking accounts at most banks. And, because brokerage firms don't have their own ATM machines, you may have to pay $1 or so for each and every transaction.

Even banks have begun to offer AMAs. First Union was the first bank in this game with its CAP acocunt, which has a $15,000 minimum and offers 10 money market funds, as well as brokerage commission discounts. Other big banks, such as Bank of America, Chase Manhattan, and Wells Fargo, are rapidly following suit.

Indeed, ground zero of *any* smart family's finances is getting organized. This chapter will tell you how to streamline your finances, how to get some respect from your bank, cut down those credit card costs, and, finally, get out of debt.

Do Your Banking Online

It's no wonder that most large banks and many smaller ones now offer online services: Each online transaction costs the typical bank one cent, according to a 1996 study conducted by Booz-Allen & Hamilton. Compare that with 27 cents for each ATM transaction and $1.07 at a teller's window. But online banking isn't good just for banks: It's great for anyone who hates the sight of a huge pile of bills. With online banking, it takes only about half an hour each month to keep up your finances.

There are other benefits. Imagine it's 4 A.M. and you need to make an emergency stop-payment on a check. Normally, you'd have to call your bank during business hours or make a trip to the branch itself first thing in the morning. With online banking, you can stumble over to your computer in the middle of the night (when the realization most likely strikes) and stop the payment with a couple of mouse clicks. Need a cash advance on your credit card by Monday morning before the bank opens? Get online and instantly advance money from your credit card to your checking account. Better yet, are you in the market for a home equity or personal loan? Say good-bye to those high-and-mighty loan officers you once kowtowed to. Now it's just you and your home computer when you apply online.

To begin online banking, you must have Internet access, which costs around $20 a month. Some banks charge check-paying fees, as well as a monthly service fee. But you're saving the cost of stamps—and a lot of time.

Security is probably the one issue that prevents potential customers from opening an electronic bank account. But electronic banking is quite secure these days. Many Internet and PC banks have a security system with three main components: a password to log on with, a firewall, and 128-bit encryption technology. A firewall works like a guard's gate outside a maximum-security penitentiary—nobody gets in unless they have the appropriate password.

Your money's worth

P rograms like Microsoft Money and Quicken have made it immeasurably easier to track your finances. Which one should you buy?

Worth it: Quicken Deluxe 98 ($49.95) is so easy to use it's amazing. Once you've set it up, the software program will balance your checkbook and reconcile it with your bank statement every month. With the click of a button, a detailed balance sheet of your entire portfolio—updated daily, via an Internet linkup that costs $15 or $20 a month, depending on which Internet service provider you use—pops up on the screen. Click another button, and the program calculates your net worth.

Not worth it: Microsoft Money 98 Financial Suite does many of the same things. But one big difference is price: The software costs $60, then you have to shell out another $9.95 a month to link to the Internet through Microsoft Investor. Plus, while Quicken has partnerships with several brokerage firms, including Schwab, Fidelity, E*Trade, Smith Barney, and Waterhouse, Microsoft Money has only two (Schwab and E*Trade).

The 128-bit encryption technology is a data scrambler so sophisticated the U.S. government considers it paramount to national security.

If you become so enamored of online banking that you don't mind forgoing a local branch altogether, check out *Atlanta Internet Bank (www.atlantabank.com* or 888-256-6932). Except for a small office in suburban Atlanta, this bank exists only on the Web. With its SuperValue checking account, you have unlimited check writing and electronic bill paying for $4.50 a month—and the account yields 4 percent interest. You can waive that monthly fee if you keep $10,000 at the bank. Atlanta Internet offers a one-year CD at 6.05 percent (that's almost a full percentage point better than the average one-year CD across the country), and money-market accounts that yield 5.5 percent—three percentage points better than average.

The downside? All deposits have to be made by mail (except direct deposit from your employer). The toll-free help line is open only on weekdays from 6 A.M. to midnight and Sundays from 1 P.M. to 10 P.M. And while you get a Cirrus-compatible ATM card for free, you could end up paying $1 or more every time you use it. So far, Atlanta Internet Bank isn't compatible with Quicken or Microsoft Money, but plans are underway.

Get Some Respect from Your Bank

Never before have you so depended on the services of a good bank. The sheer volume of checks, ATM withdrawals, and bills that pass through your hands when you become a parent would make a veteran accountant throw up his hands in despair. You want your bank to give you online banking, competitive rates, fast customer service, an adequate number of ATMs, and a willingness to negotiate on those annoying charges. There's one way to make them want you as a customer: Give them all your business.

Banks make most of their profits on only about 20 percent of their customers—the people who keep a large amount in checking, hold a mortgage with the bank, and even bounce a check now and then. The average customer, however, is a different story. A bank earns about $180 a year on a person who keeps $3,000 in checking and visits the ATM seven times a month, a sum nearly wiped out by the cost of processing and mailing monthly statements.

Your goal is to give the bank a choice between cutting you a break on loans, monthly fees, and interest rates or losing your business. Consolidate as many accounts as you can at your bank. If you've got a CD somewhere, transfer it to your bank. If its rates are competitive, transfer your credit card and mortgage to your bank. The more accounts you open, the more leverage you have.

Your Credit Cards: The Only Ones You Need

The typical family has nine different credit or charge cards; three to four of them have average balances of $1,750 each. The annual interest on these cards alone is enough to buy four round-trip tickets to Disney World. OK, two round-trips to Paris. Get the point?

Every family needs to have exactly two credit cards: a low-interest/low-annual-fee card, used for large purchases (a new refrigerator, your winter vacation) that you absolutely must pay off over time; and a perk card for the regular expenses. Perk cards give you freebies like frequent-flier miles, dollars toward a car, or cash back for every purchase. Because perk cards typically come with interest rates that would make a loan shark happy, it's important that you pay off the balance every month.

Beware one thing: Credit card companies are beginning to penalize clients who pay off their balance, depriving them of interest revenue. Some charge an annual $25 fee. Others are reducing the freebies: Customers who carry a balance with Banc One's Travel Plus Visa (800-366-2265) still get one frequent-flier mile for every dollar spent. Those who pay off their balance each month, however, must now charge $3 to earn one mile.

Now take a close look at your current credit card deal and see how it compares to the ones below. Of the 495 million cards out there, not many are worth the plastic they're printed on. Our junk mail recently turned up the Forbes Platinum MasterCard. Its teaser rate of 4.9 percent skyrockets up to 13.99 percent within a few months. Can you say "bait and switch"?

THE BEST LOW-INTEREST-RATE CARDS

Ideally, in the interest of making yourself a valued customer, you should try to get this credit card from your bank. Or you can always try to haggle your current card's interest rate down. *Smart-Money* staffers recently called several credit card companies and bargained the interest rates down on nine credit cards. For one of our testers, Chase Manhattan slashed the rate on its Visa from 18.9 to 11.5 percent.

One of the best low-interest cards around is from Wachovia Bank in New Castle, Delaware (800-241-7990). Its *Prime for Life Visa* is locked in at prime rate (currently 8.25 percent), though it has an $88 annual fee. Wachovia's *Prime Plus Visa* has an $18 annual fee, and its interest rate is prime plus 3.9 percent.

Both *Bank Rate Monitor (www.bankrate.com)*, an industry publication, and *CardTrak (www.ramresearch.com;* 800-344-7714; or send $5 check or money order to CardTrak, P.O. Box 1700, Frederick, MD 21702) publish lists of credit cards with interest rates in the 11–12 percent range. You can also search the database of *Get Smart (www.getsmart.com* or 800-438-7276) to find the card you want (perks, low-interest rate, consolidation of debt, etc.).

THE BEST PERK CARDS

This is a little trickier. First, make sure the perk is something you already need or use—only 15 percent of customers on average make use of the freebies they've worked so hard to accumulate. One of the best deals going is a *General Motors MasterCard* (800-947-1000), which credits 5 percent of the money you charge on your card toward the purchase or lease of a new car. You can save up to $500 a year for seven years. The catch is that you have to be in the market for a new car sometime over the next few years and be willing to restrict yourself to GM cars.

Second, get a perk card that matches your spending threshold. If it takes five years to accumulate enough miles for a plane ticket, maybe you'd be better off just getting a card that offers rebates on tanks of gas. With that in mind, here are some suggested perk cards:

If you charge $500 a month. A *Toys "R" Us Visa* (800-207-8472) from the Chase Manhattan Bank allows rebates of only 1 percent on general purchases, but you get 3 percent back from purchases at Toys "R" Us and Babies "R" Us stores. Bear in mind that these

---

The going rate: The cost of a checking account

Banks don't make a whole lot of money on a checking account. Unless, that is, you fail to toe the line. In their neverending effort to improve their bottom line, banks have come up with a laundry list of sins for which you pay handsomely. Here's what the average check bouncer will pay in a bad month:

	Williamsburg, Va.	Chicago	Los Angeles	Fayetteville, Ark.
Other ATM fee	$ 1.50	$ 1.50	$ 1.25	$ 1.50
Bounced check fee	$ 29.00	$ 25.00	$10.00	$25.00
Stop-payment charge	$ 25.00	$ 25.00	$10.00	$15.00
Bad-check deposit fee	$ 5.00	$ 4.50	$ 4.00	$ 0.00
Replacement ATM card	$ 0.00	$ 5.00	$ 0.00	$ 0.00
Extra copy of statement	$ 3.00	$ 2.50	$ 3.00	$20.00
Overdraft protection (per year)	$ 20.00	$ 25.00	$ 0.00	$ 0.00
Monthly maintenance fee	$ 9.00	$ 20.00	$ 9.00	$ 7.00
One hour of accounting help	$ 20.00	$ 15.00	$ 0.00	$10.00
TOTAL	$112.50	$123.50	$37.25	$78.50

stores have among the best prices on strollers, playpens, and other child-rearing staples. Or try the *Citibank Driver's Edge Card* (800-456-4507), which gives 2 percent rebates on all purchases (with a maximum of $500 a year, or $1,500 total) toward the purchase of any new car. You may also want to look at *GE Rewards Master-Card* (800-437-3927), which will give you back up to 2 percent of your charges or $140 annually at this spending level.

If you charge $1,000 or more a month. Now you're in frequent-flier territory. *Prime Preferred Visa/Mastercard* from Huntington National Bank in Columbus, Ohio (800-480-2265), has a good deal: You pay a $39 annual fee, an additional $25 for the frequent-flier club, and a reasonable interest rate of prime plus 1 percent. For every dollar you charge you earn one point. Once you accumulate 25,000 points, you can buy a ticket on any domestic airline anywhere in the country—with no blackout dates or seat restrictions. You must purchase your ticket at least 14 hours in advance and stay over a Saturday night. The program has a 5,000 point-per-month cap, and points expire after three years.

Your next best bet is to sign up with the card that offers miles on the airline you fly most, such as *Delta Sky Miles American Express Optima* (800-759-6453) or the *First Card USA United Airlines Visa* (800-368-4535). Many airlines are joining forces, so you can use miles accumulated on your United Visa, for instance, on several other carriers.

The one drawback is that frequent-flier cards usually come with fairly stiff annual fees. But while the card companies deny that it happens, we have found card users who have been able to talk their way out of paying them. The key element is that you already fly a lot on a specific airline. If you threaten to take your business—both airline and credit card—elsewhere, some airlines are suddenly ready to deal.

Finally, keep a close watch on your monthly statement. Frequent-flier miles are getting harder to come by, and in some cases they're disappearing before your very eyes. If you're late with your check to American Express, the company will now withhold any frequent-flier points accrued over the last pay period. The only way to get them back is to call customer service and pay a $15 fee. (Miles accumulated beforehand are not affected.)

How to Get Out of Debt

There aren't many people who *don't* have too much debt. We're a nation of spenders. When we see something we want, we whip out our credit cards . . . and worry about the consequences later.

The consequences tend to kick in when you become a parent and can't afford preschool because your bills are already killing you. Don't let it happen.

The easiest way to get your debts under control is to consolidate them. If you're carrying a big balance on a variety of high-interest-rate credit cards, either transfer them to one of the lower-rate cards we've just described or take out a low-interest bank loan to pay them all off. Own a house? Many people use home equity loans or lines of credit to wipe out their credit card debt. A home equity loan is certain to have a lower rate than your credit cards, and there's an added bonus: The interest you pay, up to $100,000, is tax deductible. (It's tax deductible up to $1 million if you use the money for repairing or improving the house.)

Unfortunately, while consolidating loans at a lower rate will cut your monthly payments, it doesn't *eliminate* your debt. And if you're in a real debt crisis—that is, missing monthly payments, withdrawing retirement savings to pay current expenses—you ought to get your loan balances to zero.

There are a couple of popular strategies for eliminating debts. In the first, you get out a sheet of paper and list all of your loans, ranking them from the highest interest rate to the lowest. You then **concentrate on paying off the highest rate loan as quickly as possible,** sending in only the monthly minimums on all the other loans. Once that first debt is fully paid off, you concentrate on the next one, and so on.

The second strategy is to rank your loans from the lowest *balance* to the highest. Here your aim is to **pay off the smallest debt first.** Then once it's retired, you move on to the next largest and the next largest.

The first strategy—paying off your high-rate loans before any others—makes more sense mathematically, because you'll owe less in interest over the long term. "But for a lot of consumers, it's better psychologically to start with the smaller loans," says Steve Rhode, president of Debt Counselors of America, a nonprofit counseling firm in Gaithersburg, Maryland. "Some people, if they don't see that they're making progress, they get discouraged. And this is all about having the discipline to stick with it and not get discouraged."

WHAT IF YOU CAN'T PAY EVEN THE MINIMUM BALANCE?

If that's the case, consider professional help. But not just any old help. Some debt counselors—particularly those promising "quick fixes" to your problems—will encourage you to file for bankruptcy protection.

It's true that personal bankruptcy is an increasingly popular way for people to wriggle out of financial problems, but believe us: It should be your last resort. Filing for bankruptcy doesn't "wipe your slate clean," as some promise. It will definitely affect your ability to get credit in the future, and it could even hurt your chances of getting a job. "Bankruptcy is what we call the 10-year mistake," says Rudy Cavazos, a counselor at the Consumer Credit Counseling Service of Houston. "It is reported on your personal credit file for 10 years as a public record. Lenders look at these people as [bad] credit risks, having no capacity to understand finance."

Choose a nonprofit, state-licensed agency, like Debt Counselors of America (800-680-3328) or Consumer Credit Counseling, the biggest and best-known outfit, with some 1,400 offices nationwide. (For the Consumer Credit Counseling office nearest you, call the National Foundation for Consumer Credit at 800-388-2227.)

For a small fee (usually $20 to $60), these services will help you get your debts under control. They'll set up a simple debt-elimination plan like the ones we just described above, or, if your finances are really a mess, they'll take over. They will contact all your creditors and work out a repayment plan; you then send one bill a month to the counseling service, and it sees that your creditors get paid.

Apart from the convenience of having just one monthly bill to worry about, there's another important bonus: These counseling services have clout. Typically they can get lenders to waive their late fees and drastically lower the interest rates on the money you owe. It's not unusual to see your interest rates cut to as little as 8 or 9 percent. Sometimes lenders will even drop their interest rates to zero, says Jack Girgenti, vice president of Consumer Credit Counseling Service of Connecticut. Why would they want to do that? Because getting back the money they've lent you, even without interest, is better than getting nothing at all.

Sandy Larson, a Connecticut educator, says her trip to Consumer Credit Counseling was "the best thing I have ever done." She and her husband, David Gilmore, also an educator, had run up $18,000 in credit card debts and were having trouble making their monthly minimum payments. They met with a counselor, who had them hand over their credit cards—and then dramatically sliced the cards to pieces. "You can't use credit cards anymore," the counselor announced. "If you want to buy something from now on, you'll have to use cash."

Next the counselor had Larson and Gilmore make a list of all their monthly expenses. Anything they could live without, they would have to forgo. "We cut out the newspaper, cable TV, bottled water, the number of restaurants we were eating at," Larson recalls. "It wasn't hard to come up with $500 a month in savings." That money would go to Consumer Credit Counseling every month, and it would pay the couple's credit card bills.

Finally, their counselor contacted all six of their credit card companies to negotiate reduced interest charges and get them to waive some late fees. Within three years, Larson and Gilmore were free and clear of credit card debt. Vows Larson: "I will never, ever use another credit card again."

BAD CREDIT BLUES

Using a counselor to work out a repayment scheme does have one potential drawback: In some cases, lenders tell the credit-rating bureaus that you've had to undergo credit counseling (it shows up on your report as a "Code 7," says Rhode). But that's not as bad as it might sound. Let's say you've paid off all your debts and now you're ready to take out another loan. When lenders look at your new credit report, which do you think they'd rather see—someone who paid off all his earlier debts, even if it took a negotiated repayment plan, or someone who skipped out on debts by filing for bankruptcy protection?

Whatever you do, avoid "credit repair" clinics. For a fee, these companies offer to clean up any bad marks on your credit report. They don't deliver. They *can't*. According to the Federal Trade Commission, no one can remove accurate information from a credit report.

However, if there's information in your file that you dispute, the law does allow you to request a reinvestigation, with no charge. Thus, everything a credit repair clinic can do for you, you can do for yourself for little or no cost. According to the Fair Credit Reporting Act, you're entitled to a free copy of your credit report if you've been denied credit, insurance, or employment within the last 60 days. Otherwise, it costs $8 in most states. To get a copy, contact:

- Equifax (800) 685-1111; *www.equifax.com*
- Experian (888) 397-3742; *www.experian.com*
- Trans Union (800) 888-4213; *www.transunion.com*

You can either ask the credit agency for a dispute form or submit a letter explaining why you think the report is wrong, along with any proof.

Ten Things Your Financial Planner Won't Tell You

1 *If you want a custom fit, call your tailor.*

You have in mind a master plan that effortlessly meets each of your specific financial needs, from the kids' education to your vacation home to your blissful retirement in the sun. That's what financial planners are offering, and it helps explain why theirs is such a booming business. But some planners rely on a handful of boiler-plate plans and simply slot their clients into the one that best fits their needs.

2 *Don't be fooled by my 'fee-based' title.*

"Fee-only" financial planning has become quite the buzzword in recent years. For good reason: Unlike traditional planners, who get paid on commission, fee-only planners take a flat fee or a percentage of your assets. The idea is that they have less of an incentive to sell you specific products. But in fact, the largest group of financial planners are "fee-*based*"—in 1996 they controlled 38 percent of the market. What's the difference? Fee-based planners take upfront fees—but some get a commission as well if they sell you certain products.

3 *I like to keep you in the dark.*

It seems like a reasonable enough request: Planners should inform clients of every commission they earn, including the sources and the amounts. Registered investment advisers are required by the Securities and Exchange Commission or their states to show their clients a form called ADV Part II. But this document only asks planners to declare *whether* they get money from sources other than the client—not the amounts or sources of commissions or referral fees.

4 *I disguise my commissions.*

Some mutual fund companies pay a "trailing" fee to advisers who put you into their funds—and even some fee-only planners may be taking advantage of it. While most large firms such as Fidelity, Janus, and Twentieth Century disavow this practice, many other big names don't. The Heartland Funds will give planners a "distribution fee" equal to 0.25 percent of the client's assets every year the client is in the fund. Invesco pays planners an "administrative fee" of 0.25 percent a year.

5 *I pad my pocket with "soft dollars."*

Planners bring in billions of dollars of business to brokerage firms every year, and each firm wants to make sure it gets the biggest possible piece of the action. Thus, some of them pile on the incentives, also known as "soft dollars," ranging from tickets to the opera to subscriptions to, in extreme cases, desk space, a phone, and use of a secretary. Check with your state regulator about whether or not financial advisers must disclose these extras.

6 *Manage your money? I'd sooner manage the Yankees.*

Copies of the *Wall Street Journal* and *Investor's Business Daily* are scattered throughout his waiting room. On his desk, you might even find a computer tracking the market. But does your financial planner really know anything about managing money? You might be surprised. After drawing up a plan for you, a number of financial planners will farm out the actual investing to another portfolio manager. Why should it matter to you? Duplication of fees. The math teacher down the street retires and decides to be a financial planner and then refers you to an investment adviser who then goes to the discount broker . . . and everyone collects his fees.

7 *I'm new to this business . . .*

The number of financial advisers has increased phenomenally in the last few years. Membership in the National Association of Personal Financial Advisors, a fee-only group, increased over 50 percent from 1994 to 1998. Total assets managed by financial advisers increased from $140 billion in 1993 to $370 billion in 1996, yet 40 percent of new financial advisers do not have previous financial services experience.

8 . . . and nobody's regulating me.

Because anyone can hang out a shingle and declare himself a financial planner, there is no single agency overseeing the profession. For instance, accountants and insurance agents are regulated by individual states, broker-dealers are overseen by the National Association of Securites Dealers (NASD), and money managers answer to the SEC or their individual state. A planner could be providing one or more of these services. But there is no one monitoring his service as a planner. The one federal agency that comes closest to checking financial planners is the SEC. But all the SEC is really looking for when considering an application is whether the planner has a criminal record or any SEC sanctions. It's your job to figure out whether he or she is at all qualified.

A good starting point in searching for a planner is the National Association of Personal Financial Advisors, the fee-only group, which has a directory of members listed by state (800-366-2732). At least you can be assured of some baseline qualifications: Members must have three years' experience in comprehensive financial planning and must submit a financial plan written by them for review by other members. You will also probably help your cause by hiring a certified financial planner, which at least means he or she has passed the CFP Certification Examination. Then make sure the planner is registered with the SEC or your state securities commission. The North American Securities Administrators Association (202-737-0900) can tell you how to get in touch with your state regulators and make sure your planner is licensed. The Institute of Certified Financial Planners maintains a list of certified planners (800-282-7526).

9 I can't keep a secret.

Unlike what you tell your lawyer, information held by your financial planner is not privileged. This means he or she is obligated to disclose all documents, both to government agencies such as the Internal Revenue Service and the SEC and in court proceedings. A planner undergoing an audit can request that client names and Social Security numbers be wiped out. The problem is, many planners don't realize it, or they become nervous about asking for special treatment during an examination. The best way to keep your privacy: Identify beforehand the documents that could be potentially dangerous and don't leave any copies with the planner once he or she has done your work.

10 *You don't need me.*

If you're a young parent, chances are pretty good that your finances are relatively uncomplicated. The only reason anyone needs a financial planner is if you have considerable assets beyond a 401(k) and a house. Even if you do, with just a little forethought (and this book) you can figure out your best action plan—for free.

Part 2

THE EARLY YEARS

Ever heard of Balmex? Rudolf Steiner? *Chicka Chicka Boom Boom*? Well, you will. And several million other products and services out there vying for the precious dollars of new parents like you. Nearly everything you buy in the next four years will be something you've never bought before. And it's going to cost you. We're not just talking diapers and formula. (You'll spend roughly $2,400 per kid on those two staples—but that's chump change.) The real budget busters are child care, preschool, setting up the nursery.

How do you make sure you're not wasting your money? No, you don't have to become an instant expert in everything from dermatology to children's literature. You don't have to pore through all 326 pages of Consumer Reports' *Guide to Baby Products* and endlessly surf the Net in search of bargains. You simply need to read the following chapters.

We have thoroughly researched every major expense in your first four years—from start-up costs in the nursery to child care to preschool—so you don't have to. So you can know that your money is well spent, whether it's on a $200 stroller or a $3,800 day-care center.

3

Start-up Costs

For Janet Smith, a new mother in Margate, Florida, it was the baby-wipes warmer that did it. Months before her daughter's birth, she and her husband furnished the nursery with all the essentials: $419 for a crib; $450 for a changing table and dresser; $30 for animal-dotted wallpaper strips.

Weeks before her due date, everything was complete. Or so she thought. "Then my friend down the street, who was also a new mom, asked me if I had gotten a baby-wipes warmer," recalls Smith. "When I said that I hadn't even heard of one, she looked at me and said, 'But you're not going to put a cold wipe on your baby's bottom, are you?' I went out and bought one the next day."

That's the way it is with being a new parent. You're terrified that you might be doing something wrong, or that you aren't giving your child everything a parent should, so you race around buying up everything in sight, often putting yourself in deep hock along the way.

And no wonder: The possibilities are endless. Just walk into any Babies "R" Us and take a glance at the shelves around you: whole walls devoted to bottles and nipples; car seats in every size, color, and price range; Diaper Genies that wrap up used diapers in sausage-like casings; thousands of devices to make your baby sleep (you hope) and thousands more to entertain him while he is awake.

Take it from us: Ninety percent of the stuff out there is of no use whatsoever. Most of it, in fact, was invented well after the entire baby boom generation grew up.

Let the other starry-eyed suckers get taken. In the pages that follow we help you become a savvy shopper in the baby superstore jungle. We'll tell you what to buy, what it costs, and where to get the best prices.

By the way, just in case you're wondering, you don't need a baby-wipes warmer.

Delivery

The bill is going to read nearly $7,000—or more, if there are any complications during your delivery. If you're in an HMO or another form of managed care (see chapter 9), chances are the costs of your child's birth will be fully covered. But if you have traditional indemnity insurance (the kind where you can choose any doctor you want) you may have to pay your doctor at least half of his total fee before the baby is born. You won't get reimbursed until after the birth. And when you are reimbursed, it'll only be for 80 percent of the doctor's cost.

Maternity Leave

The pitifully inadequate Family and Medical Leave Act entitles you to take 12 unpaid weeks off per year from your job, without losing your benefits or your job status, to care for a newborn or adopted child (or a sick relative). Check with your employer to see if it offers additional maternity leave benefits; some actually offer paid maternity leave (and even paid paternity leave). Otherwise, you may be eligible for short-term disability benefits. Coverage varies, but most policies pay 60 percent of your salary for six weeks. To extend their maternity leave, many women also use up vacation, sick days, or personal days they've accrued.

The Nursery

WHAT YOU SHOULD KNOW BEFORE YOU BUY

Most of the nursery gear you buy now will, in two years, become unnecessary (a crib) or unbearable (that wallpaper strip of dancing bears). This didn't stop parents from spending $4.3 *billion* in 1997 on things like stroller-car seat combos and mobiles with educationally correct designs. Rule No. 1? Invest only in the essentials.

Start by arming yourself with a safety checklist for each of the items below. Most items, as well as a list of most product recalls, appear on the Consumer Product Safety Commission's website. (Go to *www.cpsc.gov*. From there, click on Library, then CPSC Publications, then Children's Furniture.) If you don't have Internet access, write to the Office of Information and Public Affairs, Wash-

---

Best winter jacket

L ands' End hooded squall parka (800-734-5437; from $64.50 for toddlers). Yes, it's more expensive than one you'll get at Target. But it's worth it: Insulated with Thinsulate, it's warm enough to withstand all but the bitterest cold days without a sweater underneath. Yet it's lightweight and thin enough that your kid can clamber around the jungle gym. The outer shell is made of thick nylon that keeps out the wind, lined with soft Polarfleece. The squall has three pockets, an attached hood that allows for an additional hat if necessary, a cinched waist to prevent updrafts, knit cuffs that easily fit under a pair of mittens, and it extends to mid-thigh—helpful when sitting on sleds.

   Unlike nearly every other clothing maker, Lands' End doesn't change its colors and patterns every year; it sticks to a few classic solids, from green and red to cobalt and yellow. If matching mittens and hats get lost on the playground, you can call up and order a new set. The jackets are roomy enough to last most kids two winters and sturdy enough to be passed on for another couple of years. Added bonus: They're machine washable.

---

ington, DC, 20207 and ask for a free copy of "The Safe Nursery, A Buyer's Guide."

Safety information on car seats and air bags, including a long list of recalls, is on the National Highway and Traffic Safety Administration website (*www.nhtsa.dot.gov* or call 800-424-9393).

Also look for items with the Seal of Voluntary Certification, sponsored by the Juvenile Products Manufacturers' Association. While the JPMA is hardly an unbiased source, it has obvious interest in making sure its members' products are safe (think punitive damages). One note: Be suspicious of combo items like Child Craft's 3-in-1 convertible crib (it starts out as a daybed, then a crib, and finally a full bed). They tend to have more breakable parts, they're heavier, and when you think about it, do you really want a double bed that looks like a crib?

After you've bought the basics, kiss your pride good-bye and borrow everything else. If we don't mention it below, chances are you can easily get by without it.

WHAT YOU SHOULD BUY

Crib. In the Penneys from Heaven catalog from JC Penney, there are 22 kinds of cribs, ranging from a "Shenandoah slat crib" (for

$300) to a Cosco red tubular-steel frame crib ($130). Stay simple: **Child Craft** has been making cribs for more than 80 years, and all of its cribs come with the JPMA's safety seal. **Model #13301 Sleigh Crib** (about $265) has the essentials: Both sides can be lowered for easy access, the mattress can be placed at four different levels, it's on wheels, and the simple design doesn't scream with attitude. It is made of smoothly polished solid maple and comes in several finishes. Any inexpensive, firm innerspring mattress like **Serta's Extra Firm with DuraSpring Plus** (about $40) will do; we're talking 40 pounds max by the time your kid graduates to a bed. By the way, most kids grow out of a bassinet in eight weeks, so skip it.

Car seat. You've got to have one. In fact, hospitals won't let you leave the building unless you have the baby in a car seat. **Century** and **Evenflo** have both been making them for years (around $60 for an infant size). The only point of a car seat is safety, so avoid expensive extras like plaid padding that matches your car. They also don't last long; you will have to buy three car seats by the time your child reaches 40 pounds (infant, toddler, and booster).

Look for ones with a T-shield that rests on the baby's chest when he's strapped in, or a five-point harness. Most child seats are secured by seat belts; some newer ones also are held in place with a tether strap, a length of seat belt webbing that stretches from the back of the car seat to a metal plate (the tether anchor) bolted to the car's frame. Many cars have predrilled holes for tether anchors; check your owner's manual. If yours doesn't, your dealer ought to be able to install one for you.

Best washer/dryer

You and the laundry are going to develop a very close relationship. So it's worth ponying up for the Maytag Neptune set (about $1,400; 888-462-9824). You'll save money in the long run. Most washers use about 40 gallons of water per load; the front-loading Neptune uses 25, saving the average user up to $100 per year in water bills. The Neptune also extracts 30% more water in the spin cycle than the average top loader, so you'll save money on your dryer. The dryer comes with with a moisture sensor, which means it shuts off automatically when the clothes are dry, saving even more electricity.

The reference shelf

Most child-rearing books range from the painful *(When Your Child Drives You Crazy)* to the pathetic *(101 Ways to Make Your Child Feel Special).* But there are a handful of classics that you will want at close range from the moment you find out you're pregnant. With this library, you should be able to survive almost any crisis parenting can—and surely will—send your way.

Your Baby & Child: From Birth to Age Five by Penelope Leach (Knopf, 1997). Tells you pretty much everything you need to know about caring for an infant, as well as basic stages of development to age five. Straightforward and unsentimental, Leach thinks common sense is the best defense against parental anxiety.

Touchpoints: Your Child's Emotional and Behavioral Development by T. Berry Brazelton (Addison-Wesley, 1992). This generation's Dr. Spock, Brazelton is a Boston pediatrician who's written several books for parents. *Touchpoints* helps you navigate and revel in those moments (six weeks, four months, three years) when seismic leaps in growth appear.

Baby & Child A to Z Medical Handbook by Miriam Stoppard (Perigee, 1992). Comprehensive yet slim, this is the ideal book to consult when a mysterious blister or sudden fever appears. Best of all, it has a diagram of each part of the child's anatomy, with a list of various possible ailments and symptoms, so you can get a head start on figuring out what the illness is. It also tells you what to expect when you visit the pediatrician.

The Perfectly Safe Home by Jeanne Miller (Fireside, 1991). Covers babyproofing inside and out, first aid and CPR instruction, lists of harmful plants, poison prevention tips, and detailed safety checklists for products.

The Gesell Institute of Human Development Series by Louise Bates Ames et al. (Delacorte Press). Developed from research done at the Gesell Institute in New Haven, Connecticut, in the 1950s, these eight guides *(Your Two-Year-Old: Terrible or Tender, Your Three-Year-Old: Friend or Enemy,* etc.) help parents manage each stage of development with equanimity.

The Magic Years by Selma Fraiberg (Scribner's & Sons, 1959). Written by a professor of child psychoanalysis at UCLA and a disciple of Sigmund Freud, *The Magic Years* takes you inside the mind of a young child, from the newborn's gradual awakening to the preschooler's sexual awareness.

The Measure of Our Success by Marian Wright Edelman (Beacon, 1992). A blueprint for creating a family life based on shared morals and values by the president of the Children's Defense Fund.

Above all, don't get a used car seat. You never know if it was in an accident and suffered a hairline crack—or if the model was recalled.

Baby carrier. Baby carriers are those little backpacks that you wear on your front, making you look a bit like a kangaroo. (If you've got a big baby, they can be brutal on your back.) But if you're going to be doing anything with your hands while carrying the baby—shopping, say—carriers come in awfully handy.

Despite its hefty price tag, the **Baby Bjorn** (about $70), on the market for more than 25 years, is the best. It's made of durable cotton without formaldehyde, is machine washable, and, most important, all adjustments can be made from the front. You can get it on and off by yourself, and you may even be lucky enough to transfer a sleeping baby to her crib without waking her. Newborns ride facing your body, while older infants face front for a better view.

Stroller. Strollers take a beating (how smooth is *your* sidewalk?), and for the first few months anyway, your baby's spine resembles spaghetti; thus she needs a sturdy, durable stroller with strong back support and the ability to recline nearly flat. You'll spend anywhere from $200 to $300 on a quality stroller: Look for one that is foldable (with one hand, if possible), has reversible handles so that you can walk with the baby facing you or the street, comes with swivel wheels that lock and washable upholstery. Finally, get one that is as lightweight as possible. **Peg Perego's Amalfi, Maclaren's Concorde,** and **Aprica's Calais Royale** have all or most of these features, and cost less than $250. When the baby gets older and doesn't need the same strong back support, you may also want a cheap (less than $50) foldup stroller, available from any discount store, such as the **Graco LiteRider Stroller** from Wal-Mart. They're lighter, simpler to maneuver, and a lot easier to toss in the trunk when you're going on a trip.

Changing pad. You won't want to change diapers on your bed (or *your* spine will end up resembling spaghetti). But instead of springing for a $200-plus changing table, pick up the **Basic Comfort EZ-Change** ($26), an indented foam pad with a soft, waterproof-lined cover, and attach it to a dresser. Unlike other models, the EZ-

What to read to your kids

There are over 100,000 children's books in print, and most of them are about as inspired as *Old MacDonald Has a Farm*—a series of pictures accompanied by, you got it, the lyrics to the song. Short of reading every book in the store, how do you know which are worth the price (the average hardcover is $16 a pop) and which aren't? The single best way to fill your kid's bookshelf with books both of you can stand to read over and over is to develop a relationship with a bookstore in town that specializes in children's books. You will pay a little more, but they stay in business by keeping their customers happy.

Or you can do some research on your own and put together a running list every time you pass by Barnes & Noble: Check out the American Library Association's website *(www.ala.org)* or call for a recommended children's reading list (800-545-2433). The **Children's Literature Web Guide** *(www.acs.ucalgary.ca/~dkbrown/index.html)*, run by the Doucette Library of Teaching Resources at the University of Calgary in Canada, has lists, reviews, and commentary of books for kids. **Children's Literature Newsletter** *(www.childrenslit.com* or 800-469-2070) is a good source for short reviews written by librarians, authors, and illustrators of new books. Along with selling books online, *www.amazon.com* keeps comprehensive lists of children's classics, award winners, and best-sellers. Through a feature called Amazon.com Delivers, you can enter age specifications, and the company will periodically e-mail you reviews of the best new and recently recommended books that meet your criteria.

One shortcut is to look for award winners. The **Caldecott** and **Newbery** medals, the most prestigious prizes for kids' books, are chosen by separate committees of the American Library Association. The Newbery medal is given each year to a book that tells a great story, such as *A Wrinkle in Time* by Madeleine L'Engle. The Caldecott is presented to a book with wonderful illustrations, such as *Where the Wild Things Are* by Maurice Sendak. The library association's website *(www.ala.org)* has a list of the winners from the last several decades. Other distinguished awards include the **Coretta Scott King Award,** presented annually to a black author and a black illustrator; the **Mildred L. Batchelor Award,** presented annually to an outstanding translated book for children; the **Boston Globe-Horn Book Award,** administered by **The Horn Book Magazine** *(www.hbook.com)*. Bear in mind, however, that some award winners may be too offbeat or dark for your kid. They're chosen by a committee of adults, who sometimes err on the side of "original."

Beware, too, publishers trading on a good name. The original *Madeline*, by Ludwig Bemelmans, is a classic; a subsequent video spin-off, *Madeline and the Toy Factory*, "based upon characters created by Ludwig Bemelmans," is dreck. *The Cat in the Hat* (1957) and *Fox in Socks* (1966), by Dr. Seuss, are a delight; Dr. Seuss's more recent works, such as *Oh, the Places You'll Go* (1990) drone on with none of the originality and wacky humor of his earlier books.

Finally, think twice before you sign up for Children's Book of the Month Club or similar ventures. They seem like a busy parent's dream come true, until they start sending books that you don't want (like *Oh, the Places You'll Go*). Then you have to go through the annoying process of packing up the book and getting to the post office on your lunch hour.

Change has an elastic safety strap to keep squirming infants from falling off.

High chair. You want one that can move easily, has a substantial tray, and won't tip over. The **Peg Perego Bravo** (about $130) has all the essentials: a T-strap safety belt to keep the baby from falling out, an H-shaped base to keep the high chair from tipping over, sturdy swivel wheels, a safety lock for the wheels, plenty of easy-to-clean padding, six adjustable height positions, and a removable tray.

Baby monitor. **Fisher Price** makes the Direct Link Privacy Monitor (about $40), which consists of a base picking up any sounds from the baby's room, and a satellite speaker to carry with you anywhere in or around the house. Unlike some other models, it doesn't pick up your neighbors' conversations—or broadcast yours.

WHAT YOU SHOULD BORROW

Rocking chair. Forget the famed $300 Dutalier maple or cherry glider. It may indeed last forever, but unless you're into Danish modern, it will never match your living room once it's no longer needed as a nursery accessory. Surely your parents, friends, even a used-furniture store has an old rocker that you can use for those moments when you just can't bounce in place for another minute.

Toys. Your baby will only use toys like a baby swing, a Baby Gym, or Exersaucer (stationary walker) for a month or less.

Cute baby furniture. Your kid will grow out of dressers or little tables and chairs, and especially toddler beds, before you finish making the credit card payments.

Breast pump. Forget the manual ones; they take forever, if they work at all. **Medela** makes a good line of electric pumps (like the Pump'N Style, $280), and if you can't find a friend to lend you the machine, rent one from a nearby drugstore (usually for about $140 for three months). Don't worry, it's sanitary: A new set of plastic accessories can be bought at any drugstore that sells medical devices.

Baby jogger and full-frame backpack. They are expensive ($200 and up) and, unless you're a fanatic jogger or hiker, they won't get much use. Besides, have you looked at all the stuff crammed into your garage lately?

WHERE YOU SHOULD SHOP

If you don't live near a **Babies "R" Us** (check out *www. babiesrus.com* for store locations), head for **Wal-Mart, Kmart,** or a local baby-furniture discount store. Compare prices with those of **Baby Catalog of America** (800-752-9736 or *www.babycatalog. com*), **Penneys from Heaven/J.C. Penney** (800-222-6161), or **ibaby,** an online discount store (888-847-2229 or *www.ibaby.com*). Whatever you do, avoid cute boutiques: When we checked, Child Craft's crib (#13301), in a honey oak finish, was $249.99 at Babies "R" Us in Commack, New York. How much did it cost at Burlington Coat Factory in East Hartford, Connecticut? $264.75. How much at The Baby's Room in Waterbury, Connecticut? $284.95.

For baby staples—everything from formula to pacifiers—try your local drugstore or supermarket, which often deep-discount these items in the hopes that you'll also buy the fetching bottle-and-bib set on display.

What's a Parents' Choice Award?

If you haven't already seen it, you will. Browsing through a bookstore or a toy store, a gold, silver or "approved" Parents' Choice award will catch your eye, and you'll wonder, *Says who?* Parents' Choice Foundation is, in its words, a "nonprofit service organization" and grants "the only children's media awards with absolutely no commercial ties." Started in 1978 by a group of mothers who were as bewildered as you are by the array of products out there, the foundation bestows awards on children's books, toys, videos, TV, computer programs, audio recordings, music, online services, and multimedia. On its board are the requisite celebrities (Julie Andrews) and movers and shakers (child psychologist Robert Coles), but many top experts in the field are also actively involved in the organization: Peggy Charren, founder of Action for Children's Television and Jane Yolen, a popular children's book author, among others. Do these awards guarantee that a particular product is perfect for your kid? No. But at least it's *something* to help you choose from among, say, 15 otherwise indistinguishable boxes of kids' software.

The Closet

WHAT YOU SHOULD KNOW BEFORE YOU BUY

Infant clothing is now a $19 million business—up from $4 million in 1980—primarily because parents can't resist dressing their children as if they were dolls or miniature alumni. You can get corduroy overalls for a 12-month-old at Oilily for $116. Or a pretty little white cotton sweater for a 12-month-old at Jacadi for $48. Or a pair of multicolored tights at Hanna Andersson for $16. Tempting though it is to buy all those adorable clothes, understand that (1) kids grow much faster than you think, (2) if there is a purple Magic Marker under the same roof as that white sweater, the two shall meet.

A few things you don't want to learn the hard way:

• Buy almost nothing in the 0–6 months category. Most babies grow out of this size before they're born.

• Beware **Baby Gap.** Yes, the Gap has simple, practical designs, decent prices (though not the lowest), and sturdy jeans for preschoolers. But their colors are often so peculiar that the clothes only match (surprise) other Gap clothes. Entering the Gap is like stepping into quicksand. You go in for a pair of socks and find yourself surrounded by so many inviting displays of matching hairbands and sailor-boy hats that you can't resist, and pretty soon your $4.95 errand has turned into a $100 blowout.

• Never buy mail-order shoes. It's impossible to get the right size, and unlike a pair of pants, you can't just roll up the cuffs.

• Mail order will save time, but almost never money. You have to pay shipping charges as well as (often) sales tax. Plus, catalogs tend to be high-end: The Hanna Andersson catalog justifies its high prices with comments about "the very best quality fabrics" and "practically indestructible" jumpers. You don't need indestructible. You need it for the next few months.

WHERE YOU SHOULD SHOP

Start with discount stores like **Caldor** and **Target.** You can get three all-cotton onesies (made by Gerber) at **Kmart** for $8.99. At **Saks Fifth Avenue,** they're two for $20. Socks, underwear, paja-

Your money's worth

I t doesn't matter if you've got a boy. Nearly every kid, boy or girl, spends hours playing with a toy kitchen, or at least long enough for you to read the newspaper. And if you get the right kitchen, it will be around for the next kid. If you don't, you'll be back at Toys "R" Us next Christmas.

Worth it: Little Tykes Family Kitchen, $79.95 (800-321-0183). It's 38 inches wide and 40 inches tall, so you'll never have too many pint-size cooks in this kitchen. Made of heavy molded plastic (Little Tykes' parent company is Rubbermaid), it takes less than half an hour to assemble and—unless your kids are sumo wrestlers—it'll never come apart. Features include a sink that holds two gallons of water, a microwave, a stovetop with two burners, a two-shelf oven and a built-in high chair for feeding baby dolls. Accessories include plenty of dishes, pots, pans and utensils, plus the obligatory cordless phone for chatting while fixing dinner.

Not worth it: Kitchen Fun Center, made by Amav Industries and sold through the Young Explorers catalog (800-239-7577), $77.95. First of all, it takes a long evening to put it together, starting with the center structural support and ending with the stovetop knobs. Anything that has to be put together by a couple of bickering parents can fall apart, and this kitchen does. The door handles repeatedly come off with the yank of a three-year-old, leaving them to holler out for help. The cordless phone (which comes in 3 parts) breaks within days. The recycling receptacle—operated by a foot pedal—will last about 30 minutes in the presence of an enthusiastic stomper. And when we ordered one, it arrived with several utensil hooks already broken.

mas, slippers, tights, hair accessories, jeans, turtlenecks, T-shirts can all be bought at most superstores, even at some discount drugstores.

Get remaining clothes and outerwear (if you can't borrow them) at your local **J.C. Penney** or **Sears,** which has a KidVantage program where you get a 15 percent coupon for every $100 spent. If you're a mail-order junkie, the following companies have reasonably priced and well-made clothes: **Lands' End** (800-356-4444), **L.L. Bean** (800-341-4341), **Biobottoms** (800-766-1254).

For holiday clothes, go back to the discount store or to **Children's Orchard** (800-999-KIDS or *www.childorch.com* to find out store listings), a nationwide chain of 85 stores selling upscale used children's clothes and furniture.

The real world: The parent trap

A day or two after your baby is born you head to the drugstore, lightheaded from exhilaration and lack of sleep. It is precisely at this moment that you become, from the drugstore industry's point of view, a "diaper-destination shopper." Your mission? A jumbopack of Huggies. Your purchases? A clever-looking pacifier/thermometer, a teeny nail-clipper, a squishy rattle shaped like a hippo, three different kinds of kids' Tylenol (you're not sure which is the right dose)—oh, and the Huggies. The store's take? Zip on the diapers; they're loss leaders. On the rest, up to 40 percent profit.

Bingo. Another parent snagged by the colossal juvenile products industry.

You are a ripe target. Blind with love, you will buy whatever it takes to care for your tiny, helpless infant—and you don't have a clue where to start. This is not lost on advertisers. "Young families, especially new parents, are one of the most responsive consumer groups to promotion," trumpets the website for Madison Direct Marketing, a Greenwich, Connecticut, firm that specializes in targeting new parents. One of its most requested services is providing mailing lists of new parents, which it gets from hospitals, pharmacies, and public health records.

Why? Because today's parents buy more stuff than ever before. Despite the fact that the birth rate has remained stable, $4.23 billion was spent on nursery gear in 1996, up 400 percent since 1980. Spending on children's books was up 600 percent in the same period; on children's clothes, up 340 percent. A recent survey by Black & Decker found that new parents receive more small kitchen appliances (21) than brides do (a mere 18).

With each child's birth triggering so many sales, it should come as no surprise that infant-product manufacturers have figured out a lot about you.

First of all, they know that new parents today have more disposable income than previous generations: We have fewer kids per family, and we have them later, when we're earning more money.

The baby industry also knows that in your time-poor state you're more susceptible to hype than ever before. Drugstores target diaper-destination shoppers—one of many "categories" developed several years ago by the drugstore industry (soda-destination shopper is another)—by "trying to draw them into the baby care department," says Marie Griffin, editor of *Drug Store News,* a trade magazine. "When you've got something of the magnitude of a new baby in your life, it's like anybody who's got a new thing. You're a little bit more susceptible in those early days." Hype is so important to the juvenile-products industry that companies squabble ferociously about even the silliest ads. In the fall of 1997 Playtex, the market leader in sippy cups, sued newcomer Gerber over its ad campaign. Playtex's lawyers actually had to try to prove—in U.S. federal court—that 50 percent of infants do *not* prefer Gerber's cup over theirs. (Playtex lost; the judge was apparently swayed by Gerber's "evidence.")

Manufacturers know today's parents believe in "the overarching notion that technology helps civilization move forward," says Sam Craig, chairman of the marketing department at New York University's Stern School of Business. In other words, we'll try *anything* to make this exhausting and time-consuming job easier. Why else would anyone buy the White Hot

Soft Bite "safety spoon," which turns color when the food's too hot for Baby's mouth? Or Playskool's 1-2-3 highchair, which is impregnated with Microban, a substance that supposedly protects children from nasty bacteria in tainted food? (The EPA eventually forced Playskool to stop making claims that Microban prevents disease.)

Above all, the baby industry knows that you feel guilty. "These are guilt dollars," says George Rosenbaum, chief executive officer of Leo J. Shapiro, a Chicago-based market research firm. Now that most families have two earners, "parents are pouring money into children to make up for the lack of time they spend with them. They're substituting dollars for their own time." Companies know that you'll splurge on Troll's Book of the Month Club instead of making trips to the library. That you'll buy a set of Sleeping Partners' all-natural cotton crib sheets in understated celadon chambray for $200, to make up for the fact that Daddy hasn't been home before bedtime all week. That the certainty of receiving another stuffed animal makes all those business trips a little easier for junior to bear.

So what's a besotted, bewildered, guilt-ridden parent to do? *Don't buy on impulse.* Two thirds of baby accessories—especially the ones emblazoned with a frolicking Pooh Bear or Mickey Mouse—are bought without advance planning, according to *Drug Store News.* "During those urgent late-night diaper runs," says one parent from Virginia, "I often found myself scanning other baby products, buying an item or two that I felt almost helpless to resist. My impulse buys were always fun stuff—like the little purple choo-choo train that makes a choo-choo noise if you press it in the right spot. Why would such a toy be hanging in the Safeway right next to the baby bottles and diapers? Safeway is not a toy store, after all. But they know what parents are made of—very weak stuff." So the next time you go out for diapers? Leave your credit card at home.

The Toy Chest

WHAT YOU SHOULD KNOW BEFORE YOU SHOP

Young children will play with just about anything you hand them, so there's no need to go overboard on, say, a $300 trainset for your 2-year-old. Get what your instinct tells you is safe and fun.

WHERE TO SHOP

Shop at superstores like Toys "R" Us or local discount toy stores like KMart and Caldor's; even drugstores carry some toys at a discount.

If you'd rather get through life with as few visits to a toy store as possible, order toys online or through mail order when everyone's asleep. Start with **Oriental Trading Company** (800-228-2269), which has great prices on Halloween costumes, small toys, and party supplies. A few other catalogs with good prices: **Discount School Supply** (800-627-2829), **Constructive Playthings** (800-832-0224), **Toys to Grow On** (800-542-8338), **The Great Kids Co.** (800-533-2166), and **Sears** (800-775-5555). Online, try **Toys "R" Us** (*www.toysrus.com*), **Holt Educational Outlet** (*www.holtoutlet. com*), and **eToys** (*www.etoys.com*). When you need that special toy, such as a gift for your boss's kid, try the **Museum of Fine Arts** catalog (800-225-5592).

By the time your kid is three or four, take a detour to an art, music, or sporting goods store. There aren't any "toys" here, but there are plenty of things—pastel crayons, rhythm sticks, pint-size hockey gear—that will thrill any preschooler and even teach him something useful.

The Archives

In 20 years, you will have more pictures of your baby than the Pentagon has of Iraq. Not to mention miles of videotape of the baby hitting such milestones as, say, lifting her head.

WHAT YOU SHOULD KNOW BEFORE YOU SHOP

Camcorders. These are better than ever. They're smaller, lighter, and (for basic models at least) more affordable. They are, however, incredibly confusing to buy. Most electronics companies have recently been fighting an all-out battle of bells and whistles, taking what was once a relatively simple and reliable appliance and jamming it full of perplexing features like "high definition image sensors." Ignore most of it. Most camcorders have all the basics (autofocus, automatic exposure control, power zoom, remote control, battery backup). There are only a few features worth paying extra for: image stabilization, which evens out standard jitters; flipout viewscreen if you wear glasses; and, if you're ambitious, advanced editing features or the ability to record in stereo. Beware digital anything: Digital zoom "just makes the image bigger and more watered down," according to Lancelot Braithwaite, technical editor of *Video* magazine. Besides, a digital camera is simply too expensive ($2,500 and up) for chronicling the preschool play.

Cameras. Today's high-tech point-and-shoot cameras have more in common with advanced professional cameras than they do with the old Instamatics. Even a photophobe can now snap good shots. There's only one problem: There are almost 500 to choose from. According to *National Geographic* photographer Bob Sacha, the ordinary user will be perfectly happy with a point-and-shoot that costs less than $200. Sacha points out, however, that while there are few differences among the point-and-shoots in this price range, design varies greatly. This is key. If it's small enough to take with you everywhere, "you're much more likely to have it with you when something interesting happens," Sacha says. And forget about paying extra for a "red-eye reduction" feature. They don't work. (Get your subjects to look slightly away from the camera, or use black-and-white film.)

The going rate: The cost of getting baby to sleep

Parents perform comical rituals every night trying to nail down one reliable method to get the baby to sleep. Here's what it costs to bring on Mr. Sandman in four cities around the country.

	Charlotte	Houston	Phoenix	Seattle
Pacifier	2.49	1.97	3.00	0.99
Nightlight	4.49	5.99	4.99	5.98
Baby Go To Sleep music therapy (makes heartbeat sounds)	12.97	12.95	13.99	12.95
Dex Mommy Bear teddy bear (makes heartbeat sounds)	19.99	19.99	19.99	24.00
Pali Desiree rocking crib	429.97	399.99	509.99	409.99
Baby Bjorn infant soft carrier	69.97	70.99	74.99	69.95
Initial consultation with a sleep specialist	220.00	250.00	185.39	190.00
Dutalier Glider Rocker	489.99	349.99	409.99	399.99
Blankie	15.99	17.99	15.99	19.95
Graco Swing-o-matic	49.99	49.99	49.99	49.99
Little Me sleeper pajamas	21.99	15.99	18.00	19.95
Tylenol Extended Relief—100 caplets (for your headache)	8.79	7.89	9.29	6.89
Dr. Ferber's *Solve Your Child's Sleep Problems* book	12.00	12.00	12.00	12.00
Dr. Sears' *The Baby Book* (when Ferber hasn't worked)	21.95	21.95	21.95	21.95
Total	1380.58	1237.68	1349.55	1244.58

WHAT TO BUY

Camcorders. Our picks: **Canon**'s basic point-and-shoot 8mm camcorder (about $400). If you want a flipout viewscreen, image stabilization, and the crisper picture that you get from a Hi8 camcorder (and you have a new TV with a comb filter that will show the difference), get **Sony**'s low-end Hi8 camcorder (about $1,000). The only drawback to 8mm and Hi8 is that you must plug the camcorder into an outlet on your VCR to play tapes, and on older VCRs this outlet is in the back. Compact VHS tapes, on the other hand, can be inserted directly in the VCR (with an adapter). **Panasonic**'s midrange VHS-C camcorder has all the standard features, as well as an image stabilizer and a viewscreen (about $900).

Cameras. The **Yashica T-4** (about $160) has an excellent Zeiss lens, while an **Olympus Stylus** (about $110) is so small that it can fit into the palm of your hand. Another good lightweight camera is a basic point-and-shoot from **Pentax** (about $170).

4

The Child Care Challenge

Forget about the guilt. The real issue with child care is money. How can *anyone* afford it? Sure, the U.S. Census Bureau estimates that the average family with college-educated parents pays only $93 per week in child care. But if you can find a decent arrangement that cheap, we'd be amazed. Fact is, you will probably end up spending much more per week—$150, $250, even $500—not to mention paying for considerable add-ons, such as an extra television for the live-in nanny, daily transportation costs to the day-care center, Christmas presents for the neighbor who looks after the kids. In cash, after taxes.

But just because child care is expensive doesn't mean it's good. Anyone who's read a newspaper in the last few years knows that child care is shaping up to be the Achilles heel of the American workforce. Seventy percent of mothers with kids under 18 work, according to the Department of Labor, and 54 percent of mothers with kids under 1 work. But as we're marching off to the office, we're being bombarded with the news that by age 5, it's all over. Powerful brain scans have revealed that by the time she's 3, your baby's brain has formed about 1,000 trillion connections—or not. It just depends on what she does all day.

There's the rub. In a landmark study coordinated by the University of Colorado, researchers found that 74 percent of all day-care centers studied offered mediocre care. Another 12 percent were actually dangerous. And what did the parents think? Ninety percent rated their kid's day-care center "very good." Either these parents are in serious denial (a distinct possibility) or they just don't know any better.

Truth is, it's hard to know better. There are no federal guidelines or regulations for child care. States have licensing requirements for most child care centers, but many of these are laughable:

South Carolina, for example, allows 1 adult to take care of *10* two-year-olds. Nannies are unregulated, period. So parents go on their instincts and hope for the best. The teacher is friendly, the nanny is warm, the woman down the street is a good egg—cross your fingers and sign up.

Don't do it. Somewhere near you there is a better option available. You just have to know what to look for. Thoughtful inquiry now will save you months of frustration and fury later. ("Since when did *Rugrats* become an educational tool?") It will take some time: "You really have to sort the wheat from the chaff," says Oakland mother Diana Measham, who spent nearly six weeks looking for the perfect place. "There is no service that helps you. You just have to do it yourself."

With the following information, no matter which child care option you favor, you can confidently determine what is required, what is negotiable, and what is simply unnecessary. In other words, what's worth your ten, fifteen, or twenty-five thousand dollars a year, and what isn't. In fact, if you end up knowing that every penny you spend on your kid's care is worthwhile, all that working-parent guilt should evaporate. Well, some of it, anyhow.

How much does child care cost?

More than you ever dreamed you'd pay. Here's approximately what you'll pay per week to have someone else care for your darling little 3-year-old.

	Day care	Family care	Full-time Nanny
Buffalo	$120	$105	$320
Chicago	$140	$135	$350
Minneapolis	$180	$160	$450
Tampa, Fla.	$107	$ 97	$425
San Francisco	$170	$138	$480
Albuquerque	$120	$ 95	$350
Seattle	$165	$141	$475
Bozeman, Mont.	$115	$100	$300
Washington, D.C.	$166	$ 78	$450
St. Louis	$125	$ 90	$350

Day Care: Child Care Out of Your Home

There are about 6.5 million kids in the United States whose parents pay to have them watched during the day, according to the Census Bureau.

Most attend **day-care centers,** which are licensed businesses that are not located in a home. A few of these kids are lucky enough to be in corporate day-care centers, which are usually near the office. Many others are in **family day care,** provided by a neighbor or friend in her own home. Family day care, at least in theory, seems more intimate and easy to manage; it's also cheaper. On the other hand, it is often an off-the-books arrangement and unregulated. According to the Children's Defense Fund, 41 states do not require family day care providers to have any training whatsoever prior to opening their doors for business.

What Are the Advantages of Day Care?

First, it's much less expensive than a nanny. In many cases, you're not dependent on a single person, who can get sick and leave you stranded. If the center is near your office, there are no extra transportation costs, and you can drop by anytime. And while there is plenty of evidence that bad day care hurts kids, there is also research to indicate that kids may possibly do better in high-quality day care than in any other situation. A study by the National Institute of Child Health and Human Development found that top-notch day care improves a child's cognitive and language skills, and—key point here—gets him ready for school. As Susan Laskaris, a mother of three kids in Newton, Massachusetts, puts it, "In this day and age of having [only] one and two kids in a family, it's nice to have exposure to having to share and being part of a group, and to realize that you're not the center of attention all the time."

Day Care: What You Should Pay For

An open-door policy. Centers should welcome parents at any time, especially prospective customers. Spend at least half a day at each place; remember, this is where your kid will spend *all* day. Look for telling details: Are walls covered with kids' art? Are there laminated newspaper clippings proudly displayed on the wall? Any degrees or awards posted? What's on the bulletin board? Any messages to parents? Any *friendly* messages to parents? Are kids engrossed in something, crying, staring into space? Is it especially loud or eerily quiet?

For a good day-care center evaluation checklist to bring along to prospective centers, get "Finding Good Child Care: The Essential Questions to Ask When Seeking Quality Care for Your Child, Information Guide 19" from the Child Care Action Campaign (212-239-0138; or write Dept. S, 330 Seventh Ave., 17th fl., New York, NY 10001).

The right credentials. There are two private, mostly industry-sponsored associations that give their seal of approval to child care centers. The National Association for the Education of Young Children (NAEYC) accredits day-care centers; the National Association for Family Child Care (NAFCC) accredits family day care. Each has a careful application process that looks at every aspect of the center. The problem is, fewer than 10 percent of all centers have been accredited, primarily because it's a new phenomenon.

How to lower the costs of child care

N othing is going to make child care cheap, but there is one excellent way to shrink that weekly hit: a dependent-care flexible spending account, something many employers now offer.

With these accounts, your family can set aside up to $5,000 in pretax salary, as long as the money goes toward qualified child care expenses. Pretax means you don't pay any taxes on this $5,000. If you're in the 28 percent tax bracket, that equals a tax savings of $1,400. (Important caveat: You forfeit any money left in the account that you don't withdraw by the end of the year.)

If you spend significantly less than $4,800 in your dependent-care flexible spending account, or if your employer doesn't offer one, you may be able to take advantage of the Child Care Tax Credit. This will reduce your taxes by as much as $480 for one kid, $960 for two (or even more if your income is under $28,000). You need IRS Form 2441 and Publication 503: Child and Dependent Care Expenses. They're available from 800-TAXFORM, or you can download them at *www.1040.com* or *www.irs.ustreas.gov*. Some states also offer their own credits, so make sure your tax preparer knows exactly how much you've spent on child care.

Still, you can see who they've accredited by checking out their web-sites *(www.naeyc.org* and *www.nafcc.org)* or by calling and asking for a list. The NAEYC's number is 800-424-2460, ext. 333; the NAFCC can be reached at 800-359-3817.

Next, look for a state license. As we mentioned, some states don't exactly have the most rigorous regulations. But the way we see it, some regulations are better than none at all. To see how your state licenses child care providers, visit the State Profiles page of the National Child Care Information Center website *(www.nccic. org),* run by the Department of Health and Human Services. This site also has local numbers you can call to check on any complaints or infractions.

Some states have started to grade day-care centers—to link state funding to quality. Oklahoma, for instance, now has a star system, in which a 3-star center will get more state money than a 1-star center; New Mexico rates centers gold, silver, or bronze.

Child Care Aware (800-424-2246) is a nonprofit group that can refer you to local accredited family and day-care centers, as well as information on state rating systems, licensing, how to find out if there have been any complaints, and more.

A staff that doesn't bolt the minute there's an opening at the local McDonald's. Not too many people make less than a child care worker. The average wage is slightly less than $7 an hour. That's $12,000 a year. Less than a third get health insurance. Hardly a package to attract your best and brightest. Nor your most dedicated: On average, 36 percent of the typical day-care center's staff turns over every year, according to the Child Care Action Campaign. This is downright unhealthy, especially for infants and toddlers. A national study by the Center for the Child Care Workforce found that children who were in centers with a high turnover rate were less competent in language and social development than others.

A staff with training. OK, so they don't all need to be Ph.D.'s. But the administrator should have had some postgraduate coursework, and each teacher should have had some post-high-school child-development training. Every single adult (including volunteers) on the place should be certified in CPR for both infants and toddlers.

A staff that likes kids. Does the staff truly seem fascinated with the behavior and attitudes of children? Do they hold the babies as

---

Au pairs

It's a working parent's dream: a peppy foreign college-age woman who will take care of the kids for about $230 a week. In exchange for this small stipend (which includes transportation and tuition costs), several thousand families a year get 45 hours of live-in baby-sitting and "light housekeeping." But remember, translated from the French, "au pair" means "as an equal," not "do as I say." These young women are really here on special au pair visas as much for their enrichment as they are to serve your needs. Moreover, plenty of the women who work as au pairs don't have the faintest idea how to take care of children all day, and they end up frustrated and unhappy.

Au pairs work best with families who have school-age kids, families who have a full-time nanny for the baby and need a more stimulating companion for older children, or families who have parents working at home.

Here are the agencies that sponsor au pairs:

Au Pair in America (Greenwich, CT): 800-727-2437
AuPair Homestay (Washington, D.C.): 800-479-0907
EurAuPair (Laguna Beach, CA): 800-333-3804
Au Pair Care (San Francisco, CA): 800-428-7247
EF Au Pair (Cambridge, MA): 800-333-6056
Interexchange Au Pair (New York, NY): 800-287-2477
Au Pair Program USA (Salt Lake City, UT): 800-574-8889

---

much as possible? Do they encourage kids' language skills by talking to them a lot? Do they foster independence in a nonthreatening way? Are children treated calmly, with respect and affection? Does the provider listen to what children say? Does she bend down to talk to the kids? Does she have an intolerance for verbal or physical violence?

Try to gauge the motive of the provider: Is this a career or just a way to make some extra cash? In her search for a good family day care provider in the Oakland area, Diana Measham was turned off by providers "who wanted to start their own business, and this seemed like a convenient one to start. They were more interested in the corporate aspect of it, not the kids."

No criminals on staff. Don't be reassured by a blanket statement on background criminal checks. Most centers do only statewide

checks, and some can't even legally do that. The FBI can do a nationwide check, but it's time-consuming and not always thorough
(depending on states' willingness to comply). Ask the administrator, in detail, how the center checks applicants out. Also, call your
state licensing board and ask whether there have been any complaints about the center, or whether centers are obliged to follow
hiring procedures that rule out dangerous criminals.

Enough staff. A day-care center's child-to-staff ratio, according to the
University of Colorado researchers, "is the most significant deter-
minant of quality." The National Resource Center in Health and
Safety in Child Care, part of the Department of Health and Human
Resources, recommends the following:

Up to 24 months: 3:1 in groups no larger than 6.
Up to 30 months: 4:1 in groups no larger than 8.
Up to 35 months: 5:1 in groups no larger than 10.
3-year-olds: 7:1 in groups of 14.
4- and 5-year-olds: 8:1 in groups of 16.
6- to 8-year-olds: 10:1 in groups of 20.
9- to 12-year-olds: 12:1 in groups of 24.

A safe and healthy environment. Nose through the kitchen, sleeping
area, bathroom, and diapering area. Ask the provider about emergency procedures, fire drills and prevention procedures, transportation procedures, outdoor safety precautions, rules about releasing
children to adults. Even if you can't inspect everything, keep your
eye open for telling details. Susan Laskaris, the mother from Newton, Massachusetts, never worried for an instant about safety in
her family day-care center. Along with the regular childproofing
that any house should have, "the door automatically locks whenever you close it. The yard isn't just gated, it has a gate so high
even climbers won't be tempted."

Make sure there are measures in place to limit the germ exchange, like separately labeled wipes and diapers for each kid and
strict handwashing policies. Handwashing, according to the Centers for Disease Control and Prevention, is the single best way to
prevent infectious diseases.

Liability insurance. Ask to see policy certificates. Day-care centers
should have standard business owner's property policy. Family-

care centers also need Family Child Care Liability and Accident Insurance, which is different from general business liability insurance. Homeowner's insurance does not cover a family child care business.

A forgiving policy regarding tardiness. Your life is crazy enough as it is; you don't need regular drag races through town to get to the center at *exactly* 5 P.M. Many centers have extended hours for nominal fees, or even a half-hour grace period.

Day Care: What You Shouldn't Pay For

A good reputation. As we've seen from the University of Colorado study, today's parents aren't exactly rocket scientists in the child care department. A good reputation doesn't hurt, but don't rely on it.

A fantastic facility. You want safety, love, stimulation. Not a "subliminal lesson in complex geometry" written up in *Metropolis* magazine and designed by Steven Ehrlich Architects, like the on-site day-care center for Sony Pictures Entertainment in Culver City, California. Sure it would be nice if all day-care centers were state-of-the-art, but good care depends on people, not buildings.

Specially designed or brand-new toys. Anyone who's seen a kid play with the box while the present lies untouched knows that kids can be taught with the contents of a kitchen drawer.

A rigid environment. All those important brain synapses can't be connecting if the provider is constantly forcing the kid to line the squares up the *right* way.

A brand name. Companies like KinderCare, Children's World Learning Center, and Bright Horizons are working hard to become a brand you can trust. Still, only two-thirds of Bright Horizons centers are NAEYC-accredited, as are around 50 percent of Kinder-Care and Children's World Centers. (The companies say they're working on 100 percent accreditation.)

Your money's worth

Yes, you need to pay your nanny taxes. But who's going to do all the paperwork?

Worth it: Having your accountant file your nanny taxes for you. Cost: about $100, on top of what you're already paying him to do your return.

Not worth it: Doing the paperwork yourself. Cost: Free, not counting a reduced life span. This is what it entails:

1. Get Immigration and Naturalization Service Form I-9 (to order, call 800-755-0777 or download from *www.ins.usdoj.gov*) and have your employee fill it out. Keep it in your files, so the INS can see it upon request.
2. If your nanny doesn't have a Social Security number, she can get one by filing Form SS-5 (to order, call 800-SSA-1213).
3. File for an employer identification number with Form SS-4 (order this and all other IRS forms and publications from 800-TAX-FORM or download from *www.1040.com* or *www.irs.ustreas.gov*).
4. If you decide to withhold income taxes (you don't have to), your nanny has to fill out state and federal forms, including Form W-4 for federal taxes. To figure out how much to withhold, get IRS Publication 15, Circular E. Contact state offices for state forms and withholding information.
5. Fill out and attach Schedule H to your 1040. FICA (Social Security and Medicare taxes) equals 15.3 percent of your nanny's wages. You are required to pay half and withhold the other half from her salary; or you can pay it all. If you decide to pay your employee's share of FICA, you include this (but not your half) in taxable wages. Starting in 1998, you may have to pay an estimated tax penalty if you do not prepay the household employment taxes (usually by increasing federal tax withheld from your paycheck).

    FUTA (federal unemployment tax) equals 6.2 percent of the first $7,000 of your nanny's wages, but if you also paid state unemployment taxes, you may receive a substantial credit. Local state offices have unemployment forms, instructions, and tax rates; some of them still require quarterly filing.
6. Notify your nanny that if she qualifies for an earned income credit, she can receive up to 60 percent of the credit in advance with her pay during the year. She'll have to fill out Form W-5.
7. Encourage your nanny to file a 1040 or 1040EZ. Even if she's paid no income tax, if she has a child she may qualify for the earned income credit, which may erase any tax owed.
8. Give one copy of a completed W-2 to your nanny by the end of January, send another, along with the W-3, to Social Security Administration by the end of February.
9. Contact your state office to see if and how you must pay workers' compensation.
10. If this isn't *crystal clear,* get IRS Publication 926, Household Employer's Tax Guide.

The Nanny: Child Care in Your Home

The most exclusive, expensive, coveted—and unregulated—child care in existence is a private baby-sitter or nanny. Only a tiny sliver of working parents—no more than 5 percent—have private in-home caregivers, though this percentage tends to be higher in metropolitan areas.

WHAT ARE THE ADVANTAGES OF A NANNY?

When you've got the right nanny, you've got a stable caregiver who can form crucial bonds with your child. Of course, there's also the luxury of having someone who can schlep your kid to classes, playdates, and appointments, not to mention the obvious plus of housekeeping help. Costs only go up incrementally when you have more children; with day care, the cost can double. If you treat her right, a nanny can become a third parent to your child. The key is finding the right one in the first place.

WHAT TO LOOK FOR IN A NANNY

A good education and/or professional experience. When you drop your child off at a day-care center, there's a team of people there to help out if something goes wrong. But a nanny is on her own. Thus you need someone who's smart and experienced enough to think fast on her feet in an emergency, in addition to being able to sympathetically break up fights among siblings.

A warm, sunny, can-do personality. Ask a prospective nanny why children like her, why she likes caring for kids. Ask her to describe her former charges and see if she values trust, self-esteem, and independence in children.

A rave review. This is someone who will be unsupervised, in your house, alone with your children. If you are relying only on unknown references, you absolutely must talk to them in person. Too many parents have later discovered that a "reference" whom they talked to on the phone was really a cousin making stuff up on the spot.

A neatnik. If she is organized and neat, your life will be a lot easier. If she isn't, you'll spend Saturday mornings picking wads of Play-doh out of the rug, and realizing, at an inopportune moment, that you're all out of diapers.

An English speaker. Some parents get all excited at the prospect of their child growing up bilingual, until they try to explain to their nanny how to get to the playground. As you will have daily instructions, she must be fluent in English.

Similar views on discipline. First, ask her if it's ever necessary to hit a child. Then ask how she would handle various situations: a sibling fight, sharing disputes, tantrums, innocent mischief.

CPR and safety training. You can always pay for her to take a course later, but if she's already done it, all the better. In any case, ask her some basic safety questions: What do you do if a baby chokes? What safety precautions do you take when you iron? When you

---

The going rate: The cost of separation anxiety

E ventually your three-year-old will stop wailing "Mommy!" at the day-care center door. Until that day, moms are often emotional car wrecks. Here's what it costs to walk out the door when your kid is screaming.

	Fort Worth, Tex.	Norfolk, Va.	Olympia, Wash.	Topeka, Kan.
The Sacrificial Mother by Carin Rubenstein	$ 22.95	$ 22.95	$ 19.51	$ 20.65
Cover Girl Marathon waterproof mascara	$ 3.67	$ 4.19	$ 3.68	$ 4.09
Flents earplugs (box of 12)	$ 2.37	$ 4.29	$ 0.99	$ 2.99
Color photo calendar of kids from Kinko's	$ 22.95	$ 29.95	$ 29.95	$ 29.95
15-minute call to Grandma in Fort Myers, Fla.	$ 3.75	$ 3.75	$ 3.75	$ 3.75
One hour of adult therapy	$170.00	$150.00	$100.00	$100.00
One-pound box of Godiva chocolates	$ 30.00	$ 33.00	$ 30.00	$ 32.00
Wallet-sized reprints (12)	$ 39.00	$ 15.00	$ 20.00	$ 25.00*
Kleenex (box of 250)	$ 1.50	$ 1.99	$ 1.88	$ 1.74
Tums (3 rolls of 36 tablets)	$ 1.57	$ 1.69	$ 1.56	$ 1.79
Eye compress	$ 2.57	$ 4.89	$ 4.24	$ 5.99
TOTAL	$300.33	$271.70	$215.56	$227.95

*for 14

clean? When you're at the playground? What do you do if someone rings the doorbell? How do you answer the phone? What do you do if there's a burglar? Fire? Have you ever used an alarm system? Have you ever been in an emergency with a young baby? What did you do? Do you know how to swim? If you're bathing the kids and the phone rings, what should you do? (Answer: Never leave the kids alone in the tub.) Finally, a nanny should recognize symptoms of common childhood illnesses.

For a more complete list of safety and health issues to discuss with your nanny, visit the National Child Care Information website *(www.nccic.org)* and click on Health and Safety in Child Care.

KEY QUESTIONS TO ASK YOUR NANNY'S PREVIOUS EMPLOYER

1. Why did she leave your household?
2. Did she ever baby-sit for you on weekends or when you went away on vacation? (If not, why not?)
3. How would you describe her?
4. What are her strengths and weaknesses?
5. Did your children like her? Why?
6. What did she do if your child suddenly got sick?
7. Did she do any cleaning? Cooking? Housework? Did she resent having to do this work?
8. How did she handle it when the baby cried? What about a toddler's temper tantrums or older kids' sibling arguments?
9. Did she ever discipline your kids? Over what? How?
10. Did you ever feel she was less than on top of the situation?
11. How did she handle your feedback or criticism?
12. What frustrated you about her most frequently?
13. Did you ever get into disagreements? Over what? How were they resolved?
14. Did she like to initiate active games with your kids?
15. Did she prefer to play outside or inside?
16. Was she tidy in her own room? Around the house?
17. Does she have any odd personal habits?
18. Did you meet any of her friends? What were they like?
19. How did she answer the phone/the door?
20. What did she do if she got sick? How often did that happen?

21. Was she prompt in the morning? Was she flexible about staying late or working overtime?
22. Did she ever lie to you? About what?

THE HIDDEN COSTS OF HIRING A NANNY

A nanny spends her days in your fabulous house, driving your fabulous car and helping out at your child's fabulous birthday party. Naturally, she expects fabulous perks. As one mother of three children put it, "Our nanny's birthday is a national holiday in our house, complete with the day off, presents, and a ritual celebration the night before."

Here's what you may have to pony up for, either to please your nanny or protect yourself:

Health insurance. It's expensive—anywhere from $50 to $220 a month—but you might offer to pay half of it. Many parents report paying for the medical costs of their uninsured nanny out of guilt anyhow. Call either your local HMO or the official insurance rep for the International Nanny Association: Eisenberg Associates in Boston, 800-777-5765. They can also arrange for disability and retirement benefits for your nanny.

Workers' compensation. This is a legal requirement for employers in many states; you may have to add a separate rider to your home-owner's policy to cover a nanny for an average of $10 to $25 a month. If you forgo workers' comp and your nanny injures her back hoisting your toddler, she can sue for damages.

Music, gym, art classes for the kids. Because few nannies take it upon themselves to stimulate the child as much as you will want.

Gifts. On her birthday, for her kids, when you return from vacation, and naturally, at Christmas. That doesn't include a Christmas bonus, which varies from half a week's pay to a week's pay.

Overtime pay. Standard baby-sitting rate in your area, from $5 to $10 an hour, for all those late nights at work.

Household Employment Taxes. Yes, we know a lot of people don't pay nanny taxes. But they should. All in all, it totals up to about another 17 percent of her salary. (For more information on filing your nanny's taxes, See "Your money's worth" on page 53.

Personal umbrella insurance. If you don't have this extra liability protection already, you should get it, now that a nanny and her many friends will be traipsing through your house (see Chapter 11, "Safeguarding Your Assets" for more information).

Car insurance. If part of your nanny's job is to drive the kids around in your car, make sure you inform your insurance rep. You may pay a premium to have her listed on the policy, but if you fail to tell your insurance company and she cracks up the car, you may not be covered. If she only drives your kids occasionally, with your permission, she may automatically be covered with no extra charge.

Infant and CPR training. The American Red Cross offers a five-hour Infant and Child CPR course for $50 (*www.redcross.org* has details); so do many local hospitals.

A contract. It should spell out general job duties, without being so specific that you can't ask for something (like ironing) that's not mentioned. It should discuss holidays, vacation, sick days, benefits, hours, salary, overtime, tax obligations, probationary period, frequency of review and terms of dismissal.

5

Harvard or Bust

What do you remember about your very first school experience? Back in the '50s and '60s, preschool—or nursery school, as it was known then—revolved around finger painting and play dough, sandbox struggles and show-and-tell. Your parents probably chose the preschool that was closest and cheapest. That's if they chose at all: Few American families opted to enroll their children in preschool back then, preferring to let the little ones stay home tied to mommy's apron strings.

Today 65 percent of children are attending preschool at the ages of 3 and 4—and some are starting as young as 18 months. Several states have recently adopted mandatory preschool programs, and others are expected to follow. Current research suggests that preschool is key to later learning. A recent study by the Carnegie Corporation proposed "universal access" to good programs for three- and four-year-olds, based on the fact that the brain learns easiest and best during the first few years of life, when it is growing fastest and making essential and permanent interconnections. Don't believe it? Children's brains double in weight by their first birthday and are three-fourths their adult size by the time they are 3.

The question is what sort of preschool—and there are more than 100,000 in the United States—you will choose for your child. Chances are you won't think much about it until you're on the playground with your adorable toddler and you hear other parents discussing the preschools in town. Reggio Emilia? You thought it was a cheese. Waldorf? You thought it was a salad. Suddenly you're plunged headlong into a hunting process you didn't think would hit until college.

Depending on where you live and the cutoff dates for entering elementary school in your town, each of your children may spend up to three years attending preschool. With tuition starting at about $2,000 and climbing as high as $8,000—on top of any child care costs—preschool is bound to take a heavy bite out of your budget. Your goal is to make sure all those dollars are spent on the best program for your child's needs.

Readiness, Not Reading

The point of preschool isn't to teach your child how to read and write at the tender age of 3. It's all about developing the crucial readiness skills that will enable him to succeed when he enters kindergarten. There's going to be plenty of time for the ABCs and 123s later. A good preschool focuses on expanding children's social, emotional, physical, and cognitive faculties—not on rote drilling that can stifle his exuberance and curiosity. As a recent announcement by the National Association of Elementary School Principals put it, "Children in the three to eight range acquire knowledge in ways that are significantly different from the way older children learn. Younger children learn best through direct sensory encounters with the world and not through formal academic processes. . . . Young children acquire knowledge by manipulating, exploring, and experimenting with real objects. They learn almost exclusively by doing, and through movement."

How Young Is Too Young?

Given the benefits of preschool—and weighing them against the costs—it's tough figuring out when your child should start. Many educators agree that 3 is the ideal age. At that point, most children can handle separation and toilet training, two major issues affecting school attendance. A 3-year-old is also usually willing and interested in doing things for himself, like putting on his own jacket and boots, or cleaning up a pile of toys. While some experts feel that 2-year-olds can get a lot out of a few hours of preschool each week, in many cases it's too stressful for children that young to be away from their regular caregivers. Hence the increasing popularity of "Mommy & Me" programs, which allow toddlers to socialize in their parents' presence.

Judging a Preschool Program

It's critical to begin hunting 6 to 12 months before your child will enroll, as the best programs fill up early. Check your local library, town hall, or community center for a list of all preschools in the area. Talk to friends and neighbors, but don't rule out—or accept—a program based on their opinions. Different schools suit different children. While a boot-camp atmosphere might suit the rambunctious boys next door, it could be all wrong for your artistic daughter.

It's essential to visit several preschools, so you have ample opportunity to compare. When you tour a program, make plenty of mental notes and then jot them down as soon as you leave. You want to consider both the individual pieces of information and your overall impression. Following are the elements of a good preschool:

A safe, comfortable, and appropriate physical environment. Everything doesn't have to be brand-new or state-of-the-art. But it does have to look as though someone who really understood children put the facility together. Some of the best preschools are conducted in the tightest spaces with the scarcest resources. The Roseville Community Preschool, held in a tiny concrete bungalow outside Sacramento, California, is widely hailed as a model program. Its director, Bev Bos, instructs parents to dress kids in old clothes that can get trashed while the children dye Easter eggs in November and

---

How much does preschool cost?

Here's what it costs to send a 3-year-old, five mornings a week from September to June, to an NAEYC-accredited preschool in six cities around the country.

Bluebonnet Montessori, Austin, Tex.: **$3,720**
Transitional Learning Center, New Rochelle, N.Y.: **$3,355**
Preschool Experience, Newton, Mass.: **$3,236**
Peach Tree Montessori, Ann Arbor, Mich.: **$4,590**
10th Street Preschool, Santa Monica, Calif.: **$4,950**
The Putnam Indian Field School, Greenwich, Conn.: **$7,345**

Which program is right for your kid?

Montessori. Reggio Emilia. "Developmentally appropriate practice," or DAP. As you look through brochures and listen to preschool directors prattle on, you'll get tossed a lot of mysterious terms. With more and more kids attending preschool, more and more kinds of preschools are popping up, many of them incorporating elements from several different philosophies. The first step in determining which is best for your kid is to know what all the terms mean:

Developmentally appropriate practice. Many preschools today emphasize a "child-centered" or "developmentally appropriate" curriculum. All this means is that the children, through their actions and requests, help direct the action. Instead of a nursery school teacher plotting out the day's events ahead of time, each morning is loosely structured into, say, "play time" and "snack time." Within those periods the teacher tends to follow the kids' lead. If a group of kids start to play with the toy kitchen, the teacher will enter into the play with them, perhaps seizing the opportunity to talk about cooking or nutrition.

Montessori. The Montessori method is developed from the work of Dr. Maria Montessori, an Italian doctor in the early 1900s who observed children free to do whatever they wanted in a well-ordered physical environment. She discovered that the kids returned to a "normal" state: They exhibited spontaneous self-discipline, love of order, concentrated attention, and interest in intellectual activity. Montessori schools today, to various degrees, aim to duplicate the environment of Dr. Montessori. Teachers are encouraged to "control the environment, not the child," to look at the child as an "unknown entity" and to allow the child's true nature to freely emerge. Unlike other nursery schools, Montessori classrooms often mix children of different ages. The International Montessori Accreditation Council (IMAC) was organized in 1994 as an umbrella agency and is the official accrediting body for Montessori schools.

Reggio Emilia. A few American preschools model their curriculum on the early childhood program in Reggio Emilia, Italy. For the past 25 years, this affluent northern Italian community has committed 12 percent of the town budget to providing high-quality child care for children 6 years old and younger. The central element of the Reggio Emilia approach is the emphasis on children's symbolic languages, including drawing, sculpture, dramatic play, and writing. Another important ingredient is parental involvement. The role of the environment is also key; Reggio Emilia teachers refer to the environment as "our third teacher" that fosters a sense of community. Classrooms open to a center piazza, kitchens are open to view, classrooms are connected with passageways or windows. Small groups of children are often involved in long-term projects, such as acting out a play. Teachers are encouraged to improvise and respond to children's predisposition to enjoy the unexpected.

Waldorf. There are about 125 Waldorf preschools in North America. They are based on the program developed by Austrian philosopher Rudolph Steiner in 1919. If you explore the Waldorf option, you will inevitably encounter the word *anthroposophy,* from the Greek for "human wisdom." Don't let the multisyllabic jargon throw you off. Steiner simply believed in awakening each child to his or her own "inner nature," so prizing imagination and freethinking above all else. Academics are deemphasized during the early years, and there is a great emphasis on the oral tradition; children learn to write before they learn to read. One unusual feature of Waldorf schools is that children, if they continue on, stay with the same teacher for 8 years in order to promote understanding and encouragement of each child's individual character. Waldorf schools also incorporate "eurythmy"—specific movements that correspond to particular musical notes or sounds, the idea being that it enhances coordination, as well as the ability to listen.

make snowballs out of shaving cream. A glimpse into Roseville's gleeful classroom shows that children feel happy, warm, and secure in the special little world she has created.

When you visit preschools, use your instincts as a guide. Are there cozy small sofas for children to curl up on? Are there toddler-sized potties and sinks so going to the bathroom won't be a struggle? Are there windows at ground level so kids can see what's happening outside? Are there a variety of play materials in decent shape? Are classrooms laid out in an interesting manner, with special areas for building, painting, dressing up, and other activities? Is the play-

14 key questions to ask a preschool director

1. What is the student/teacher ratio (7:1 is ideal)?
2. How do you compose a class? Are boys and girls balanced?
3. What sort of background do the teachers have?
4. Does the staff participate in continuing education programs?
5. Are you licensed by the state? Do you have national accreditation?
6. What are the curriculum's major elements?
7. What are your goals for each age group?
8. How do you handle separation?
9. How do you handle discipline?
10. How can parents get involved?
11. How are admissions decisions made?
12. May we talk to parents of children at your school about their experiences?
13. Are parents welcome to observe classes in session?
14. How is information exchanged with parents? Are there written reports, conferences, etc.?

ground in good condition, and is the equipment manageable for the youngest children?

A professional and nurturing staff. Like child care workers, preschool teachers run the gamut, from experts with graduate degrees to warm bodies whose alternative is flipping burgers. Preschool pay runs around $14,000 for starting full-time instructors to $24,000 for experienced teachers—so it's not surprising that it's hard to attract and retain good candidates. Ideally every staffer should have completed some coursework in early childhood education or be enrolled in a nearby college with a child development department. A good preschool encourages teachers to continue their education, and often pays for a portion of their tuition.

On a tour, pay close attention to the teachers' style. Are they dressed in sweats, splattered in paint, and clearly loving it? Are they kneeling down to the childrens' level to engage them fully? Is there a mix of younger and older teachers working together? Teachers should appear busy but calm; if they can't serve juice and crackers to 16 kids without snapping, then they're in the wrong place.

A fearless leader. Just as the president of a college or the headmaster of a private school sets the tone, so the preschool director embodies

---

Your money's worth

The minute your kid hits preschool, you have to label everything in sight: an extra set of clothes to stay at school, jackets, mittens, just about everything they wear out the door.

Worth it: Clothes Personalizer ($22.95, from Perfectly Safe, 800-837-5437). This palm-size stamper couldn't be easier to use. You insert whatever it is you're marking, squeeze, and it prints your kid's name in indelible black ink. It's good for 5,000 imprints and allows two lines of 15 characters each.

Not worth it: Iron-on labels (available at most stationery stores, for about $5 per 100). The problem is, they tend to peel off after only a few washings. Sure, you can always get around that by sewing them instead of ironing them on. But don't you have better things to do?

the program's spirit. Although her decisions may have to be ratified by a board of trustees consisting of parents, her influence is evident in every area of the school environment. Is she so entrenched in traditional methods that she isn't open to new ideas? Is she a strict disciplinarian who can't tolerate rambunctious kids? Does she hire only those teachers who conform to her standards? Many pre-schools are run by charismatic individuals who become legendary in their communities. It's important to meet the director on your visit, and spend a few minutes asking her about the program. You'll quickly get a feel for whether her style suits your family.

A high-quality curriculum. What do kids actually do at preschool? Anything that encourages active learning. Activities and experiences should include indoor and outdoor free play; gross and fine motor skills development; creative arts; music and movement; dramatic play; cooking; science and discovery; nature; sand and water play; and age-appropriate field trips. It's a long list, but consider the average preschooler's attention span. Few kids can color or build with blocks for half a day. A typical schedule should allow for structured and unstructured time, ideally in 15- to 30-minute intervals.

The right credentials. Naturally your child's preschool should have a state license, though as is the case with day-care centers, it's a lot easier to get a license in some states than in others. A better measure of a preschool's quality is whether it has been accredited by the National Association for the Education of Young Children. NAEYC sponsors a voluntary yet rigorous accreditation process in which it evaluates nearly every aspect of a preschool. You can find which schools have the stamp of approval in your area by visiting the group's website (*www.naeyc.org*) or by calling 800-424-2460. Unfortunately, only a tiny percentage of preschools have been accredited so far, though many more are in the process.

Getting In

Once you've found a few appealing preschool options, it's time to apply. The admissions process at many preschools is first-come, first-serve. Pay a $25 fee, fill out a sheet of paper, and you've got a spot. But in every community there are a handful of programs that require testing and interviews. No, your child needn't master a foreign language or draw like Degas. But he may need to demonstrate that he can sit still and pay attention during a brief story; get involved in playing with dolls or trucks or other toys; and respond appropriately to a few simple questions asked by an adult. You'd be surprised how much a preschool director can discover about your child during a half-hour observation.

Paying the Price

Given the importance of a quality preschool, you'll probably wind up paying more than you intended. How much? Possibly $3,000 or more for 5 mornings a week. Don't panic: There are ways to soften the blow to your wallet. Most tuition prices are based on a 5-day week; you might prefer to send your child 3 days a week, if it's an option, and save 40 percent of the cost. Some preschools offer tuition payment plans and/or financial assistance. Some even provide scholarships for a few promising children.

The going rate: The cost of a birthday blowout

N ow that Junior's circle of friends includes a whole new crop from preschool, the perfect party—for 30 or so kids—doesn't come cheap. After all, you may have to pony up for, well, a pony. Here, a sample tab for the coolest bash on the block:

	Albany, N.Y.	Austin, Tex.	Nashville, Tenn.	Sacramento, Calif.
Inflatable trampoline (a.k.a. "Moonwalk")	$178.00	$150.00	$130.00	$125.00
Streamers (500 feet)	2.59	1.15	3.59	3.25
Piñata (without candy filling)	10.97	9.95	9.50	9.99
Magician (40-minute show)	100.00	85.00	125.00	95.00
First-aid kit	11.99	7.69	14.98	7.79
Face painter (one hour)	110.00	75.00	52.00	95.00
Cotton-candy machine rental	91.70	86.00	52.00	35.00
Paper towels (12 rolls)	13.80	9.48	21.48	8.28
30 hot dogs and buns	12.84	9.54	9.72	9.84
Kool-Aid (3 gallons)	1.80	1.74	1.80	1.80
Bubble gum ice cream (2 gallons)	30.00	39.80	35.96	39.96
Chocolate cake (from bakery)	24.95	32.00	26.75	29.95
Mylar balloons (one dozen)	42.00	36.00	36.00	37.20
Extra-strength Tylenol (24 caplets)	3.99	4.19	3.99	3.79
Total cost	634.63	547.54	522.77	501.85

Once you've agreed to fork over thousands of dollars to a pre-school, what if your kid hates it? What if you get transferred? What if he gets dismissed for biting another student? Most of the time you're on the hook for the whole year's tuition. But an increasing number of preschools are doing what private schools have long done—offering tuition insurance. A typical tuition-refund plan costs about 3 percent of tuition. If your school has a policy with A.W.G. Dewar (781-380-8770), for instance, you'll be reimbursed for 100 percent of the unused yearly fees if your child withdraws due to a physical disability. If a child withdraws for nonmedical reasons (such as moving) parents receive 60 percent. Tuition insurance has become popular enough that some preschools will automatically bill you for it unless you request otherwise.

Ten Things Your Child's Preschool Won't Tell You

1 *We've got revolving doors.*

Given the low salaries and lack of benefits, preschool teachers often jump ship when a better offer surfaces. But some schools do have a knack for hanging on to talented teachers, by providing more competitive financial packages and/or an excellent work environment. Ask the director what percentage of faculty have been on staff for five or more years. If the answer is less than half, you're in the wrong place.

2 *Training? What Training?*

While the National Association for the Education of Young Children administers accreditations for preschools, no specific certification is required for teachers. Some have graduate degrees in early childhood education; others' chief qualification is weekend babysitting. Many preschool teachers are working toward their master's at a local college. The point is dedication to a professional career. If a preschool encourages faculty members to pursue their own education in the field, it's committed to high standards.

3 *We haven't changed our curriculum since Eisenhower left office.*

Remember the cute Thanksgiving turkey you made in nursery school by dipping your hand in brown paint? Or the bracelet you made out of colored macaroni? You may find it charming when your child comes home with the same projects—or you may wonder if there's anything new under the sun. When screening schools, inquire about curriculum change. Does the director belong to any organizations that keep her abreast of the latest developments? Are teachers free to deviate from the standard pattern? Can they freely improvise according to the children's interests? Flexibility and progress are keys to a successful program.

4 *Working mothers are pariahs.*

Want to get involved with your child's class? Want to get plenty of feedback from his teachers? It's not going to happen if you're a working mother and all class meetings and conferences are held smack in the middle of the morning. Moreover, many schools put up notices rather than send home memos—so if your caregiver takes the kid to school that day, you may not have a clue as to what's going on. Talk to parents at the preschool and find out how—or if—working mothers can participate in activities. Ask if they hold parent/teacher conferences in early mornings or evenings. Some schools hold events in the evenings to encourage both parents to attend. Also make sure your caregiver will be welcome at functions hosted by and for parents.

5 *Our facility is a petri dish for disease.*

If your child hasn't been exposed to group day care, expect her to bring home at least half a dozen colds during the first year of pre-school, along with a couple of ear infections, a case of strep throat, and a virus or two. Check the school handbook for the policy on bringing sick children to school—or sending them home. Then ask the director about absentee rates and about any recent epidemics and how they were handled.

6 *Tuition costs are only the beginning.*

So you're paying $3,000 in tuition. Now you've got to finance a slush fund for all the extras: teachers' gifts, mothers' coffee, bake sale, book fair, field trip fees, and so on. Then there's the annual appeal, to which you'll be expected to make at least a minimal contribution. And don't forget the fund-raising gala, where you can open your wallet half a dozen times (tickets, auction items, raffles, etc.) Odds are you're looking at $500 or more on top of that $3,000 bill.

7 *We weren't kidding about potty training.*

In most states, by law, unless a facility is licensed to change tod-

dlers' diapers, teachers are not allowed to do this dirty job. Some
schools stipulate this in your contract, stating that your child will
have a certain length of time (usually 6 to 8 weeks) after school
opens to complete potty training. Meanwhile, if your kid soils his
underpants, you'll be called to drive over and clean him up. Should
Christmas roll around and your kid is still in Pampers or pullups,
he can be kicked out.

8   There's nothing voluntary about volunteering.

You might have your hands full with work and family. But some
preschools believe every parent is an extra set of helping hands.
Can you serve as a chaperone on a field trip? Sell books at the book
fair? Bake cookies for the holiday party? Festoon crepe paper for
the fund-raiser? If you intend to drop your kid off and head for the
office (or the gym), these are not the schools for you.

9   Our admissions "policy" is quid pro quo.

More and more top preschools have agonizingly long waiting lists.
How do you crowbar your way in? Don't be fooled into thinking
that your little sweetheart can secure a spot based on her adorable
qualities alone. It helps to know a trustee or a heavily involved
parent. It helps if your name is DuPont. It also helps if you have a
specific skill to offer—many preschools could use a pro bono lawyer, nurse, accountant, or financial adviser. Don't hesitate to let the
admissions officer know how you could "participate" in the school
community.

10   Special needs aren't diagnosed or treated.

Privately funded preschools, unlike public elementary schools,
have no requirement or provision to actively look for children with
learning disabilities, speech disorders, or behavioral abnormalities.
Many preschool teachers overlook these problems, expecting them
to gradually disappear before kindergarten. If you suspect your
young child—or your child's classmate—needs special attention,
don't count on his preschool teachers to acknowledge or treat the
problem.

Part 3

THE BIG-TICKET ITEMS

If there's one thing that's worse than driving a lousy car, it's driving a lousy car with kids in it. Staying in a crappy hotel room is bad enough; with kids it's torture. And watching your kid's science fair project disappear when the computer crashes will make you long for the days of dioramas and papier-mâché.

Face it. You can't afford to be an ignorant consumer. The sea change that occurred the moment your child was born seeps into every aspect of your life. You need to get smart about what car and computer you buy, where you go on vacation, even whether or not you buy a cell phone. But major purchases require major research, even more so now that there's one more person laying a claim on your every dollar. Armed with the following information, you'll be able to quickly develop a strategy to spend less than you thought and get more than you bargained for.

6

Curbing Your Cash Flow

It will happen. The kids will finally be wrestled to bed and your mind will start to wander. If only we didn't have to pay for preschool, you'll think, we could go to Venice for two weeks—just the two of us. Or buy one of those home spas. Or put the money into an early retirement account.

Too late. Preschool it is. Unfortunately, trade-offs loom large in the middle years. There will come a time when you have to forgo Disney World to put some money in a college fund, or you may have to live in a house you're not wild about because it's in a good school district.

Still, you *can* keep the trade-offs to a minimum. How? Focus on the big purchases. You don't have time to track every dollar that flows in and out of the house, but if you do your homework where it matters—buying a car, for instance—you'll probably have enough left over for that trip to Disney World.

Or better yet, that trip to Venice.

Here's what you need to know about four of the biggest—and potentially most confusing—expenses you'll have to face.

Deals on Wheels: The Best Strategy for Buying (or Leasing) a Family Car

OK, so you've given up your dreams of driving a sleek late-model sports car. For now. What you need is safety, reliability, and room for a couple of car seats—and no sticker shock.

You've got two things going for you: the used-car market is better than ever, and whether you buy or lease, the Internet is a godsend.

WHICH CAR DO YOU WANT?

As you look for a car, bear in mind its true costs. Don't just look at the price. The real cost of owning a car has less to do with its initial price than with factors like how much maintenance and repair the car needs, how much gas it uses, how expensive it is to insure, and—significantly—how much it depreciates before you sell it or trade it in.

If you want to research cars on your own, a great place to start is **Microsoft CarPoint** (*www.carpoint.msn.com*). Choose from among several categories, and as you make your selections, Car-Point produces a list that meets your specifications. Click on one of the cars, and you get in-depth coverage.

As you narrow in on a few favorite models, check out **Intelli-Choice** (*www.intellichoice.com*). This California company offers well-researched projections of what cars will cost you to own over time. One negative: You have to pay for some of the IntelliChoice data.

You may want to check how a prospective purchase did on a recent government crash test by visiting the **National Highway Traffic Safety Administration**'s website (*www.nhtsa.dot.gov*). If you're in the mood for it, you can even download a movie of your model crashing into a wall.

GETTING THE BEST PRICE

Next, arm yourself for negotiations. (Whatever you do, don't pay the "sticker price" that's pasted on a car's window. Unless you are buying a Saturn, which has a no-haggle policy, the sticker price is fiction; you are expected to negotiate.) **Kelley Blue Book** (available at your library or at *www.kbb.com*) and **Edmund's** car buyer's guide (at your library or *www.edmunds.com*) can give you "dealer invoice prices," or what the dealer paid for the car, not only for base models but also for each individual option. Edmund's site also has data on the "holdback" money that manufacturers pay to dealers for every sale, information that will certainly add to your leverage during negotiations. Or you can hire a service to get much of this information for you, like Long Beach, California–based **Fighting Chance** (800-288-1134 or *www.fightingchance.com; $24.95* and up) or **Consumer Reports New Car Price Service** (800-933-5555; $12 and up).

Now that you know what the dealer paid for the car and how much it will cost to own, you're ready to negotiate. Or not. If you really can't face a car sales rep in person, find a buyer's agent who will do your negotiating for you. **AutoAdvisor** (800-326-1976 or *www.autoadvisor.com*), a Seattle car researching and buying

---

What's the safest car on the road?

These are confusing times for people who want to buy a "safe" car. The same auto executives and bureaucrats who insisted for years that we should all pay extra for vehicles with one, two, or even more air bags, plus antilock brakes, now tell us that we should be allowed to disable the air bags because they might hurt our kids. And they're even confiding that those fancy computerized brakes don't make much difference.

What is safe? Does anybody know? Do you head for a Volvo or Saab with a vague impression that Swedish cars are sensible and safe? Score one for relentless safety salesmanship.

The fact is, bigger is better. The larger the car, the safer you are. On this, the numbers and most of the experts agree. "The bottom line is you want to trade size for anything else," says Virginia Commonwealth University economics professor and auto-safety researcher George Hoffer. One of the first researchers to argue that air bags and antilock brakes were overrated, Professor Hoffer routinely annoys insurance industry and government safety experts with his unorthodox opinions. But on this, he's mainstream.

"You take a car that is large, and it has a built-in advantage in multicar crashes," says Kim Hazelbaker, senior vice president at the Highway Loss Data Institute, a research arm of the insurance industry known as HLDI (pronounced "Hildy").

HLDI's safety rankings use a scale where 100 is average. They're scored a bit like golf: the lower the number, the better. So, for example, a score of 34 for injury claims means there were 66 percent fewer accidents involving injuries for that model than average. According to the latest statistics, the models with the best records for injury claims are: Ford f-250 series pickups (38), the Buick Roadmaster wagon (39), GMC 2500 series 4×4 pickups (40), the Chevy Suburban 1500 (41), GMC's Yukon 4×4 (43), GMC's 1500 four-wheel drive (43), and the Oldsmobile Cutlass Ciera (44).

When it comes to fatalities, a much less frequent occurrence, the most recent data show these cars as the five safest: Ford Windstar van (25), Mercury Sable wagon (29), Lexus ES 300 (30), Cadillac Fleetwood (32), Volvo 850 (32), and Chevy Lumina APV (34).

For information on how other models have fared, call the Insurance Institute for Highway Safety—parent group of HLDI—at 703-247-1500, or visit its Web page at *www.hwysafety.org*.

service, for instance, guarantees the lowest price available. It'll cost you $155 to $395, but at least you can be confident it's working in your behalf. Online services, such as **AutoVantage** (*www.netmarket.com*), have a similar deal. **Auto-By-Tel** (*www.autobytel.com*) can also eliminate some of the haggling, but eventually they still hand you off to "accredited" dealers with whom you eventually have to deal in person.

If you truly hate haggling with car dealers, consider a new strategy: negotiating by fax. Take Mark James, a Houston software consultant. When he decided to go shopping for a Plymouth Grand Voyager, he composed a terse letter ticking off the options he wanted, the colors he was willing to accept, and a fairly detailed estimate of the dealer's invoice price (that is, the price the dealer paid to Plymouth to get the van on the lot), and he fired it off to the fleet or sales manager of 15 dealers in and around Houston and Dallas. He soon had quotes from 5, and ended up paying just $100 over invoice—about $2,500 off the sticker price.

COMING UP WITH THE MONEY

Unless you pay cash, you've got three options: Financing from the car manufacturer, from your bank, or from a credit union. The bank with your checking account is likely to give you a break— especially if you have the monthly payment automatically deducted. Some lenders offer "balloon payment" financing. After the term, you can pay a hefty balloon payment and keep the car, refinance it, or return it.

While most banks still charge more for used-car loans, many are making the same rate available for both used cars and new cars. Bank of America, for instance, eliminated the half-percentage-point spread between its new- and used-car rates. The DOT Federal Credit Union in Poughkeepsie, New York, which once limited its used-car loans to three years, now lends money for five years for some used cars. Ford Motor Credit has gotten more flexible about terms as well.

Don't have a lot of cash for a down payment? Bank of America and some credit unions will now go as high as 100 percent.

On the other hand, maybe you don't even want a car loan at all. Several lenders, including many credit unions, have started offering

Best piano-shopping strategy

You're convinced that your five-year-old's relentless humming betrays a fervor for Mozart. Or you've heard about all the scientific research linking early piano training with improved brainpower. Whatever your reason, if you enlist your kid for piano lessons and he actually likes it, be prepared to add a very large item to your shopping list. A decent upright piano costs between $2,500 to $4,000; grand pianos start at about two and a half times more. But there are alternatives.

For parents who fear that playing "Chopsticks" is as good as the kid's going to get, renting is a good option. Many piano retailers offer plans that allow you to rent a piano on a monthly basis; some even let all or part of that money apply toward the purchase of a piano. Westport/Fairfield Pianos and Organs in Fairfield, Connecticut, for example, rents out about 150 pianos, including vertical Yamahas and Young Changs, at $75 a month. The delivery and pickup fee ($75 each) must be paid up front, but you'll get credit for the first six months' payment ($525), which you can then redeem against the price of a new or used piano.

Used uprights sell for an average of $1,500; baby grands for $4,000 to $6,000. But you should bring the piano teacher with you to evaluate the instrument's quality. Or call the Piano Technicians Guild (816-753-7747) and ask for a tuner-technician in your area who can go with you (fees vary). Used pianos may be either rebuilt or reconditioned. Rebuilt means a complete repair and replacement of necessary parts, resulting in a piano that should measure up to similar new models by the same manufacturer; reconditioned means a piano has been repaired and adjusted for its maximum performance. Chickoring, Baldwin, and Steinway are all good brands to look for.

If you're buying new, Baldwin has long been the poorman's Steinway, which is no doubt why it was the best seller in 1997. Juilliard students use Yamaha uprights. Another label to consider, according to Marc Silverman, chairman of the piano department at Manhattan School of Music, is Petrof from Czechoslovakia. The company offers good factory-made pianos with some handcraftsmanship.

In any case, don't lowball this purchase. Julie Whaley, spokeswoman for the Music Teachers Association, says that if you give the child the best piano you can afford, he's more likely to grow to love it. "It's important for children to have quality instruments," Whaley explains. "If it doesn't sound right, they'll become discouraged."

"auto equity" products that let you borrow against your home to finance your car. You'll get the home-equity rate, plus all the tax advantages that a second mortgage affords you, and the bank won't require a home appraisal, since it views the automobile as the primary collateral.

Whatever kind of loan you get, you'll want a bumper-to-bumper warranty, which is available on most new cars these days.

How to pay for private school

D rugs. Crime. Teachers who can't spell, much less interest your kids. Yes, public schools have taken their share of hits lately. So we're never surprised when we hear parents talking about going the private school route.

Let's hope they're prepared to pay up.

Generally, religious schools are the least expensive; Catholic school tuition can be under $2,000 for elementary school students. Nonsectarian schools tend to be more expensive; exclusive schools cost the most. For a student entering in September 1998, the tuition at Blessed Sacrament School in San Diego, California, was $3,640 for a fourth-grader. That same fourth-grader would have had to pay $6,200 to go to Delmar Pines private elementary school. If he'd gone to exclusive Francis Parker in nearby Mission Hills, the tuition would have been $9,500.

Financial aid and scholarships. While there are no federal programs for private school financial aid, there is definitely money out there. In the 1996–97 school year, 906 member schools of the National Association of Independent Schools awarded $464 million of need-based financial aid to 17 percent of their students, with the average award being $5,494. Roughly a third of the schools offered $13.3 million in merit-based scholarships, with an average of $2,228. In other words, your best, and usually only, resource for aid during these years is the school itself. The school financial aid office should be able to give you the details about how much money the school has to offer, how you might qualify for it, and any information on outside funding sources (such as local scholarships) that are available.

Your first step will be to fill out a Parent Financial Statement (PFS) form, issued by the School and Student Service for Financial Aid in Princeton, New Jersey. Even if you're applying to more than one school, you only need to fill out one form—the SSS will send copies out to the various institutions. Which is lucky for you, because the process is arduous. One couple in Brooklyn, New York, recently got aid for their twins, who were entering sixth grade at Packer Collegiate Institute, a nearby private school. "The form teases apart your finances in an incredibly detailed way," says the twin's mother. "We thought we'd just look at our tax forms and fill in our incomes, but they want to know all sorts of things you might not be reporting on your taxes, like child care or other household expenses." It took them one entire weekend.

SSS will process your information and come up with an estimated family contribution, which gets sent on to the school. Various factors contribute to this assessment—among them, your income, assets, family size, your age, and the number of children attending tuition-charging schools. Also included are any assets in your child's name. If you're divorced or separated, the noncustodial parent may be asked to fill out a separate form, but this differs from school to school.

Schools do have the power to recalculate your contribution, and may do so based on issues like how much you think you can actually pay, or the cost of living in your area. This was a big help for the Brooklyn twins. Packer took into account the fact that living expenses in Brooklyn are much greater than elsewhere, their Mom says. "They definitely recognized the increased burden of paying two tuitions," she adds.

Loans. Beware a snazzy new breed of loan designed specifically for kids in private school. True, they are convenient, and it's fairly easy to get approved. The catch: "Frankly, these private school loans aren't great deals," says Mark Kantrowitz, the creator of the Financial Aid Information Page *(www.finaid.org).* In fact, many will cost you far more than a bank loan.

Take the Plato Junior loan offered by Educap Inc. It's "a convenient, flexible and affordable loan program," its marketing materials promise. Well, convenient, perhaps. But affordable? The rate is prime plus 3.7 percent—that worked out to 12.2 percent in mid-1998—and there's a 6 percent "origination fee" just for taking out the loan. Let's say you borrowed $10,000 this way. Pay it off in 60 installments over five years and you've coughed up over $4,000 for the loan. By comparison, a $10,000 home equity loan through First American Bank in Chicago recently carried an 8.5 percent interest rate; pay it off in five years and the interest is just $2,300. Even a comparable unsecured personal loan from the same bank carried a more attractive 11.75 percent rate. The lesson? Unless a special school loan beats a home equity or personal loan at your own bank, forget it.

SHOULD YOU BUY USED?

Last time we checked, the average new car lost 15 to 20 percent of its value the moment you nosed it out the dealership door. Which helps explain why the used-car market is booming: Four million cars hit the "preowned" market in 1997, up from 3 million in 1995, according to J.D. Power and Associates, a market research firm.

If you choose used, look for **cars with warranties.** A number of automakers, including Lexus, Toyota, GM, and Nissan, are promising to make buying a used car less of a gamble: They offer extra warranty protection on what they call "certified" used cars. Certified cars are usually less than four years old and typically are coming off lease or were part of a corporate fleet. And unlike some warranties sold by dealers, these warranties are good anywhere in the country.

How can you be sure what a used car is really worth? Again, check out **Edmund's** and the **Kelley Blue Book** for reasonable retail prices for your area.

SHOULD YOU LEASE A CAR?

Conventional wisdom says that if you lease a car, you'll have nothing to show for your money when the term of the lease is up.

But that ignores the "opportunity cost" inherent in buying: The money you pay up front for the car could be bringing a healthy return as part of your investment portfolio. Conversely, if you foresee owning the same car for seven years or more, you'll save money by buying. That's because with a lease, you walk away from a car just when depreciation slows and—under long-term financing—equity begins to build.

Here's what you should know before you decide.

THE ADVANTAGES OF LEASING

Low down payments and monthly payments. Even though many advertised lease deals assume a down payment, you can often get the dealer to limit or even waive it just by asking. You may only have to come up with $1,000 to $2,000 for fees, the first month's payment, and a refundable security deposit. Sales tax is usually paid monthly. If you buy a car and finance it, you could easily put 10 percent of the purchase price down, as well as 6 percent to 8 percent sales tax—perhaps $3,400 on a $30,000 car. Monthly payments on a lease are low, since you are only paying off the car's depreciation—not its full value.

Easy turnover. Assuming your car is in good shape when your two or four years are up, just stroll in to the dealer, hand over the keys, and drive out with a brand-new car and a fresh lease arrangement. You don't have to bother with selling the car or haggling with a dealer over trade-in value.

The summer vacation

Can't figure out where to take the kids? Your answer is likely to be on the Great Outdoor Recreation Pages website *(www.gorp.com)*. It has everything you need to know to plan your outdoor vacation to parks in the United States and around the world, from where to go, whom to call, what to bring (and where to get it) and what to do once you're there.

Another great source of ideas is *Family Travel Forum*, a newsletter with trip suggestions, as well as reviews of travel gear such as kids' carry-ons (212-665-6124 or *www.familytravelforum.com;* $48 for 10 issues).

Bigger tax write-offs for business use. If you are deducting a portion of your car's depreciation from your taxes, which you can only do if you are using the car for your business, you will be able to deduct substantially more if you lease. Interest paid on loans to purchase a car is not deductible. But when you lease, you can deduct depreciation as well as the implicit financing costs. The IRS does, however, limit depreciation deductions for certain luxury cars.

Flashy wheels. You get to drive a new, or nearly new, car all the time. This can be a real plus, especially when two or three years of spilled juice and hauling bikes have taken their toll on your car.

THE DISADVANTAGES OF LEASING

No equity. Unlike traditional financing, you can't look forward to the day when the payments will stop and you can drive your own car free and clear.

Lack of flexibility. You pay a big penalty if you want out of the lease before the full two- or three-year term—possibly several extra months of payments. If you foresee a move, more kids, a divorce, or a new job, or you don't have a clear idea where you will be in two or three years, don't lease.

Mileage penalties. Most leases charge an extra 12 or 15 cents for each mile you drive over a certain limit. Typically the lease agreement grants 15,000 miles per year. One way to avoid the mileage charge is to buy more miles at a reduced rate up front. (If you drive substantially less than the agreed-upon miles, however, you may be paying for depreciation you are not causing.) Also, you'll have to pay for any damage to the car beyond normal wear and tear when you turn it in. If you routinely cart around carpools of kids, a few dogs, and an entire beach party, there's a good chance you will inflict damage that you'll have to pay for later. Ironically, you should also consider buying if you keep your car in immaculate condition. That way you can build up some equity and take advantage of its spotless interior.

Insurance may come up short. If you total a leased car or it gets stolen, your insurance will only reimburse you for the car's market value, which might not cover what you still owe on your lease. You can

What you should know about amusement parks

Only suckers pay full price. While you're waiting in line at the entrance gate, go through your wallet and pull out every credit card and organizational membership ID you can find. Chances are that at least one of them will cut the cost of entry. Discounts flourish at theme parks because admissions account for only part of their revenue. At Six Flags Great America in Gurnee, Illinois, for instance, American Automobile Association membership gets you $4 off admission every day except Wednesday—when it's $12 off.

They're too popular. Show up at the theme park of your choice after 11 A.M. and you might not even get into the parking lot. If you do, you might not be able to get onto your favorite rides. Want to stay one step ahead of the crowds? You'd better have a plan. Hit all the most popular rides first thing, before lines have formed. Find out when the place is the least packed—and it's not when you might think. At Disney World in the summer, for instance, weekend crowds tend to be relatively sparse, since most families drive to Florida, leaving the weekends for traveling rather than touring.

It doesn't pay to spend the night. While families who stay at Disney World have advantages, like early admission to a different theme park each morning, they pay a steep premium. Although nightly rates at Disney World start at $74 for a double, those rooms get snapped up quickly. The next-cheapest accommodations start at $129 and go up to more than $1,000. Tack on airfare and meals, and you might as well be taking the kids to Rome. Are there cheaper rooms? Yes. There's a Comfort Inn and a Ramada Inn, situated just 2 and 6 miles, respectively, from Disney World's main gate, with discounted room rates of $46 and $42. Restaurants outside the gates tend to be a lot cheaper, as well.

You can buy your way to the front of the line. At Universal Studios in Orlando, $110 will get you 5 VIP hours and preferred access to 7 attractions. At Disneyland you can buy a 5-day Flex Passport ($68), which will get you into the park 90 minutes early one day, or you can spring for a private VIP Tour ($240 per person for 4 hours) in order to swing plum seats at the most densely packed performances and, reportedly, get faster access to rides. Steven Weil, a retailer from Fair Lawn, New Jersey, forked over extra dough so he, his wife, and two of their kids could enjoy the privilege of strolling on Universal's red carpet. "There was a woman leading us around," Weil says. "We were a small group of about 10 people, and she took us through back doors, through side doors, to the head of every line. We got a lot of dirty looks, but we didn't care—we didn't have to wait on line. It was well worth the money."

Don't assume it's safe. While serious injuries at amusement parks are rare, some states—Missouri, Montana, North and South Dakota, Alabama, and Kansas—do not regulate rides at all. A handful of others—California, Rhode Island, Washington, D.C., and Mississippi—regulate traveling carnivals but not permanent ones. Probably the safest states are Florida and Pennsylvania, both of which employ full-time inspectors who do nothing but evaluate rides for safety. Still, if it looks dangerous, don't take a chance. Some of these rides, especially water slides, "require strength, physical agility, and control," says

Anne McHugh, an attorney who has represented injury victims. "Yet there is the attitude that it's all safe. They sell this as amusement, entertainment, and fun. There's an illusion that it's safe for a 5-year-old, a pregnant lady, and an 85-year-old man."

buy extra "gap coverage" to protect against this (some lease deals include it automatically).

HOW TO NEGOTIATE THE BEST CAR LEASE

Auto lease talk, whether in a newspaper ad or a lease contract, is a language unto itself. Capitalized cost reduction, residual values, money factors—this balderdash doesn't just seem as though it's intended to give car dealers an advantage over you. It is.

"This is a $100 billion business designed to keep people from doing what's in their best interest," admits Drew Talbot, a director of marketing of Oxford Resources, one of the largest independent lease-financing companies. "The newspaper ads are going to confuse you—they are basically designed to confuse you. The large print giveth, the small print taketh away."

But really, lease agreements needn't leave you confused. We'll explain here the main things you need to know. Then, to confirm that you're getting a good deal, fill out the leasing worksheet below. It'll show you the true bottom line: the net interest rate on your deal.

Forget the monthly payments for now. Your dealer will try to distract you with all kinds of talk about "low monthly payments." Ignore it. The first thing you need to do once you've decided what model you want to lease is negotiate the purchase price of the car. Even though you're not buying the car itself, you have the opportunity to negotiate its price down, which—as we explain below—will ultimately cut your monthly payments and your total cost of leasing. Approach this like you would any car negotiation. Find out what the dealer paid for the car—known as the "invoice price"—either from a book at the library such as *Pace Guides* or a website such as *www.edmunds.com* or Cendant Corp.'s consumer site, *www. cuc.com*. Negotiate up from the invoice price, allowing the dealer a reasonable profit. The best negotiators will get within a few hundred dollars of the invoice price on a high-volume or inexpensive car, or within $1,000 on a pricier model. Once you settle on a price, stick with it.

You should also find out the car's "residual" value, or what it's expected to be worth when you give it back, by checking out CarWizard on *www.leasesource.com*. In every case, make sure you're in a closed-end lease, which prevents the residual value from changing over the life of the lease.

Understand how all the numbers are tied together. Your monthly payments on a lease will essentially pay for three things: (1) the depreciation in the value of the car while it's in your possession—in other words, the difference between the purchase price and the preset residual value of the car; (2) the interest on the money it took for the finance company to buy the car from the dealer; and (3) the dealer's profit.

That means your monthly payments can be reduced in several ways: first, by lowering the purchase price through negotiation or by applying a manufacturer's incentive to the cost of the car; second, by raising the preset residual value, which is often negotiable; third, by lowering the interest rate—which is usually the result of a manufacturer's incentive program. The key is to get the dealer,

---

Brace yourself

Abby Wilberding of Grosse Pointe, Michigan, made her first trip to the orthodontist when she was 6. Her father, Frank, figures he's looking at a 6-year course of treatment costing more than $4,000. "Orthodontia used to be much more reactive," he says. "Once your teeth were in, the doctor would straighten them out. But now they do a lot of strategic work to make room for permanent teeth before they come in."

Luckily, orthodontists aren't going to demand all the money up front. Jeffrey Geller of Pueblo, Colorado, is typical in that he gets 25 percent of his fee up front and then lets parents pay off the rest in installments. However, if you've got $4,000 laying around and want to pay off your bill all at once, that will earn you a 10 percent discount.

Frank Wilberding has another way to knock a full third off the price of orthodontia: his employer's flexible-spending account. Each year, he can set aside $2,000 from his salary, pretax. That money can be used for nonreimbursable medical expenses, including orthodontia. So far, he's saved $800 in taxes.

the carmaker, and the finance company to sacrifice their profits in order to lower your monthly payment.

But watch out, because there are ways to lower monthly payments that require them to sacrifice nothing. They may get you to pay part of the leasing costs up front. It's called a down payment, or in leasing terms, "capitalized cost reduction," and it can make all the difference in the world. Sure, the monthly payment is low if you hand over $2,500 or trade in your used car, worth $3,000, before driving out the door. Don't let the low monthly payment fool you into thinking you got a deal. Likewise, some dealers will

---

The going rate: camping out

There are some parents who relish the thought of packing the family in the van, driving straight through the night to a national park, spending days locating bear tracks and nights getting to know the terrain of a small patch of ground intimately. Then there are parents who figure camping out is a hotel without cable-TV. All kids, however, want to go. Here's what it will cost:

	Vail, Colo.	Portland, Ore.	Washington, D.C.	Madison, Wis.	Montgomery, Ala.
Deep Woods Off bug repellant	$ 4.63	$ 5.99	$ 4.39	$ 5.99	$ 3.90
Four Patagonia Cinchilla Polarfleece vests	$ 296.00	$ 296.00	$ 296.00	$ 200.00	$ 340.00
Five pounds honey (to distract bears)	$ 9.35	$ 9.99	$ 9.65	$ 11.45	$ 9.70
Dr. Bronner's soap	$ 4.00	$ 4.00	$ 4.00	$ 4.00	$ 4.00
Two small lightweight Gregory Reality backpacks	$ 430.00	$ 430.00	$ 430.00	$ 430.00	$ 430.00
Post-trip chiropractor fee	$ 44.00	$ 47.00	$ 65.00	$ 40.00	$ 35.00
North Face Cumulus Tent	$ 395.00	$ 395.00	$ 385.00	$ 395.00	$ 395.00
Motorola Talkabout plus one walkie talkie	$ 149.00	$ 135.00	$ 136.00	$ 135.00	$ 159.00
Petzel Micro Headlamp	$ 24.00	$ 24.00	$ 24.00	$ 24.00	$ 29.95
Deck of cards	$ 2.49	$ 2.09	$ 1.89	$ 2.50	$ 1.89
Swiss Army Knife (Huntsman)	$ 40.00	$ 42.95	$ 33.00	$ 33.00	$ 47.00
Five pounds trail mix	$ 19.95	$ 22.95	$ 17.45	$ 17.95	$ 33.95
Glad Trash Bags (15 tall kitchen)	$ 2.59	$ 2.00	$ 2.09	$ 1.85	$ 1.99
Nearest hotel room	$ 101.76	$ 101.76	$ 101.76	$ 101.76	$ 101.76
Totals	$1522.77	$1518.73	$1510.23	$1402.50	$1593.14

raise your residual value (thus reducing the amount of depreciation you're paying for) if you promise to drive the car only 10,000 miles a year. Everyone's happy, right? Yeah, if you don't mind leaving your car at home for your next summer vacation—or later shelling out the thousands of dollars it will cost you if you've driven more miles you contracted for.

Compute the net interest rate. If one expensive add-on pops up every time you push another back down, how can you evaluate how good a lease deal you're getting? By boiling all the variables down to a single number that can be compared across various lease deals. Modeling our system on IntelliChoice's, we calculate the net interest rate, which essentially measures how much you are paying above the cost of depreciation.

Here's how to evaluate your net interest rate: Compare it with the rate that banks offer on auto loans. Unless the net interest rate is as good as or better than the bank's—incentive leases will often beat the bank by three or more percentage points—consider walking away from the deal.

A. Monthly payment. Don't include taxes or license fees. $_____

B. Capitalized cost. The negotiated price of the car minus any
   dealer and manufacturer discounts. $_____

C. Net capitalized cost. The negotiated price minus any down
   payment (a.k.a. cap cost reduction) and minus the value
   of any trade-in. $_____

D. Residual value. The preset value of the car at the end of the
   lease. $_____

E. Lease term. Number of months.   _____

F. Subtract D from C. How much the car will depreciate in
   value during the term of the lease. $_____

G. Divide F by E. How much the car will depreciate per month. $_____

H. Subtract G from A. The amount of interest you will pay per
   month. $_____

I. Add C and D. $_____

J. Divide H by I. The so-called money factor.   _____

K. Multiply J by 2,400. The base interest rate.   _____

L. Multiply any up-front "acquisition fee" by .0044 for a 24-
   month lease   _____,

by .0032 for a 36-month lease   _____,

by .0026 for a 48-month lease.   _____

M. Multiply the lease-end "disposition fee" by .0036 for a 24-

   month lease   _____,

   by .0022 for a 36-month lease   _____,

   by .0015 for a 48-month lease.   _____

N. Add K, L, and M. Your NET INTEREST RATE; compare it with

   your local bank's auto loan rates.   _____%

Biting the Bullet: Computer Shopping Strategies

Some expenses are brand-new to the 1990s, like the cost of cyber-space. Lynn and Doug Borck, parents of two in Chappaqua, New York, resisted getting a computer until their daughter was in fifth grade and their son in third. Lynn admits: "We were the last hold-outs." That first machine set them back $2,000. But when their kids asked about going online to help do their homework, the Borcks quickly determined that their three-year-old computer was obsolete. The new one cost $2,500, for starters. Increasing the number of outlets in their home office and enlarging their fuse box was another $450. A designated modem line cost $25 a month. And then they had to fork out $19.95 a month to their Internet provider.

If your kids are 4 to 7 years old, you can probably spend a lot less than the Borcks. Instead of going top-of-the-line, get a low-priced model and see how much it really gets used. If you spend the minimum now, you won't feel so guilty if it gathers dust. Alternatively, if it turns out to be the plaything of choice at your house, you can more readily justify replacing it after a year or so with a more powerful model if you don't spend too much now. Don't overspend on software, either; a lot of it gets used once and then ignored. Instead, buy a handful of titles from top developers such as Broderbund, IBM's Edmark division, or Humongous Entertainment.

Hewlett-Packard makes an excellent $900 computer. Its Pavilion model 6330 is powered by a processor that runs at 300 megahertz. It also has a 4-gigabyte hard drive, 48 megabytes of memory, a CD-ROM drive, and a fast 56-kilobit modem. Though you'll have to spend an additional $200 or so for a 14-inch monitor, the package still checks in at $1,100.

If your kids are older, say 7 to 11 years old, first check to see what kind of computers your child's school uses—Apple's Macintosh or a Windows PC. If you're lucky, your school or your employer may even offer a discount-purchase program. Often, for instance, schools will purchase computers at an education discount and allow parents to buy the computer from them.

For Windows users, **Compaq's Presario 5020** offers a 300MHz Intel Celeron processor, as well as 64MB of memory and a large 8GB hard drive. It also gives you a fast CD-ROM player and a 56-kilobit modem. This machine sells for about $1,100, but Compaq offers a $100 rebate if you sign up for its Internet-access service. A 15-inch Compaq monitor, with built-in stereo speakers, lists for about $300.

For fans of Apple's Macintosh, the computer maker has finally joined the low-priced derby. And its first offering is a stunner, the slick **iMac.** This all-in-one unit includes a 15-inch monitor, CD-ROM player, 4GB hard drive, 56-kilobit modem, 32MB of memory, and a 233MHz processor. And it's housed in a sleek, translucent case that allows you to see its innards. The price: a very competitive $1,299.

In their teenage years, kids start to get serious about computing—probably much more than you ever will be—so get them a serious machine. You might as well spring for one of the newer Intel processors in the hopes that the computer will last a bit longer than this season's Nikes. And a big screen will make homework, as well as games, more of a pleasure.

Gateway, the highly regarded mail-order house, offers the well-equipped midrange G6-350 PC for $1,900. It's powered by Intel's Pentium II processor, and comes with 64MB of memory—all your child is likely to need unless she starts designing 3-D molecules. The package also offers a 17-inch monitor, just about as big as you'd want on a home machine. It comes with a DVD drive, which plays conventional CDs as well as those new digital video disks, a 56K modem, and a big 10GB hard drive.

As for the **extras,** it's up to you. Most families don't really *need* a color printer or color scanner, but they can be lots of fun if your kids are into making invitations to family parties, place cards, birthday cards, and so on. Unless you want high-speed, professional-quality printing, you're best choosing an inkjet printer like the **Hewlett Packard DeskJet 722C.** It retails for around $299, and for family purposes, the printing quality is fine. Higher-end laser printers, such as the well-regarded NEC Superscript line, typically go for $399 or more. Scanners? A stand-alone model, like the **Visioneer PaperPort Strobe,** fetches around $250. This is a favorite of *SmartMoney* computer columnist Walt Mossberg. But before you buy, check out **HP's 380 OfficeJet** model, for $399. It's an inkjet printer, a copier, and a scanner all rolled up in one.˘

Eventually, as the Borcks found, you have to go online. Which means you need an **Internet Service Provider** (ISP). A company called **Concentric** (800-939-4262) earns top marks from the staff

---

Your money's worth

Unless you actually like the Spice Girls, you're going to want to get your kid her own ministereo. Fortunately, today's minisystems are real stereo equipment, and can double as portable backup tunes on the family vacation. But who has the time to learn about "virtualizers" and "velocity-sensitive rotary encoder volume control"? We took a shortcut and asked Tom Horrall, technical director at Cambridge, Massachusetts–based Acentech, one of the nation's premier audio and acoustics consulting firms, to look at a handful of stereo minisystems and tell us which one was the best buy.

Worth it: Panasonic's SC-PM 15 (about $300). A sleek, single-disc player with one auto-reverse cassette deck, it weighs only 11 pounds. The speakers are encased in particle board, which is "a good material because it tends to dampen resonances" and prevents buzzing or ringing. It comes with a remote control, an alarm clock, radio, and both bass and treble controls. The CDs are loaded on the front, which means it can be tucked into a bookshelf. Best of all, it has few extras, which means it has fewer parts to break—a nettlesome problem when it comes to electronics.

Not worth it: Sony's MHC-RX70 (about $480). A bulky nightmare of oddly contoured black plastic, this may grab the attention of your kid with all its blinking lights and buttons. The contraption's outrageously complicated primary control "looks a bit like the interface on my satellite receiver," noted Horrall. But with this many parts, you'd better memorize the repairman's phone number. The biggest flaw, however, is the plastic speaker case, which Horrall said "tends to ring."

of *SmartMoney*'s website (*www.smartmoney.com*). Concentric is fast, reliable, and you'll pay $19.95 for unlimited service, with no start-up fees. If you want to save some cash, you can prepay six months, at $17.95 per month. And if you're only going to be logging on for a few hours a month, you can also select a $7.95 per month option. The plan covers five hours, after which you'll pay $1.95 per hour. Other *SmartMoney.com* favorites: **Mindspring** (800-719-4332) and **IBM Internet Connection** (800-821-4612).

Talk Is Cheap: Low-cost Strategies for Keeping in Touch

With both parents at work and the kids shuttling from school to soccer to ballet to playdates, you'd like to buy everyone a cell phone to stay in touch. But you can probably get away with spending a lot less.

If all you want is a gadget that will let the kids leave messages for you, get a beeper. Beepers are not a whole lot bigger than a matchbox these days, and you can usually rent one for $10 a month or so, including service in your region (national coverage will run you $16.95 a month). The monthly fee generally entitles you to 300 to 500 messages per month before any additional charges kick in. The big beeper companies will let you receive pages of up to 16 or 20 digits, so you and your family can make up codes for different messages, such as 911 for emergency or 730 to say you'll be on the train at half past seven.

If you don't mind spending a little more than $10 a month, consider an alphanumeric pager, which can take both text messages and numbers. **PageNet** (800-724-3638 or *www.pagenet. com*), for instance, offers alphanumeric service for $15 a month. Your beeper will have an e-mail address, and people can send notes directly there. You get 100 alpha transmissions and 300 numeric per month. For another $10 a month, you also get 50 operator-relayed messages.

If you can't stand one-way conversations and you stay fairly close to home most of the time, get a digital phone. (The two main types of phones are digital and analog. The main difference: Analog, at this point, is available in more places. If you travel a long ways from a metropolitan area, for instance, you may not be able to use a digital phone.)

Phones usually cost $100 plus when you sign up for a service such as the 30-minute-per-month plan from **Sprint PCS** (800-455-4551 or *www.sprintpcs.com*) for $16.99 a month. Then you can just leave the phone turned on when you go out. Most phones will remain on standby—ready to take a call—for at least 60 hours. You can recharge it at night. One feature worth considering is offered by **PrimeCo** (800-774-6326 or *www.primeco.com*) or **Powertel** (888-611-6119 or *www.Powertel.com*), which gives you the first minute of any incoming phone call free. With lots of other companies, the incoming calls count against your monthly air time.

If you travel a lot, get a digital phone with voice mail, like one of the **Nokia 2100 series** (around $150) or a palmsize but pricey **Ericsson** (around $300). Yes, a digital phone can't make calls in some remote parts of the country, but it can still receive voice mail when you're out of range. Your concern is roaming charges, or the fees you get nailed with when you leave your home service area. PrimeCo and Powertel don't levy any roaming charges within their networks—but most other providers do. With providers such as Bell Atlantic, these charges can run as high as $1 a minute outside the network. Some companies, such as Sprint, will reduce roaming charges and long-distance fees for an extra charge a month.

Finally, if you absolutely must be reachable (and cost is no object), get a so-called dual-use phone. The **Nokia 6100** (around $300) or the **Qualcomm QCP2700** (about $200) are covered by digital service until you travel outside the coverage area. Then the phones automatically switch to analog (which was the original cell phone network). These analog calls can rack up big bills, though, even as high as $2 a minute in some cases.

On the Road: The Best Strategy for Affordable Family Vacations

With three built-in school vacations per year (winter, spring, and summer), you've got lots of opportunities to travel. Problem is, so does everyone else. Family travel accounts for 74 percent of all vacation travel in the United States, and 88 percent of all families with children take the kids on vacation.

In no other spending category, however, will lack of advance planning cause costs—and the chance of disappointment—to rise so quickly. Here are six ways to decrease the bickering in the back-seat *and* the front.

CHOOSE THE RIGHT HOTEL

Beware the latest in hotel industry come-ons: Kids' programs. Some hotels will offer all kinds of kid-friendly activities, but in plenty of cases "they probably gouge you for it," notes Ed Perkins of *Consumer Reports Travel Letter.* Some resort or hotel child care services, for example, charge up to $70 for a seven-hour "day."

Before you automatically assume a kids' program will solve your baby-sitting problems, ask a lot of questions: What is the ratio of adults to children? What emergency procedures are in place? How are the counselors trained or certified? Does every counselor know CPR? What is the scheduled list of activities? Are children broken up into age groups? Then ask yourself a question: Why did you bring the kids along if you want them to be in day care all day?

Look carefully at "family packages," too. While some are great, many of these deals are anything but. Some brag that they'll put the kids up for free—as long as they stay in your room. Travelodge essentially charges you extra for the privilege of sharing a regular-size room with a childish motif and a VCR setup. On the other hand, **Holiday Inn** (800-465-4329) has Kidsuites in some hotels, where the markup is usually less than for two rooms, and you get a kitchenette and private playroom/bedroom area with bunk beds. **Radisson** hotels (800-333-3333) offers parents 25 percent off the second room. **Sofitel** (800-763-4835) in Europe often offers steep discounts for a second room for the kids.

GET A GREAT DEAL ON YOUR HOTEL

First rule: Never pay a hotel's "rack rate." This rate, the hotel's official price for the room that it prints in brochures and on the inside of your room door, is almost always negotiable. No matter what the first quoted price is, always ask for something cheaper. With your business card in hand, request a corporate rate. Then inquire about any specials. If you're flexible, ask if the rate could be lowered if you came or left a different day. If all else fails, try using a hotel reservations service, which buys hotel rooms in bulk and sells them at a discount. Among them: **Hotel Reservations Network** (800-964-6835 or *www.hoteldiscount.com*), **Central Reservation Service** (800-548-3311 or 407-740-6442), or **Quikbook** (800-789-9887).

GET THE BEST AIRFARE

Now that the FAA recommends putting toddlers in car seats (as opposed to on your lap), more and more airlines are offering discounts for kids: **American Airlines** gives a 50 percent discount on domestic flights for kids under 2, and other major carriers are following suit.

If getting a decent fare—but not the absolute lowest one possible—is your goal, find a good travel agent and stick with him or her. Travel agents won't always get you the best deal on a flight (they have to make money somehow), but they will get you one that's reasonable. And the process of using a travel agent can save you time.

But if getting the *lowest* possible fare is your objective, then you're going to have to do the finagling yourself. The key is flexibility (that, and staying over a Saturday, which is the single best way to reduce your airfare). Ask your ticket agent if you'll get a better fare if you leave at a different time of day, or on a different day altogether, or fly from a different airport, or to a different city. Another way to cut your fare is to forgo nonstop flights. Finally, if you're making plans at the last minute, shop on *www.priceline. com*. You can tell them where you want to fly, tell them how much you'll pay, give them your credit card number, and they'll let you know in an hour if they found a flight at your price.

RENT THE RIGHT CAR

Hoping to rent a car big enough for the whole family? That may be harder than you think. Skyrocketing demand for vehicles like minivans, coupled with an overall tightening of the auto-rental market, has left national rental companies in, dare we say it, the driver's seat during peak travel times. "Make your reservations early," advises an unsympathetic-sounding spokesman for National Car Rental, "and don't expect any bargains."

Do you have any alternatives? Actually, yes. If you don't need the emotional safety blanket of a brand that advertises nationally, you may be able to find what you want—and at a better-than-average price—at smaller and even local auto-rental outfits that specialize in particular vehicle types.

If you're traveling to Disney World, for instance, you can rent a minivan for $200 a week with **Specialty Auto Rental** (888-871-2770), with locations in Orlando and Miami. Similarly, **Florida Auto Rental** (800-327-3791) charges around $285 a week, with 200 free miles. How does that compare with **National Car Rental**? About $350.

Because these smaller outfits don't advertise nationally, you'll have to do a little legwork to find them. The easiest way: Dial up one of the Web's many Yellow Pages–type services (*www.switchboard.com*, for instance, or *www.bigyellow.com*) and search under Rental Cars in the city you're visiting.

One caveat: Local companies frequently offer less flexibility when it comes to options such as picking up a minivan in one city and dropping it off in another. Tom Parsons, editor of *Best Fares* magazine, recommends booking as early as possible and doing a lot of comparison shopping in the hope of stumbling across a bargain. (His magazine's free website, *www.bestfares.com*, includes daily updates on rental deals, which frequently come and go in the blink of an eye.)

Ten Things Your Kid's Summer Camp Won't Tell You

1 *There's a terrorist loose in your child's cabin . . .*

At one overnight camp in Wisconsin, a bully was so mentally abusive a few summers ago that campers nicknamed him "the Nazi." But the really scary part, say parents, was that he was also their counselor. "He was mean to the point that the kids were in fear," adds Neil Gantz, the parent of one camper. At one Rhode Island camp in 1996, the accusations were even more frightening: The alleged sexual abuse of several campers by a counselor sparked state legislators to sponsor a bill requiring summer camps to conduct background checks on staff using state agency databases. The accused predator, it turns out, had been fired from a previous camp for inappropriate sexual behavior.

Only a handful of states require such background checks, notes the American Camping Association, based in Martinsville, Indiana. Yet the databases used don't reflect records from all state agencies, or even those from other states. In fact, the Rhode Island camp did run criminal checks on its staff applicants, says the camp's executive director. But allegations about the counselor weren't made available. To be more secure, ask camps about their screening procedures, both legal and otherwise, before sending your kids.

2 *. . . but we were short on staff.*

With camp enrollments rising steadily by 7 to 10 percent each year, the demand for good counselors is higher than ever. But frankly, a camp counselor's job has become a hard one to fill. That's because many university students—the staple of camp staffs—are now looking elsewhere for summer jobs. And the big reason is money: A typical 8-week salary for a regular overnight bunk counselor ranges from just $1,000 to $3,000. A lack of student talent is forcing camps to look elsewhere for staff members. According to the ACA, some 13 percent of the total staff of day and overnight camps is now recruited overseas. But that can create a problem of its own, notes one camp director in Pennsylvania's Pocono Mountains, as some foreign counselors bail out midsummer to travel the United States on their cultural exchange visas. "I know of a camp that lost 30 to 40 people one summer," he says.

3   *Training? What training?*

When choosing a camp, you count on the fact that the waterfront director is certified by the American Red Cross or another certifying body. You expect camp bus drivers to have a commercial driver's license. In short, you expect that the counselors will know how to . . . well, counsel. And, in fact, to be accredited by the ACA, camps must meet the group's counselor training requirements, which include a minimum five-day orientation for resident staffers, who receive instruction in first aid and search-and-rescue procedures and other training. Keep in mind, however, that only 26 percent of the 8,500 recognized camps are accredited by the ACA, which means that camps may or may not have training procedures in place.

4   *Warning: We may be hazardous to your health.*

Shana and Alan Denenberg sent their daughter Lexi to a suburban Philadelphia day camp in the summer of 1996, figuring Lexi would be busy with activities like arts and crafts and dancing. The Denenbergs were wrong. During the course of the 8-week program, Lexi spent much of her time with doctors instead. First she developed a viral wart on her lip. Then came a bout with mononucleosis, which was topped off by an ear infection so severe that it required surgery. "I sent her to camp for the whole summer, and the only thing I got was doctor bills," Shana Denenberg complains.

Indeed, camps can be a breeding ground for health problems ranging from lice and broken bones to, in one recent case, an epidemic: In July 1996 more than 50 children and counselors fell prey to a contagious stomach virus at a now-closed New Jersey summer camp. One way to gauge the general health conditions of a camp, suggests Marge Heller of Student Summer, a New Jersey–based camp advisory firm, is to do a quick inspection of its on-site medical facilities. "If I go to camp and see 800 kids in an infirmary, I'm suspicious," she says.

5 *Welcome to the Hot Zone.*

No doubt camp is a great opportunity for kids to explore the great outdoors, but some of the most popular camp locations—the northeastern states, Minnesota, Wisconsin, and northern California—are also havens for ticks that carry Lyme disease. The problem, say experts, is that while reported cases of Lyme disease rose 18 percent nationally last year, camps may not be doing enough to protect their charges. Though the Lyme Disease Foundation in Hartford, Connecticut, sent out letters to roughly 100 camps two summers ago offering educational advice and materials, the organization's chairwoman, Karen Forschner, reports, "We haven't had any kind of response from them."

6 *No insurance, no fun.*

Like practically everything else you remember from your childhood, the summer camp experience has changed. Gone are the days of diving boards, water slides, and trampolines. Field trips, water skiing, and horseback riding programs are also a thing of the past at some camps. The reason? Rising insurance rates. The average private 8-week overnight camp will spend in the range of $30,000 to $50,000 per summer for insurance alone, estimates Gordon Josey, coordinator of safety underwriters at A.M. Skier, a camp insurer based in Hawley, Pennsylvania.

7 *And to your left is Stalag 17.*

Camp is camp, right? Wrong. Every camp has a different structure, and it may or may not be a good fit with your child's temperament. Just ask Lisa Collier Cool, who sent her 6-year-old twins to Mount Tom Day School/Day Camp in New Rochelle, New York. Housed in a large mansion surrounded by beautiful grounds, the camp seemed perfect. What she didn't ask was whether campers would get to enjoy any downtime. Cool claims that her twins rushed from one 45-minute activity to the next, with the counselors always yelling at them to "hurry up." By day's end, she says, they were practically sleepwalking into bed. Mount Tom director Mel Tanenbaum is surprised: "We are laid-back here," he insists. "But if you have 350 kids and you don't have structure, you'll have chaos."

8 *Our prices are negotiable . . . really negotiable.*

True, some of the most exclusive camps don't give you much wiggle room when it comes to summer tuition, but others want to bring your little darlings aboard so badly that they'll cut deals—big deals. And those breaks can be even larger if you're sending more than one child to camp. Of the 10 overnight and day camps we phoned at random, in fact, half were willing to discount their summer fees by up to 50 percent—after a bit of prodding on our part. Real bargains loom if you're willing to wait until the last minute, since 75 percent of all cancellations occur in June. In addition to scholarships and multichild discounts, camps routinely offer price reductions for early enrollment. You can bring those prices down even further if you're willing to barter: Often a camp will welcome a parent's medical or other skills in exchange for cheap—or free—tuition.

9 *Your kid'll get an "education," all right.*

Requiring counselors to be of a certain minimum age is no guarantee that they'll meet the minimum in character and judgment. We talked to 12 women who, when they were in their very early teens, dated counselors who were in their twenties. If, in letters and phone calls home, you get a whiff of counselor-to-camper harassment or even gentle flirting, take it seriously.

10 *We squeeze our bug juice daily.*

Bear patties, mud pies, mystery meat floating in a bath of ketchup. The institutional fare at many summer camps is far from gourmet. But is it edible? Sara Sherrod, a 15-year-old camp veteran from New York City, watched a bunkmate chew a broccoli stalk as a "huge, disgusting, white worm" crawled out. "We were always finding bugs and weird, gross types of things in our food," Sherrod exclaims. Along with its legendary rap for rotten taste (and unsavory additives), camp food can also be bad for your health. "By gosh, we wouldn't serve this stuff at home, because it's loaded with fat," says Robert Christensen, a consultant with the Camp Doctor in Chesterbrook, Pennsylvania, a firm that designs healthy menus for camps. Fresh food—especially fruits and vegetables—isn't a priority for many camps, which typically spend just $5 to $7 per camper, per day, on food. "And that's for three meals," Christensen says.

Part 4

HOME TRUTHS

Just wait. Within a year of your first child's birth, every square inch of your home will be swallowed up with toys, books, snowsuits, mountains of diapers, you name it. Small wonder that over half of all prospective first-time home buyers are either parents or about to be parents, according to Bruce Hahn, president of the American Homeowners Foundation, a Virginia research and education group.

But to the uninitiated, house hunting is akin to entrails-reading. What's a "diverse" neighborhood? Which school district is better? What's the upside of using a buyer's broker?

For much of the postwar generation, home buying was nothing like it is today—because it was so hard to go wrong. You liked the house, you bought it, and every year it got more and more valuable. But anyone who's watched the swings in housing prices in the last decade knows that it's anyone's guess what the market will be doing when it's *your* turn to sell.

The upshot: You need the right house at the right price.

This section will guide you through the house-buying process: finding the right town, dealing with brokers, evaluating school districts, taking your search online, and closing the deal.

Then, we'll help you figure out how to pay for your dream house. Choosing the wrong mortgage can have far-reaching consequences not only for your short-term cash flow but also for your long-term financial health. We've assembled a comprehensive guide to getting a home loan, no matter what your financial situation.

Choose right, and your home will be your child's admission ticket to the school district of your choice. A pool of cash to be borrowed against when college tuition rolls around. A capital-gains freebie to fund your retirement. Choose wrong, and your single biggest asset will become a money pit.

7

Buying a Home

No matter what's going on in the market, buying a house can land you on an emotional roller coaster. You look through some ads, march off to see a few houses, fall in love with one, and spend the next 7 days agonizing over every aspect of your life, from where you're going to put your grandmother's antique desk to the balance in your checking account.

Then the deal falls through.

Before you even reach for the real estate section of a local paper, read the following chapter. We'll help you avoid the pitfalls of the ever-changing market, from picking the right town to hiring a home inspector you can trust.

Your Kind of Town

Consider this tale of two houses: The first, a three-bedroom, two-and-a-half bath, center hall colonial in Maplewood, New Jersey. The second, a three-bedroom, three-and-a-half bath center hall colonial in Short Hills, just a few miles away. The houses couldn't have seemed more similar. They had the same clapboard siding, comparable mature plantings, identical black shutters. Inside they were both in impeccable shape. But the house in Maplewood was on the market for $211,900, while the one in Short Hills listed for $404,000.

Was one extra bathroom worth double the price? Hardly. The big difference between these homes—a scant 10 minutes away from one another by car—is the schools. Children who live in the Maplewood house are enrolled in the South Orange-Maplewood system, eventually attending Columbia Senior High. Children in the Short Hills house end up at Millburn High.

And that, statistically speaking, is a big deal. In 1997, 98 percent of seniors at Millburn passed the New Jersey proficiency test; only 93 percent at Columbia passed. And 91 percent of seniors at Millburn go on to four-year colleges. At Columbia, that's true of only 74 percent of the senior class. SAT scores? Millburn students averaged a combined 1190. Students at Columbia: 1020.

School district mania is a national obsession, driving up house prices in "good" districts, deflating them in areas where the schools are seen as lacking, dominating the lives of anxious parents who worry that the "wrong" decision will spell disaster for their children, not only in the competitive world of education but also in their careers, their lives.

The National Association of Realtors notes that a good school district is one of the big four reasons people decide on the home they buy, right up there with price, neighborhood, and commuting time.

Most parents of young children, we'd be willing to bet, make schools their No. 1 reason. So do you buy a house you like and can afford in a neighborhood with less desirable schools, or a smaller—and more expensive—house in a district with better schools?

Real estate agents are not supposed to tell clients that one school is better than another. "That would be discriminatory" and a possible violation of civil rights laws, says Maureen Doyle, an agent with Weichert Realtors in Morristown, New Jersey. But they are free to supply statistics, and they do, in spades—SAT scores, graduation rates, percentage of graduates who go to four-year and two-year colleges, student/teacher ratios, average class sizes, and more.

"Don't trust your realtors to get the good scoop," says Nancy Gill, author of A Parent's Guide to Schools in the San Francisco Bay Area. "They'll tell you to buy a house you hate because you'll get good schools. And then it turns out that they're more touchy-feely than you want. Or you get very good elementary schools, but not a great high school." When Susan and Joe Stix moved from Wisconsin to a Philadelphia suburb a few years ago, they relied on their agent, who recommended the North Penn school district. The Stixes didn't look any further. They bought a lot in Hatfield and built a $220,000 home. They could have moved to nearby Souder-

Hidden expenses: Don't get taken when moving

You know that estimate you got from your mover? It may not be worth the paper it's written on. Some crafty movers have a list of add-ons they don't bother to tell you about until it comes time to pay the bill. That's what happened to Charles E. Hodge when he moved locally in Pompano Beach, Florida. The estimate was a reasonable $560; the final bill, $1,353. When Hodge complained, the movers told him his stuff would sit in storage and he wouldn't get it back until he paid up—not only for the move but also for the cost of the locker. Hodge had to go to court to get his belongings back.

And some people think doing your taxes is a headache.

Here's what to consider before you contract for the job.

Go online. Mover Quotes *(www.moverquotes.com)* can help you plan the job. After you fill out an inventory list and the mileage of the move (accessible via a link to MapQuest), the site will turn up detailed quotes from a database of about 30 moving companies, as well as phone numbers and links to sites. While there is no guarantee that the quotes are accurate, the site does investigate customers' complaints and removes offenders.

Off-peak discounts. You may not be able to control when your move takes place. But if you do have some wiggle room, try to put it off until after Labor Day. Summer—when the kids are out of school—is peak time for movers. They'll often give discounts of as much as 30 percent once it's over.

Materials add up. Movers often sell boxes and other supplies, but not always at the lowest prices. At Moishe's, a Manhattan mover, a book box runs $3, a heavy duty dish pack is $10, and 100 feet of two-foot-wide bubble wrap is $50. At West Side Movers, just uptown, the prices are half that. If you're willing to pack with used cartons, you can save even more. Some movers will throw them in for free. Finally, stockpile your old newspapers in the weeks before you move. There's nothing more frustrating than paying movers $15 a bundle just for clean newsprint to wrap your dishes in. You're going to wash them anyway when you reach your final destination.

Negotiate for extras. Always ask for free packing tape to seal the deal. A typical move for a five-room house runs through 10 to 15 rolls of the stuff. At $5 a roll and up, that can add up fast.

Tips. Even if your moving company doesn't try to pad the bill, you still may not be off the hook. The movers themselves may try a number of tactics—from subtle complaints about how heavy your stuff is to outright threats—in order to get you to tip generously. To head off this problem, ask the moving company beforehand what its movers typically make in tips. If they hit you up for more on moving day, deflect the blame onto the home office. And if that doesn't work, by all means call the moving company. Since the money is going in the employees' pockets, not the owner's, firms are often quick to crack down on this practice.

ton and paid less, admits Susan, "but because of [our broker's] recommendation, we didn't really think about any other towns."

A few months later, the Stixes were shopping for private schools. What their broker *hadn't* revealed was that North Penn was the fastest-growing school district in the area and that the influx of new students had far outpaced the district's ability to keep up.

So how *should* you judge a school district? Test scores are still a good indicator of quality. Call and ask the local elementary school for the math and reading scores for the district's fourth-graders. Almost every state keeps these statistics, along with similar scores for eighth- and tenth-graders. For high school, don't rely entirely on SAT scores. Even the College Board, the creator of the SAT, has complained that some schools don't release scores as they are reported but instead come up with ways to boost their averages, like leaving out the scores of children who don't go to college. Besides, the SAT is an aptitude test, so what's being measured is not how much a school has taught a child but his or her innate ability—or, some critics say, his or her socioeconomic level.

Better to look at the results of Achievement Tests, taken in high school, which measure a student's knowledge in specific subjects like math, English, and history. These scores can show you how strong the honors courses are at a particular high school. Proficiency exams, which students in many states are required to pass in order to graduate, can also be a good indicator of how much students in a particular school know compared with those throughout the state. But each state defines "proficiency" differently. Ohio's test, for instance, measures eighth-grade proficiency—and that's the one high school seniors are required to pass before they can graduate.

Class size is especially important in elementary school. There should never be more than 25 children in a class; in high school that number jumps to 30. Beware: Your realtor or local district official may answer your inquiries about class size with information about the student/teacher ratio. Don't accept that number: Some schools include all their personnel—secretaries, administrators, even athletic-team coaches—and divide that into the number of students. A better question to ask is, What's the teacher workload at school? The fewer kids a teacher has, the better. It's better, for example, to teach two classes of 30 kids each than five classes with 20 students each.

Another thing to consider is the level of community-wide support for the schools—which translates into money. In the Littleton section of Denver, state funding cuts drove the district to consider asking parents to pay for school buses and add more fees for playing sports. In the Monument section of nearby Colorado Springs, on the other hand, a $14 million bond issue earmarked for school construction passed a few years ago, followed closely by a second bond issue two years later. A community that's willing to pay for good schools demands good schools.

Don't Stop at the School District

However important schools may be to you, they are not the *only* thing to consider when evaluating a town. This is a lesson Marlene Coleman and her husband recently learned. They were looking for a home in Scottsdale, Arizona, and after a while came across a four-bedroom house that looked ideal. But then they started poking around, and what they discovered was a shocker. According to some talkative neighbors, there were rumors that the city was going to significantly widen the main road near the house, making the traffic noise far worse.

Sure enough, construction started shortly thereafter, and nearly every house on the block went up for sale. The Colemans wound up in a similar house on a much quieter street just five blocks south.

If you don't feel comfortable chatting up strangers, there are plenty of other places to get information about a town you're considering. Say you were looking at Kingston, Tennessee. A visit to a newsstand or library, where you could look up back issues of the *Tennessean,* would quickly alert you to the problems local residents have been claiming are a result of the nearby Oak Ridge nuclear reservation. Among them are learning disabilities in children and health problems for everyone, which residents suspect are being caused by toxic waste being leaked into the Clinch River and traveling through the county.

Town websites are often worth looking at, too. The better ones today have a trove of information on past history, future development, and even the area's political bent. Finally, there's nothing

---

Broker-speak deconstructed

S ome homes don't need any advertising; others need . . . well, let's just call it good press. Every broker knows how to paint even the most dilapidated wreck in the most favorable light. It's called broker-speak. Read on for the translations:

Cute, charming, cozy: it could double as a playhouse for your kids

Up-and-coming neighborhood: you wouldn't want to live there if someone paid you

Rustic: imagine a cabin in the woods and add running water

Updated bathroom or kitchen: they painted the walls and the cabinets, but the stove and the fridge were Grandma's

Bedroom/study: sure, you can stick a bed in the room, but there's no closet

Handyman's special: falling apart so fast you'd be better off tearing it down

Expansion potential: blow out all the walls and you might consider living there

Close to everything: including a loud, busy intersection or the main drag

Location is everything: it's the worst house in the best neighborhood

Wonderful potential: because no one has lifted a hammer or a paintbrush since the house was built

In-law suite: the house has a separate apartment, which means you can invite your mother-in-law to live in it or you can rent it out illegally

Classic colonial: screams out 1950s and hasn't been touched since

Dramatic: has a color scheme of red and gold

Secluded or private: you'll need a tractor to get through the shrubbery in front of the house

---

like spending some time just hanging around in town. Go to a park and sit on the bench for a while, observing the other parents and their kids. Nose around the bulletin boards at the local YMCA. Drive by the high school and see what the students look like.

A Home Less Taxing

The overall composition of your community will have a big effect on how much you pay in taxes. If there are a large number of corporations in town, for instance, the tax burden on residents will probably be lower. That's partially why the property tax on a $250,000 home in Purchase, New York—headquarters for Pepsico and several other Fortune 500 companies—is lower than on similar homes in other nearby towns.

The property tax you'll owe on any given house is no secret.

How to lower your property taxes

If you have any suspicions whatsoever that your property taxes are too high, challenge them. Appealing your property-tax assessment is easy and quick; more than half the people who go before an appeals board win some sort of relief.

Sometimes just telling the assessor you think the value is off will be enough to save you money. When Thurston Freeman, for example, added a pool to his house in Lexington, Kentucky, he filed a building permit noting that the cost of the pool would be $12,000. A few years later, he realized the assessor had added the full cost of the pool to the value of his $100,000 house. Freeman collected information on similar houses with and without a pool and went to the assessor's office, arguing that the full price of the pool wouldn't show up in the market value of the home. "We reached a compromise," Freeman says. "And I saved $544 a year in taxes."

The first step is to closely read every assessment notice. Because it's not a bill, too many homeowners give the notice a quick glance and chuck it in the trash. It's only when the actual tax bill arrives that they pay attention, but by then the deadline for filing an appeal may be over and you'll have to wait until next year (you can appeal your property tax every year; each municipality has a different deadline, such as the third Tuesday in June).

Before you file your challenge, double-check a few things. Find out how your community calculates the value for the assessment—in many places, the assessment is based on a rate that is a percentage of your home's value. Next, be sure of the assessment date, which for many communities is years in the past. What you'll be contesting may not be the current value of your home, but its value at an earlier date. And remember, it's the value of the home you're challenging, not the tax rate.

You can challenge your assessment on the grounds of factual errors or on "comparables," real estate talk for similar homes' value. Factual errors—if the assessor has wrong information about your lot number, square footage, number of floors, whether or not there is a basement or a fireplace—are obviously more solid footing for protest. Comparables are a bit trickier. "My idea of what's comparable and your idea could be two different things," says Sam Forsythe, chief deputy assessor in Boulder County, Colorado.

Start by giving a local real estate agent a call. He or she will help you find three or four comparable homes and their sale price. Next, check the tax rolls to find homes as close to yours in size as possible, especially when it comes to square footage. Remember that a lousy paint job or ugly landscaping doesn't mean you'll get a break. However, serious problems such as fire damage or a lousy foundation will make a difference.

If at first you don't succeed, try again. Above the local assessor there is usually a county appeals board, and then you can generally fight again at the state level.

Of course, there are some attempts that just don't work. Josette Polzella, an assessor in Ossining, New York, recalls a woman who said her assessment should be lower because the home was haunted by Civil War-era ghosts and she couldn't sell the house at the assessed price. Polzella replied, "Until you show me comparables of other haunted houses, there's nothing I can do."

Real estate agents will have this information at their fingertips. But it's important for you to understand *how* the home is taxed—and if the tax on it will be changing anytime soon. There are two important factors to look at when you're trying to figure out how much property tax you'll actually be paying on that dream home: the home's assessed value and town's *millage* rate. The millage rate is a number that represents how much you will owe per thousand dollars of property value.

When towns want to raise property taxes, they can either change the millage rate, or they can reassess property values. So before you buy, visit the local town hall's tax assessor's office and find out if there are any major reassessments or rate changes coming up. It can make a big difference in what you pay. When Cobb County in Georgia reassessed the value of residential and commercial properties in time for 1998 tax bills, the average hike in value was 16 percent. A house that was previously valued at $40,000 will now be valued at $46,280, meaning an extra $201.50 in county property taxes. Although the town is tinkering with the millage rate to help offset the increase, it should take at least a few years before the difference begins to even out.

Take Your Hunt Online

Once you've got a few towns in mind, going online can help you narrow your choices down considerably before you hit the streets. It can also give you a good idea of what's available for your price range wherever you're hoping to buy. In addition, many websites combine real estate listings with other helpful moving information like insurance advice, agent listings, school district reports, and mortgage deals—in other words, anything that might be causing you to panic.

The website for the National Association of Realtors *(www. realtor.com)* lists over 1,000,000 homes for sale in the United States and is virtually idiot-proof. It can produce pictures of houses within 10 percent of your price in either direction, as well as a host of information about the house itself (heating systems, security systems, distance to public transportation) and the community (property taxes, lists of schools).

Other sites you might try are *www.cyberhomes.com, www. homescout.com,* and *www.realtylocator.com,* the last of which will provide you with links to websites that have listings in the state of your choice, including local realtors.

Choosing the Right Broker

After you've scanned the classified ads or the Internet, seen a few neighborhoods, and maybe even visited a couple of open houses, you'll probably want to choose a real estate broker to show you around. Why a broker? In most towns, the brokers control access to the multiple-listing services that show all the homes for sale; without a broker, you won't have a full idea of what's on the market.

The first thing you need to know about real estate brokers is that they typically work for the people selling the home—not for you. The standard practice is for the seller to hire a broker, who then takes over marketing the home and seeking out potential buyers. For this, brokers usually are paid around 6 percent of the sale price, which gives them a built-in incentive to find the seller the highest price they can.

That sounds simple enough. But as you begin to drive around town with seasoned agents, you'll quickly find that they *act* like they are, in fact, working for you. So don't get too cozy. You will probably be tempted to tell an agent the highest price you are willing to pay for a house or the down payment you can afford. Don't. The agent is obligated to pass those details on to the seller, which could hurt you in any negotiation.

Whatever you do, choose the right broker. While all brokers have access to the same multiple-listing service, the best are so plugged in that they know beforehand about the fantastic bargains about to hit the market.

Take Bonnie Golub, of the firm Holmes and Kennedy in Chappaqua, New York. On a recent tour of the area with a young couple looking to buy a home, she not only pointed out houses for sale but also had information on quite a few that were soon to be: "This couple's getting a divorce," she confided. "The husband here is getting transferred." "This couple's third child just left the nest; they'll be selling soon."

How to sell without a broker

Here are the cold hard facts. Sell your current house through a traditional real estate broker and you're probably going to pay 6 percent of the selling price in commissions. On a $300,000 house, that's $18,000. Invest that money and you've got a year or two of college tuition under your belt.

Not that most people see it that way. In 1997, only about 25 percent of homes were sold without a broker. But why pay someone to do a job that you could do yourself? Here's what it involves, along with fielding phone calls and showing the place at all hours:

Pricing your house. Charge too little and you'll always wonder if you lost money on the deal. Ask for too much and you'll "go stale" as real-estate agents put it, making buyers suspicious that something's dreadfully wrong or that the price is too high. To make sure you're in the ballpark, check out recent sales of similar homes at your local county court-house or town hall. Or spend $200 to $350 on an independent appraiser (for names, call the Appraisal Institute, 312-335-4100, or *www.appraisalinstitute.org*).

Spread the word. Your house won't be included in the multiple-listing service—a realtor-controlled database of homes for sale—so you'll have to generate a lot of traffic on your own. Buy classified ads in all your local papers, including shoppers and weekly alternative publications. Many areas have freebie real-estate newspapers that cater to people selling their own homes. List your place on the Web. (Use a browser like Yahoo! or HotBot to help you find local real estate listing services; often you'll find them linked to your city's or county's site.)

Your ads should list the basics: location, price, number of bedrooms, and any unique selling points such as a new kitchen or lake views. Be sure to mention that it's "for sale by owner" and "priced below the market."

Know what to say when a broker calls. If you allow an agent to show your house, you may be liable for his or her commission, even if you haven't signed a listing agreement. One way to avoid confusion is to have your real-estate attorney draw up a one-time-only open-listing agreement. This document should clearly state that you do not have an exclusive agreement with the agent but that you are willing to pay a fee if the house is sold to a specific buyer that the agent is referring to you. This fee is negotiable and should be included in the agreement. In some of these situations, an agent will ask for half the usual commission paid in the area but will often settle for as little as 1 or 2 percent of the purchase price.

Closing the deal. The first thing you'll need is a contract of sale—the document that shows the price you and a buyer have agreed on, the closing date, and any details of the sale such as what happens if the buyer's financing falls through or who gets the curtains. Six to eight weeks is usually plenty of time for a qualified buyer to get a mortgage. If someone asks for more time, that could be a signal that he or she will have trouble getting financing. Again, you'll probably want a good real-estate attorney to help you draw up these papers. Although many owners use copies of realtor agreements or forms found in published handbooks, laws and regulations vary so widely by county that these generic agreements often have to be rewritten at closing. Asking your attorney to review them beforehand will only cost around $100.

Nervous about going solo? Try a compromise. You may want to hire a discount broker, who charges a flat fee for marketing your property. For $799, for example, Save 6, a Maryland firm, will list a house with a photo in its local for-sale-by-owner magazine, post it (again with a photo) on the Internet, install a sign on your front lawn, and—because the owners are licensed realtors—provide you with contracts and forms and list your property on the MLS. If it sells because another realtor sees the listing in the MLS and shows it, you'll have to pay a commission, but only the half (typically 3 percent) to the agent who brought in the buyer. On a $300,000 house, that saves you $8,201, the selling agent's commission minus the $799 discount broker's fee.

How did Golub know all these things? As one of the highest-producing brokers in the area, she's often called on to do appraisals—before homes are listed. As a result, her clients are among the first in the door. "She knows how to talk to people and she knows this is an emotional kind of business," says Robin Elkin, a former Golub client who herself became a real estate agent. "You're dealing with a lot of money and a lot of emotion and different reasons for selling. Some are very happy reasons and some aren't. People that work with Bonnie trust her."

How do you find the Bonnie Golub of your community? Call up a handful of firms and ask who makes the highest number of sales in your price range. The agent who hustles is the one for you. (It's probably not worth requesting the highest-producing broker overall; if she's busy with $2 million estates, chances are she won't be bothered with starter houses.)

You may be tempted to use a buyer's broker—a fairly new breed of agent who works exclusively for you. Many agencies offer both buyer's and seller's brokers. In theory, being a buyer's agent means the broker agrees not to disclose confidential details to the seller that could affect negotiations. Buyer's brokers are supposed to be more willing to tell you the negatives about an area or a house. In most cases the buyer's broker is paid 3 percent of the purchase price, which usually comes out of the listing agent's commission. Occasionally a buyer's broker will ask you for a retainer of anywhere from $250 to $1,000, which is refundable when you buy a house.

It all sounds great. But don't assume a buyer's broker is totally on your side. A buyer's broker who's getting a commission is just as motivated to close the deal as a seller's broker—and the more you pay for the house, the better it is for them both. One more thing to bear in mind: If a buyer's agent finds you a house being sold by the owner, you are typically responsible for the agent's 3 percent commission.

Do your homework on your schools

D on't have time to call five different school districts and quiz them about class sizes, test scores, and student/teacher ratios? You ought to go online.

Start by checking out the Department of Education website for your state. Many states post statistics about student/teacher ratios, SAT scores, enrollment, and graduation rates right on the Internet. For example, the New Jersey Department of Education website *(www.state.nj.us/education)* will let you search through its school report cards for every district. Each of these lists all the vital information about a district and compares it to all other school districts in the state. There's also other helpful information posted on the site, like listings of charter schools and results of statewide proficiency tests.

If your state doesn't make that information available on the Web, you may have to pay for it. In the past few years, several companies have cropped up to supply parents with school data. Among the leaders: SchoolMatch, based in Westerville, Ohio, which puts out school "report cards" that compare a chosen district with other schools nationwide. As of mid-1998, SchoolMatch (*www.schoolmatch.com,* 614-890-1573) was charging $34 for each report. If you're in a hurry for results, you can have the material faxed to you on the same day for an extra $8.

There's so much information in a SchoolMatch report that it's practically overwhelming. For instance, each report lists the school's ranking within the national percentile in areas like enrollment, class size, student/teacher ratios, and standardized test scores. In addition to these basics, there is detailed information on school system expenditures—how much gets spent per pupil on programs like guidance counseling, library resources, teacher salaries, and building upkeep. There's also community data: property values, median household income in the district, percentage of families with school-age children, tax base information, and the average education level of local residents. At the end of the report, the school in question has a chance to weigh in, in the form of a paragraph providing any other information that might be relevant, such as details about extracurricular activities, sports, and advanced placement courses.

Hiring a Home Inspector You Can Trust

It's standard in many states to pay for an engineer's inspection before you sign a contract or put a penny down. This is to ensure that
you know what condition the house is in, and that it won't collapse
the day after you move in. The quality of the inspector's opinion is
essential—especially at a time when emotions can run high. But
there's a lot riding on this one person's opinion.

Here's the pitch: For $250 to $600 a certified home inspector
will look over every nook and cranny of a house you want to buy,
from the foundation to the roof, from the gutters to the storm windows. If the inspector finds a few small problems, you get the seller
to pay for fixing them. If there are larger problems, you walk away
from the deal or bargain down the price. And if the inspector gives
the thumbs-up, you can buy with carefree confidence.

Although real estate agents will tell you that this is a home buyer's ultimate protection, home inspection is neither a science nor,
in most cases, an art. To become an inspector you need only call
yourself one, without going through any training *at all*. And home
inspectors never guarantee their work. In fact, almost all will require you to sign a preinspection disclaimer that limits their liability to the amount of their fee.

So how do you judge an inspector's credibility? Asking your
inspector the following questions before, during, and after the job
will help ensure that you get the most for your money.

Are you a member? The only truly important credential for home inspectors is membership in the American Society of Home Inspectors. Members must pass two exams and perform 250 inspections.
To check out a particular inspector or get a list of members in your
area, call the ASHI at 800-743-2744 or check out their website at
www.ashi.com.

How often do you work? As far as on-the-job expertise, you want to
hire an inspector who has completed at least five inspections a
week for at least 2 to 3 years. Forget the builders, architects, or
engineers who do a little inspecting on the side. They don't have
the well-rounded expertise you're looking for.

How dirty do you get? OK, you don't really have to ask this question.
You can see for yourself. Even ASHI guidelines don't require its

Worksheet: How much house can you afford?

Before you waste your time looking at houses out of your price range, figure out with this worksheet how much home you can buy. (If you have Internet access, you'll find the electronic version of this worksheet—it'll do the math for you—at *www.smartmoney.com.*)

First, figure out how big a mortgage check you can afford to write each month.

1. Gross monthly income $ _____
2. Monthly debt payments $ _____
   (car loans, credit cards, etc.)
3. Monthly real estate tax and homeowners insurance* $ _____
4. Multiply line 1 by 0.28 $ _____
5. Enter line 3 $ _____
6. Subtract line 5 from line 4 $ _____
7. Multiply line 1 by 0.36 $ _____
8. Add lines 2 and 3 $ _____
9. Subtract line 8 from line 7 $ _____

Now compare lines 6 and 9. The lesser amount is the approximate monthly mortgage payment you can qualify for. To see how big a loan you can get with that payment, see the table below.

*These will be estimates, since you don't yet have an exact house in mind. Ask your real estate agent for approximate numbers.

Now you know how big a loan you can swing. But that by itself won't tell you how much of a house you can really afford. You must add in one last piece of the equation—the down payment.

1. Estimated equity in any current home* $ _____
   (today's value minus your mortgage balance)
2. Subtract closing costs** $ _____
3. Subtract repairs and improvements needed before selling $ _____
4. Subtract broker's commission (usually 6 percent) $ _____
5. Add savings you're prepared to spend on a down payment $ _____
6. TOTAL $ _____
7. Maximum amount you can borrow, based on table opposite $ _____
8. Divide line 7 by 0.80*** $ _____
9. Subtract line 7 from line 8 $ _____

Line 8 is how much house you can afford right now—with one caveat. Line 9 is the amount of cash you must put down to get the loan amount in line 7. If you don't have that much money for a down payment (see line 6), you'll have to find a lender that will let you get away with a smaller down payment. Either that or you'll have to lower your sights and buy a cheaper home. How much cheaper? Divide line 6 by 0.20. That's your top-dollar price.

*Be conservative here. Your equity may not be as great as you'd like to imagine. If you have any doubts, check around your neighborhood or at city hall to see what comparable houses are selling for.
**National averages for closing costs range from $3,000 to $8,000, depending on the size of the loan. For the purposes of this worksheet we suggest using the average of $5,500. When you've calculated how much house you can afford, you can go back and make a more accurate estimate. The rule of thumb: Closing costs add at least an additional 3 percent to the price of your home.
***We're assuming you'll need a 20 percent down payment. However, if lenders in your area will let you put 10 percent down, divide line 4 by 0.90 instead. Only 5 percent down? Divide by 0.95.

RATE	$750		$1,000		$1,250		$1,500		$1,750		$2,000		$2,250		$2,500		$2,750		$3,000	
	15 YR	30 YR	15 YR	30 YR	15 YR	30 YR	15 YR	30 YR	15 YR	30 YR	15 YR	30 YR	15 YR	30 YR	15 YR	30 YR	15 YR	30 YR	15 YR	30 YR
5.00%	95	140	127	186	158	233	190	279	221	326	253	373	285	418	316	466	348	512	379	559
5.25	93	136	124	181	155	226	187	272	218	317	249	362	280	407	311	453	342	498	373	543
5.50	92	132	122	176	153	220	184	264	214	308	245	352	275	396	306	440	336	484	367	528
5.75	90	129	120	171	151	214	181	257	211	300	241	343	272	386	301	428	331	471	361	514
6.00	89	125	119	167	148	208	178	250	207	292	237	334	267	375	296	417	326	458	355	500
6.25	87	122	117	162	146	203	175	244	204	284	233	325	262	365	291	406	321	447	350	487
6.50	86	119	115	158	143	198	172	237	201	277	230	316	258	356	287	395	315	435	344	475
6.75	85	116	113	154	141	193	170	231	198	270	226	310	254	347	282	385	311	424	339	462
7.00	83	113	111	150	139	188	167	225	195	263	223	301	250	338	278	376	306	413	334	451
7.25	82	110	110	147	137	183	164	220	192	257	219	293	246	330	274	366	301	403	329	440
7.50	81	107	108	143	135	179	162	215	189	250	216	286	243	322	270	358	297	393	324	429
7.75	80	105	106	140	133	174	159	209	186	244	212	279	239	314	266	349	292	384	319	419
8.00	78	102	105	136	131	170	157	204	183	238	209	273	235	307	262	341	288	375	314	409
8.25	77	100	103	133	129	166	155	200	180	233	206	266	232	299	258	333	283	366	309	399
8.50	76	98	102	130	127	163	152	195	178	228	203	260	228	293	254	325	279	358	305	390
8.75	75	95	100	127	125	159	150	191	175	222	200	254	225	286	250	318	275	350	300	381
9.00	74	93	99	124	123	155	148	186	173	217	197	249	222	280	246	311	271	342	296	373
MONTHLY PAYMENT	$750		$1,000		$1,250		$1,500		$1,750		$2,000		$2,250		$2,500		$2,750		$3,000	

Match your maximum monthly payment as closely as possible with the dollar amounts shown at the bottom line. Then choose a term—15 or 30 years—and an interest rate. (You can get current interest rates in your local paper or by calling a few lenders.) Where those three variables intersect is the amount you can borrow, in thousands. NOTE: If your maximum monthly payment is off the chart—$3,500, say—you can still use the table. In this case, simply find the term and interest rate you want at $1,750 a month and multiply the amount you find by 2.

members to check the "strength, adequacy or efficiency" of any "system" in the house, which includes plumbing, heating, air-conditioning, electricity—in other words, practically everything you care about. Nonetheless, every inspector will tell you he diligently assesses these systems. Some do and some don't. To tell the difference, look at what he's wearing. If an inspector shows up wearing a suit and tie, send him home. You want someone who's planning to get his hands (and knees) dirty, climbing up to the roof, scrambling around in the crawlspace, checking the basement for water stains.

How long will this job take you? Two-and-a-half hours to look over a modest three-bedroom house is a respectable number. For a larger place, expect the inspector to stay half a day or longer. And don't be afraid to tag along with a notebook in hand. The inspection serves as a crash course for new homeowners. Take copious notes, type them up, and you'll refer to them for years.

Can I see a few of your past reports? A good inspection report is chock-ful of details, indicating that the inspector looks over everything. It should read like a narrative guide to the house, recalling every step of the inspection process and offering concrete advice on maintenance and repair. A bad inspection report reads like a checklist—a signal that you've got a lazy inspector who treats every house the same way. And if the inspector is reluctant to show you any reports at all? Needless to say, that's someone you don't want to hire.

Finally, if you don't fix any major problems the engineer turns up in his report, you may not be able to file an insurance claim for them later. Say the engineer notes that the roof needs to be replaced. You figure you can live with a few leaks for a year or so. Then there's a deluge, and you've got thousands of dollars of water damage. Your insurance company may not pay a dime, says Michael Leyland, head of underwriting for Nationwide in Columbus, Ohio.

Keep a Lid on Renovation Costs

It's amazing how many houses in move-in condition suddenly require several weeks of work before you're ready to call the moving van. Here are a few points to keep in mind when you're dealing with contractors in an unfamiliar town.

Write up a contract. Do this for any job that is bigger than a few hundred dollars. Your builder may supply the contract; if not, you can get a sample contract from the American Institute of Architects (800-365-2724) or the American Homeowners Association (800-822-3215). Make sure the contract allows you to withhold 10 to 20 percent of the fee until the work is completely finished. Have a lawyer or architect look over the contract to make sure nothing is left out; or contact the nonprofit consumer group United Home-owners Association, which offers contract reviews for $26 (202-408-8842 or *www.uha.org*).

Get an architect or engineer to oversee the project, if it's a big project and you won't be on site much. That'll cost you more—maybe $200 per visit—but it should improve your chances of getting it right the first time. One New Jersey couple hired a contractor and crew to frame the second floor of their house a few years back. By all appearances, everything went swimmingly. Then the local building inspector came and noticed some serious structural problems. Among them: Braces needed to be put in around a skylight, 80 two-by-

---

Your money's worth

There's nothing like a fresh coat of paint to make a tattered house look lovingly looked-after. And it's a lot cheaper than a new kitchen. Not all paints are equal, however.

Worth it: Paying more means getting more mileage out of one can of paint. Benjamin Moore's MoorGard Low Lustre Latex, at $25 a gallon, has high-quality pigments and resins for better coverage, lasting color, and about a 10-year life span. And with 20 ready-mixed colors, you're less likely to have to resort to custom mixing, which can lead to excess blistering. Call 800-826-2623 for a local dealer.

Not worth it: At first glance, it seems as though you'll save about $10 a gallon on Glidden's Evermore Super 15-Year Flat Latex paint. But you'll need 25 percent more of it to cover the same square footage. And about the 15 years it promises on the can? Forget about it. Count on repainting in about four years.

The real world: Buying a house online

When Tom Canty went shopping for a house in San Diego in early 1998, he had one overriding concern: getting to work. The computer consultant, then based in Boston, couldn't stand the idea of sitting in his car every afternoon on the Southern California freeways, so he wanted a house convenient to more than one major route (giving him an out if one was blocked) and far away from the area's most congested spots.

But unlike most people, Canty, 33, and his fiancée, Nancy Villalobos, a 28-year-old nurse practitioner, didn't simply call up a real estate agent and ask for advice. Instead, come 8 or 9 P.M. Boston time (the height of the evening rush in San Diego), Canty would log on to Maxwell Technologies/Caltrans's Freeway Speeds website and check out the action: Was I-15 backing up near the Route 56 cutover? How was traffic heading east on I-8? The site (updated in real time) would show what was happening with a series of colored dots: green for traffic moving at 50 miles per hour or faster, yellow for 15 to 30 mph, red for bumper-to-bumper traffic. Eventually, the couple homed in on a few neighborhoods on the city's northeast side, including Mira Mesa and La Mesa, which were convenient to both north-south and east-west routes.

Canty and Villalobos didn't stop there. They knew they wanted a new home, so Canty spent hours surfing the National Association of Realtors' website, looking for neighborhoods that had the most to offer in the way of new construction. They also wanted to be able to run out for a quick dinner and a movie, so, using Yahoo!'s map service, Canty checked the areas they liked for distances to the nearest multiplex and restaurant row. All their data led them to decide on Mira Mesa.

The couple was finally ready to look for a house in earnest. Again, most people would just have gotten on the phone, called a few real estate agents, set up appointments in California, and then flown out for several weekends' worth of serious house hunting. But Canty had no intention of getting on an airplane to San Diego, ever. For one, he's terrified of flying. Besides, as he admits, he's a geek: "I'm in the computer industry. My plan from day one was to do this remotely." So Canty fired off a round of e-mail to a series of agents who were also mortgage brokers (he was after one-stop shopping), in which he explained that he wanted to complete the entire transaction in cyberspace. Tom Guarino, a local agent and owner of North America Real Estate Services *(www.buyourhome.com)*, was the first to respond enthusiastically.

Their procedure was simple: Canty and Villalobos would scour the listings on *www. realtor.com* and then, a couple of times a week, e-mail Guarino with specific houses they wanted him to visit, generally three to four bedrooms in the $240,000 range. The agent would then drive out to each house with his Epson digital camera in hand and snap photos of the interior and exterior. Back in his office, Guarino would upload the pictures to his computer, then e-mail them to Canty at his Boston office. Canty, in turn, would transfer them to his specially created home-shopping Web page, which Villalobos would check from her home computer. In this manner, the couple weeded out 10 unsuitable houses before seeing one they liked: a Mediterranean-style four-bedroom with an enormous yard for the dog Villalobos was planning to buy.

By fax the couple made an offer of $242,500. Several weeks later they closed, without ever having set foot in their new house. Today, more than a year later, Canty seems pleased with the outcome, noting that the pictures Guarino took left almost no detail uncovered. Well, except for maybe one thing. "You can't check out your neighbors on the Internet," says Canty with a laugh.

fours (to which the Sheetrock was to be attached) were missing, and the support beams had been improperly installed. If your contractor balks at having someone watching over his shoulder, think seriously about finding another contractor.

Check references on everyone who works for you. And don't take those photos in looseleaf notebooks for granted. Many projects involve input from a number of people, all of whom are eager to take credit once the job is done. Ask about a contractor's specific role in a project.

Don't consider this an investment. Bear in mind that you probably won't be able to build more than 40 to 60 percent of your renovation cost into the resale price of your home. For that reason, spending more than 25 percent of your home's value on remodeling should raise a red flag. Which improvements will pay for themselves? Updated kitchens, bigger closets, built-in bookcases, and upgraded baths—all in neutral colors, of course. Which won't? Restaurant-quality ranges. Thousand-dollar dishwashers. Humidity-controlled wine cellars. And anything overly colorful.

Ensure that the contractor has $500,000 to $3 million of insurance. This is in case of accidents or major screw-ups.

Beware expensive materials. One contractor tells the story of a couple who wanted a new marble counter for their kitchen. They were perfectly satisfied with Carrara marble, which sells for $35 per square foot—until they heard about the elegantly patterned Azul Macauba marble. It's mined in Brazil, difficult to produce, and costs at least $200 per square foot. Is it worth it? Only if you *must* have blue-veined marble. Otherwise, you're buying hype and helping your remodeler reap higher profits. Remember: Materials are

The going rate: Finishing touches

N ow that you've got your dream house, you want it to look like, well, Martha Stewart's dream house. Watch out. Emulating Martha Stewart is time-consuming . . . not to mention expensive. Here's what it costs to re-create Martha's feats of domestic derring-do.

	Charleston, S.C.	Highland Park, Tex.	Rancho Palos Verdes, Calif.	Westport, Conn.	Winnetka, Ill.
Parchment paper, 75 square feet	$ 7.25	$ 5.95	$ 2.75	$ 5.00	$ 2.19
Kitchen twine, 210 feet, for trussing	5.50	5.95	3.25	5.99	5.50
All-Clad 8-quart stock pot	214.00	198.00	198.00	214.00	214.00
Candy thermometer	8.50	3.79	3.95	2.99	5.99
Dental Floss, 27 yards, for cutting delicate cakes	3.49	2.99	3.19	3.67	3.03
Pastry bag	2.50	2.50	4.99	2.99	2.99
Melon baller	14.00	8.95	9.00	2.49	13.00
Latex gloves, 100	28.70	34.50	29.00	30.00	25.00
6 yards French ribbon, for gift-wrapping	11.94	9.00	10.50	7.50	11.10
Compost bin, yard-size	79.00	49.99	80.00	89.99	84.00
No. 22 florist wire, to tame cut flowers	0.99	0.99	1.49	0.89	0.89
Manure, 50 pounds	6.95	1.99	1.99	9.99	5.79
New wheelbarrow	92.99	80.49	59.99	114.99	99.95
Black & Decker glue gun	13.00	16.79	14.00	21.89	16.97
Martha Stewart house paint in moss, 2.5 liters	80.00	80.00	N/A	78.00	65.25
9-by-12-foot cotton canvas dropcloth	17.50	16.36	24.99	25.00	18.00
Steel wool, for garden-furniture refinishing	0.99	1.99	3.00	1.79	2.49
Pair of Wellington-style boots	53.00	59.00	59.00	62.40	59.00
Clairol ash-blonde Ultress rinse for hair	6.99	7.19	6.89	9.97	7.59
Smith & Hawken overalls (shorts)	64.00	63.86	63.86	62.54	64.16
Navy blue bandanna	3.00	5.41	2.00	2.50	5.43
Crane's calling cards, 500	137.00	137.00	151.25	137.00	140.00
Total	851.29	792.69	733.09	891.58	852.32

typically marked up by 20 percent, so the more you spend, the more the contractor earns.

Never pay a big chunk of the contractor's fee in advance. If the job's not completed to your satisfaction, your money is about the only leverage you have over him. Just ask Steve Friedman, a homeowner in New Jersey. He gave a contractor 40 percent of the money when he started a job and another 55 percent when he was about 75 percent through. At that point the contractor took a "business" trip to Florida and never finished the job. It cost Friedman $20,000 over his original budget—hiring a new plumber, electrician, carpenter, and tiler—to get his project completed. Holding back 10 to 20 percent of payment until the project is finished down to the last nail is usually enough to keep a contractor on the job.

8

Getting a Mortgage

Relax. Getting a mortgage these days isn't as hard as it used to be. Up until just a few years ago, you could count on taking a couple of months to shop around, get approved, and get your check in hand. Now it takes only a few weeks—less time than it took, perchance, to conceive your first child. Better yet, it's getting easier and easier to find a lender who's only too happy to break all the old rules. You only have enough cash for a 5 percent down payment? That's OK. Still owe lots of money on that college loan? No problem. People who wouldn't even have bothered to apply for a mortgage five years ago are now getting them—at decent rates.

Yes, it's true that most mortgages do have to conform to certain standards. Why? Most lenders bundle up all their mortgages and sell the lot of them to giant investors like Fannie Mae and Freddie Mac. Though you'll still send in your monthly check to a bank, it's really only servicing the loan; the debt is owned by these "secondary" mortgage holders. As Fannie Mae and Freddie Mac are way too big and bureaucratic to make an exception for one little loan like yours, conforming mortgages must have nearly the exact same characteristics: same interest rate, same time period, same risk profile of the homeowner.

But plenty of lenders have wised up to the fact that there are borrowers out there who don't fit the mold but are still a good risk. These lenders, which tend to be the savings and loan banks down the street, don't bother with the secondary market and instead keep the mortgages in their "portfolio" to make money on the interest. Because they don't have to sell the mortgage, they have much more leeway. If you have an iffy credit history or a promising career but little in the bank, if you're a newly minted doctor with loans up to your eyeballs, apply anyhow, advises Jane Morrow, a New York real estate attorney. Put on a suit, attach an articulate letter to your application (explaining in earnest detail the reasons for your transgressions), and take it into your lender's office by hand. "If you can find someone in the bank who's willing to shepherd you through the mortgage, the better the chance you have of getting your loan," she says.

The best news of all is that it's easier than ever to avoid mortgage brokers. Instead of paying them to search for the best rates and elbow your application into the bank, there are now ways for you to do all this on your own—for free.

Of course, applying for a mortgage will never be a breeze. It's still an annoying rite of passage for homeowners: You have to find the mortgage that fits your wallet, and you need to qualify for it. Below is a step-by-step guide to make sure you do just that.

What's the Best Mortgage for You?

Ask a couple of friends what kind of mortgage they have and you'll find yourself drowning in a host of unfamiliar terms: A 1-year ARM. A 5-year delayed adjustable. A 30-year fixed-rate. A jumbo loan. You don't need a degree in finance to know what they're talking about. It's really much easier than you think. Here's a rundown of what the different kinds of mortgages are, who should consider them, the risks involved, and where to find them.

The hidden expenses lurking in your closing costs

Interest rates are one thing. But you also have to pay closing costs, which can easily add up to 10 percent of the value of your loan. As one home buyer puts it, "everyone, from your lawyer to the state, wants a piece of your mortgage." Lenders are required by RESPA, the Real Estate Settlement Procedures Act, to give you a good-faith estimate of your closing costs when you hand in your application, and extra charges are a violation of the law. But some banks try to sneak them in anyway. We've seen messenger fees, "jumbo warehousing" fees, intangible-tax charges, even inflated Fed Ex charges.

Ask for a detailed, itemized list of your estimated closing costs when you hand in your loan application. It's required by law. Then on closing day, look carefully at the figure called "amount financed" on your settlement papers. If it does not equal the principal you are borrowing, minus any points or interest paid up front, ask your loan officer why. It could mean he slipped some fees into the amount financed and you can guess what that means: You'll pay interest on those charges, as well as the fees themselves.

FIXED-RATE MORTGAGES

What they are. Loans that carry the same interest rate for the life of the loan. Most fixed-rate loans have a repayment period of 30 years. But 15-year, 10-year, 20-year, and 25-year fixed-rate loans are also available.

Who should consider them. People who plan to live in the house for longer than 10 years. If you have found your dream house where you expect your kids to grow up, this is the mortgage for you. People who want to lock in rates and not worry about when they are moving might want to consider getting a fixed-rate loan as well.

What's better, a 15-year loan or a 30-year loan? It largely boils down to what you can afford. A 15-year loan will carry a slightly lower interest rate than a 30-year mortgage, but the monthly payments will be higher because of the shorter repayment period. For example, one 15-year loan in mid-1998 carried a 6.51 percent interest rate; a 30-year loan had a 6.81 percent rate, according to Bank Rate Monitor, a Florida-based financial information database *(www.bankrate.com).* How much higher are the monthly payments for the 15-year loan? If you borrowed $200,000 you'll pay $1,743 a month with the 15-year loan; with the 30-year loan,

Monthly mortgage payments on a 30-year loan

Rate	Payment per $1,000	Rate	Payment per $1,000	Rate	Payment per $1,000
4.50%	$5.067	6.50%	$6.321	8.50%	$7.689
4.625	5.141	6.625	6.403	8.625	7.778
4.750	5.216	6.75	6.486	8.75	7.867
4.875	5.292	6.875	6.569	8.875	7.956
5.00	5.368	7.00	6.653	9.00	8.046
5.125	5.445	7.125	6.737	9.125	8.136
5.250	5.522	7.25	6.822	9.25	8.227
5.375	5.60	7.375	6.907	9.375	8.317
5.50	5.678	7.50	6.992	9.50	8.409
5.625	5.757	7.625	7.078	9.625	8.50
5.75	5.836	7.75	7.164	9.75	8.592
5.875	5.915	7.875	7.251	9.875	8.683
6.00	5.996	8.00	7.338	10.00	8.776
6.125	6.076	8.125	7.425	10.125	8.868
6.25	6.157	8.25	7.513	10.25	8.961
6.375	6.239	8.375	7.601	10.375	9.054

Should you refinance?

M any people rush to refinance their mortgage—basically, take out a new loan—the minute rates dip below what they're currently paying. Problem is, the closing costs of the new loan can easily wipe out the monthly savings. Fill out the worksheet below, adapted from one by HSH Associates, a publisher of mortgage information, to see if you will truly save money with your new loan. To illustrate how this works, we've supplied the numbers for a hypothetical borrower with a $210,000 mortgage who's going from an 8.75% rate to 7%. One important note: This worksheet assumes that you will be refinancing into a 30-year mortgage, so you'll be restarting your payments at year 1. (If you have Internet access, check out the electronic version of this worksheet at *www.smartmoney.com;* it can calculate your savings on 15-year mortgages as well as 30-year loans.)

1. Points   1% _____
2. Cost of points (*$210,000* × *1%*) $2,100 _____
3. Application fee $150 _____
4. Credit check $55 _____
5. Attorney fee (yours) $150 _____
6. Attorney fee (lender's)   0 _____
7. Title search   0 _____
8. Title insurance $275 _____
0. Appraisal fee $300 _____
10. Inspections   0 _____
11. Local fees (taxes, transfers) $200 _____
12. Document preparation $200 _____
13. Prepayment penalty on current loan   0 _____
14. Other   0 _____
15. Total closing costs (add lines 2 through 14) $3,430 _____
16. Your current monthly mortgage payment $1,652 _____
17. Amount you are refinancing $210,000 _____
18. Payments per $1,000 (from monthly mortgage payments table on page 126) $6.653 _____
19. Divide line 17 by 1,000   210 _____
20. Monthly payment for your new loan (multiply line 18 by line 19) $1,397 _____
21. Your monthly savings (subtract line 20 from line 16) $255 _____
22. Number of months it will take you to recoup the closing costs of your new loan (divide line 15 by line 21)   14 _____

If you expect to stay in your home longer than the number of months on line 22, you should refinance.

$1,305. The bottom line: If you can afford the more expensive payments for the 15-year loan, go for it. You'll shell out less money in interest, and after just 10 years, you'll have paid down 55 percent of the equity in your home. Compare that to the equity you'll have after 10 years with a 30-year mortgage: a paltry 14 percent.

Potential traps. Fixed-rate loans are not a good idea if you're temporarily strapped for cash, because rates are often initially higher than loans with fluctuating interest rates. Also, if interest rates drop and you're locked in at a high rate, you'd have to refinance to take advantage of the lower rates.

Where to shop. A mortgage bank or lender that resells the mortgages to Fannie Mae or Freddie Mac. What you're looking for is a company that sells only home loans—a lot of them—like national lenders **Countrywide Home Loan** (800-327-9877) and **Norwest Mortgage** (800-288-3212). Also consider regional companies like New York-based **Dime Mortgage** (800-879-3463), **Fleet Mortgage** (800-255-5353) in Massachusetts, and **Nationsbank Mortgage** (800-344-0632) of Illinois. These companies have such high volume that they can offer the most competitive rates.

ONE-YEAR ADJUSTABLE-RATE MORTGAGE (ARM)

What they are. Mortgages with interest rates that adjust up or down depending on the movement in a broader monetary index (typically a short-term Treasury, the prime rate, or the Eleventh District Cost of Funds index) to which it is tied. A 1-year ARM adjusts every year. There are also 3-year ARMs, which adjust every three years.

Who should consider getting one. Temporarily strapped homeowners who must count every penny to purchase the house. The interest rate of a one-year ARM—at least in the beginning—is the lowest rate you'll find of any mortgage. In mid-1998, one-year ARMs averaged 5.61 percent, according to Bank Rate Monitor. Several banks offer even cheaper rates.

Potential traps. Rates could rise, and you'd be hit with a larger mortgage payment. Of course, rates could drop, too. But unless you're clairvoyant, you won't know which way they'll move or by how much. Take comfort in the fact that adjustable-rate loans typically have a cap of 2 percentage points for each adjustment period and a lifetime cap of 6 percentage points. So a one-year ARM at 5.68 percent can only jump to 7.68 percent after one year. And the most it can ever climb to is 11.68 percent. (That said, watch out for the rare lender that has a 10-point lifetime cap).

Where to shop. Savings and loans. The secondary market doesn't mean much to these institutions—instead, they'll write hundreds of adjustable loans and make money off the interest. For that reason, they can gamble with competitive rates. At **Capital Federal Savings** in Kansas City (800-222-7312), a one-year ARM was as low as 5.38 percent in mid-1998.

DELAYED ADJUSTABLES

What they are. Adjustable-rate mortgages that stay fixed for a period of time in the beginning—typically 3 years, 5 years, 7 years, or 10 years—and then fluctuate according to the prime rate or another index every year thereafter. Also called hybrid ARMs, they're often referred to as 3/1, 3/1, 7/1, or 10/1. Generally, the longer the initial fixed period of time, the higher the initial interest rate; a 7/1, for instance, will have a higher starting rate than a 3/1.

Who should consider getting one. Buyers who won't be in the house for more than ten years. If your job requires that you move every few years, or you're thinking you'll eventually have to move to a town with a better high school, a delayed-adjustable may offer the best rates.

Potential traps. Staying in the house beyond the initial time when the interest is fixed at a low rate—and living at the mercy of rates that could go up or down.

Where to shop. Your local savings and loan, again because it doesn't have to worry about a secondary market.

A JUMBO LOAN

What it is. A home loan that's larger than $227,150. It's also known as a nonconforming loan; conforming loans, which are for any amount under $227,150, fit the guidelines established by Fannie Mae and Freddie Mac.

Points or no points?

Fees, or "points," used to be a fact of life in mortgages. Now many lenders will let you choose—pay points and other costs up front or pay no costs and accept a slightly higher interest rate. Fill out this worksheet to see which alternative makes more sense. We've included figures for a hypothetical borrower with a 30-year mortgage of $210,000 and $3,430 in closing costs. (If you have Internet access, consider using the electronic version of this worksheet at *www.smartmoney.com;* it can calculate your savings on 15-year mortgages as well as 30-year loans.)

1. Your mortgage amount. $210,000 $_____
2. Rate you'll pay without costs.   7.50%   _____%
3. Rate you'll pay with costs.   7.00%   _____%
   a) Closing costs with this loan $3,430 $_____
4. Monthly payments with rate on line 2.
   a) Payment per $1,000 (from the "monthly mortgage payments" table on page 126) $6.992 $_____
   b) Divide line 1 by 1,000.   210   _____
   c) Multiply line 4a by line 4b. $1,468 $_____
5. Monthly payments with rate on line 3.
   a) Payment per $1,000 (from the "monthly mortgage payments" table on page 126). $6.653 $_____
   b) Divide line 1 by 1,000.   210   _____
   c) Multiply line 5a by line 5b. $1,397 $_____
6. Monthly savings from lower rate. (Subtract line 5c from line 4c.) $71 $_____
7. Amount you could earn each month on the closing costs if you invested it instead.* (Multiply line 3a by 0.00487.) $17 $_____
8. Total monthly savings. (Subtract line 7 from line 6.) $54 $_____
9. Number of months it will take to recoup the costs on the loan with a lower rate. (Divide line 3a by line 8.)   64   _____

If you expect to own your home longer than the number of months on line 9, pay the points and grab the lower rate.

*Assumes a conservative annual return of 6% for 30 years.

Who should consider getting one. Well, if you need to come up with more than $227,150, you don't have much choice, do you? Five years ago, you would have had to put 25 percent down on the house—a hefty chunk if you're talking about a $500,000 mortgage—and interest rates were about 2 percentage points higher than the going rate for a conforming loan. Today, you can get a jumbo loan with a 10 percent down payment, and interest rates are much lower. Maryland homebuyers, for example, could have gotten a 30-year jumbo loan through Countrywide Home Loans for 7.5 percent in mid-1998, compared with 7.0 percent for a conforming loan.

Where to shop. Maybe the big consumer bank where you have your checking and savings account, as it already has a relationship with you. Or try big national lenders like **Fleet Mortgage** (800-225-5353) and **Countrywide Home Loans** (800-327-9877), which are now in the business of selling jumbo loans on the secondary market and can thus offer good rates. In mid-1998 Fleet was offering fixed-rate loans up to $300,000 with just 5 percent down. For loans of up to $1 million, **First Consolidated Mortgage Company,** a Dallas-based lender (888-520-7757), only required 10 percent.

B-RATED, C-RATED, OR D-RATED LOAN

What it is. A home loan for anyone with bad credit.

Who should consider getting one. Maybe you, if you missed a Visa payment, had a run-in with a collector, or once had a lien put on a piece of real estate.

It used to be that if you had poor credit you'd pay a hefty rate for a mortgage (double the going rate for a 30-year, for example) or you wouldn't get one at all. But in the last 3 years, many smaller, less well known firms have started to write B and C loans. Of course, you still have to pay a higher rate—the worse your credit is, the higher the rate—and put more money down (25 to 40 percent, depending on how delinquent your credit).

If you want to get a preliminary idea of how the banks will view your credit history, go to the website produced by HSH Associates *(www.hsh.com),* a New Jersey–based mortgage information publisher, to find out. Its credit calculator lets you plug in where you've gone astray—a credit card bill or mortgage payment that was 90 days late, a real estate lien 2 years ago—and it will spit out your rating (A, B, C, or D).

Where to shop. Your best bet is to get a mortgage broker to help you find a home loan. It will cost you—anywhere from $1,000 to 1 percent of the loan—but these middlemen know where to look. Where to find a broker? you ask. Try the Yellow Pages or the real estate section of your local paper. If you don't want to use a broker, you could also try some of the big mortgage lenders, including **First Guaranty Mortgage Corporation** of Maryland (888-296-7000), Ohio-based **The Mortgage Source** (800-336-6026), and **Full Spectrum Lending** (800-909-8217), a division of Countrywide Home Loans.

What Lenders Want to See in Your Application

You've winnowed down your mortgage options, shopped for the ideal one, made contact with the bank officer. Now for the hard part: Qualifying.

Lenders look at your application as if it were a balance sheet—a snapshot of your financial life taken on one day. So whatever you do, don't take on new debt. Wait until you get your mortgage before you buy a new car. Pay off as much of your credit cards as you can. If your parents or grandparents are thinking of passing along any assets, you might drop hints that now would be a good time.

Specifically, here is what your lender is looking for.

A MONTHLY INCOME THAT'S THREE TIMES BIGGER THAN YOUR MORTGAGE PAYMENT

Ideally, your "housing ratio"—the percentage of your gross monthly income that you'll spend on mortgage, property taxes, and insurance—is 28 percent or lower. Some large banks such as **Chase Manhattan** in New York City (800-873-6577), however, have upped their housing ratio to 33 percent; other banks are following suit. Call up a few banks and see what their required housing ratio is. It's no secret, you just have to ask.

Even if a potential lender generally adheres to the 28 percent cutoff point, it may make an exception depending on your circumstances. Say you're a first-year lawyer at the firm, or you just got out of graduate school, or you can argue that you'll be receiving standard raises in the next few years, you can probably convince a bank to allow a higher housing ratio. Banks may also be willing to increase the housing ratio if you are applying for a jumbo loan (any amount above $227,150).

FIXED EXPENSES THAT DON'T EXCEED 36 PERCENT OF YOUR MONTHLY INCOME

The second number that your lender will look at is the "debt-to-income ratio"—what percentage of your income is eaten up by all the fixed expenses you have every month, including housing, credit cards, car loans, insurance, and child support (this number is also sometimes called the total-obligation ratio). The ideal spot: below 36 percent.

If you can't meet this number, try consolidating all your debts into a lower-interest loan. Cut out any expenses that you can. If this doesn't work, call a few banks and ask if they are willing to accept a debt-to-income ratio higher than 36 percent. Again, **Chase Manhattan** is lenient. It will accept a debt-to-income ratio of 42 percent if you make $75,000 to $150,000 a year. A salary of $150,000 or more could qualify you for a mortgage at an even higher ratio.

A 20 PERCENT DOWN PAYMENT

The bigger your down payment—20 percent or more is best—the more amenable lenders will be about letting you bump up against their expense ratios, notes Ty Taylor, loan officer at Waukesha State Bank in Wisconsin. Plus, if your down payment exceeds 20 percent, you won't have to buy mortgage insurance, which eliminates another set of eyes going over your application (see page 135, for more information on mortgage insurance).

Of course, if you can't make 20 percent, or even 10 percent, there are other options. Both **Countrywide Home Loans** (800-327-9877) and **Fleet Mortgage** (800-225-5353) offer a loan with just 5 percent down.

ENOUGH CASH IN THE BANK TO COVER YOUR CLOSING COSTS

Savings, you might be surprised to learn, aren't all that important. You don't have to have a fortune stashed away. All the lender wants to see is enough savings to cover closing costs and two or three months' of mortgage payments, taxes, and insurance.

A SHORT LIST OF CREDIT CARDS

Have lots of credit cards? You might as well list every card that you own—they'll show up on your credit report anyway, along with the balance you owe. However, if you do have many credit cards with zero balances, such as those Bloomingdale's and Sears cards you haven't used for a while, now is the time to get rid of them. While some bankers ignore them, others look at them as potential liabilities.

Shopping for a mortgage online

When it comes to mortgage-rate information, the Internet is a gold mine. **Bank Rate Monitor** *(www.bankrate.com)* surveys approximately 1,400 mortgage lenders a week to determine prevailing rates for 30- and 15-year fixed-rate mortgages and one-year ARMs. **Microsurf** *(www.microsurf.com)* lists 1,100 lenders, with a full range of mortgage options for each, and provides links to calculators that let you figure out what your monthly payments will be. (Microsurf kicks lenders off the site if they lowball their quotes.) **HSH Associates** *(www.hsh.com)* regularly updates its database of 2,500 lenders, and offers several calculators and worksheets to help you figure out your best mortgage.

If you have a reasonably standard financial situation (no recent job changes or questionable credit history), you can even apply for a mortgage online with **Countrywide Home Loans** *(www.countrywide.com)*, or other smaller, lesser-known outfits that do half or more of their volume on the Web. Two that have gotten high marks from consumers include **Mandarin Mortgage** *(www.mandarinmortgage.com)* and **DiTech Funding** *(www.ditech1.com)*.

But how do you know whether a lender you're considering is reputable? If the lender represents itself as a bank or savings institution, head over to the Federal Deposit Insurance Corp.'s website *(www.fdic.gov)* and see if it shows up on a list of federally insured banks and savings institutions. The FDIC also recommends calling your state's consumer protection divisions or attorney general's office, particularly if you're considering a financing company that doesn't fall under the FDIC's mantle. At a minimum, these offices can tell you whether you're dealing with a legitimate business.

The mortgage insurance blues

I f you can't afford to put a full 20 percent down on your house, the mortgage community won't have trouble lending to you. Quite the contrary. They'll just insist that you buy mortgage insurance to seal the deal. They'll also tell you that once you've been in the house for a while and have been able to store up enough equity to cross that 20 percent line, it's easy to drop the insurance and the payments.

The truth is, it can be anything but. It's the lender's prerogative to let you escape from the land of the mortgage-insured, and when the time comes they often balk.

On a $200,000 mortgage, with 15 percent down, a buyer's mortgage insurance will cost about $476 a year. With 5 percent down, it can cost three times as much. And depending on which insurer you go with, it may cost even more. Some insurers require an additional fee up front—on top of your monthly payment—of as much as 1 percent of your loan if you put only 5 percent down. Since your lender typically chooses your insurer, this is probably going to be beyond your control as well.

So what *can* you do? The key is to understand the terms of your mortgage-insurance obligations before you close your loan. Some lenders simply require an appraisal to prove you've paid down 20 percent of your home's value. Others require additional documentation. Get your lender to explain—in writing—what conditions you have to fulfill before you can stop paying for insurance.

A CLEAN CREDIT HISTORY

Get a copy of your credit report (it costs $8) before you apply for a mortgage. That way you can clear up any mistakes or, in a worst-case scenario, prepare a defense of any blemishes and send along a note with your application. Call Equifax, 800-685-1111, *www.equifax.com;* Trans Union, 312-408-1400, *www.transunion. com;* or Experian, 800-682-7654, *www.experian.com.*

How to Win Friends and Influence Bankers

The point here is to get your mortgage as fast as possible, with the least amount of friction on both sides. If you're that perfect borrower—or close to it—you're in luck. Otherwise, you'll have to go the old-fashioned route and rely on the phone and plain old face time with a bank officer.

If you've got a squeaky clean financial history—that is, nothing out of the ordinary in your financial or personal background (no recent divorces, no collection agency sagas)—you can usually get preapproved for a mortgage within a few days. Many homebuyers in hot real estate markets get preapproved at the same time that they start their housing search, so when that dream house comes along, their bid will be more attractive than any competing bidder without mortgage preapproval. Preapproval usually involves filling out an application, getting a credit check done, and handing in copies of tax forms, W-2s, and bank statements. Once you're pre-approved, it's unlikely that the loan will fall through, unless your situation changes drastically (like you lose your job).

By the way, don't bother getting "prequalified." All that means is that the bank has taken a cursory look at your finances and determined that you're not a total basket case. They could easily change their minds once they take a look at your credit history or anything else they don't like.

Many lenders who sell their loans on the secondary market use automated underwriting systems developed in the past several years by Fannie Mae and Freddie Mac. This means the bank can just plug the numbers from your application into a computer, and it will spit out an approval or denial within hours. Bonnie O'Dell, a spokeswoman for Fannie Mae, estimates that some 500 lenders nationwide, including **Wachovia Mortgage** (800-922-8810) and **HomeSide Lending** (800-827-7022), use their system. In addition, some top lenders such as New York–based **Citicorp** (800-667-8424) and **Norwest** (800-566-3542) have systems similar to the ones used by Fannie and Freddie. If you want a quick turnaround, ask whether your lender can give you preliminary approval within 24 hours.

If your application is less than perfect, you're better off with a lender that can promise you a real live loan officer. That way you'll have someone to complain to—and, in a perfect world, to reason with—if something goes wrong. From the moment you call to check on rates to the moment you hand in your application, here are some important tips that ought to help the process go more smoothly:

- Ask for names. Who's handling my application? Who is that person's boss? What are their direct phone numbers? If your loan officer is reluctant to hand over that information, ask to see a supervisor. Knowing whom to contact can save you hours, if not days, of frustration.

- Document everything. Sending a missing tax form to the bank? Use Federal Express or registered mail—and save your receipts. If you fax a form over, print out a transaction report when you're done. That's proof that someone on the other end actually received what you sent.
- Keep a log of all phone conversations—the name of the person you spoke with (even if it's just the receptionist you left a message with), the time the call took place, and what was

---

Your money's worth

A re nasty things being said about you in your credit report? Is a hacker up to no good with the credit-card digits he stole from your last Internet purchase? You can keep tabs on your credit without going even deeper into debt.

Worth it: Credit experts recommend consumers check their credit reports once every 1 or 2 years for inquiries, fraud, and inaccurate comments, or to close inactive charge accounts The Big Three credit-reporting agencies—Equifax, Experian, and TransUnion—provide reports free to consumers who've been denied credit.

For consumers who just want to stay on top of their credit status, each report costs $2 to $8, depending on what state you're in. They're free once a year in a few states, and twice a year in Georgia.

Credit reports can be ordered by phone or on the Internet (Equifax: 800-997-2493 or *www.equifax.com;* Experian: 888-397-3742 or *www.experian.com;* Trans Union: 800-888-4213 or *www.transunion.com*).

Not worth it: "Protect your credit . . . and your good name!" urges a recent Citibank promotion.

"Don't you need to know what is in all of your credit files?" American Express asks.

Seizing upon fear of bad credit and paranoia about identity fraud, a number of credit card companies are using scare tactics to sell their customers access to credit reports. A handful of other companies, such as Privacy Guard, QSpace, CreditComm Services, and ConsumerInfo.com, also provide similar services.

But unless you've suffered bad credit or fraud and absolutely must be kept up-to-date on your credit report, the constant monitoring and frequent reports offered by these programs are excessive and expensive. Amex's CreditAware program costs about $71 for 13 months, while Citibank's CreditUpdate plan goes for $49.

discussed. If communications begin to break down, start attaching a copy of that log to every letter. Sometimes just knowing that you're paying attention is enough to keep a lender on his toes.

The Right Stuff: Filling out Your Application

OK. So your lender is looking for perfection personified and you're . . . not? Don't worry. "Underwriters are real people, too," says Dea O'Hopp, managing director of First Guaranty Mortgage. "We've had our share of student loans, medical and family problems, and tough job circumstances." Your one last opportunity to make a good impression: your application.

Make it neat. It should be typed or, in a crunch, handwritten by someone who got straight As in penmanship.

Fill in every blank. Literally. If you're applying for a mortgage with your spouse, and a space appears for your spouse's address—fill it in (and not with the words "same as above"). Come across a question you don't think applies to you? Don't skip over it. Instead write in the words "not applicable" or just "N/A."

Attach a letter of explanation any time you feel something on your application will give the lender pause. You didn't finish college? The solution: Put an asterisk in the schooling blank and attach an earnest cover letter to your application that explains how hard you've worked to educate yourself outside of high school. Suppose you've switched jobs or moved 3 times in the past 5 years. Write a letter explaining how each time you made a switch, it was for more money or better schools for your kids or whatever the reason. (Of course, we're not suggesting that you lie on your application—that's a federal offense.)

Explain, in detail, any "yes" answers that you know should be "no." On the application you'll find several declarations: Have you ever filed for bankruptcy? Are you party to a lawsuit? A yes answer on any of them means you'll have to supply additional information on another sheet of paper. Although they all look like deal breakers, you actually can explain your way out of most of these declarations. If you've ever filed for bankruptcy protection, for example, you'll

The going rate: The cost of moving in

The closing is over and you are still stunned at the number of checks you just wrote. Sorry. It's not over yet. Here are the hidden costs of settling in to your new home.

	Austin, TX	Bangor, ME	Tallahassee, FL	Eureka, CA	Rapid City, SD
Changing 3 sets of locks	$ 67.75	$ 56.00	$ 80.00	$ 56.60	$ 50.50
Fantastik (32 ounce bottle)	$ 2.49	$ 2.39	$ 2.39	$ 3.09	$ 2.50
One-year subscription to local paper	$135.00	$161.20	$159.13	$125.30	$166.50
Visit to chiropractor (from moving boxes)	$ 70.00	$ 78.00	$ 85.00	$ 73.00	$ 30.00
Celebratory bottle of Cordon Negro champagne	$ 8.99	$ 7.99	$ 8.99	$ 8.99	$ 10.99
200 gallons of heating oil	N/A	$158.00	$176.00	$162.00	$158.00
Swing Set	$ 85.00	$ 99.99	$ 99.00	$129.00	$140.00
Animal-proof garbage can	$ 17.88	$ 9.96	$ 9.67	$ 12.99	$ 9.76
Plastic rake	$ 4.77	$ 4.97	$ 4.76	$ 6.99	$ 4.76
Mailbox	$ 10.00	$ 5.47	$ 5.46	$ 5.95	$ 4.87
TOTAL	$401.88	$583.97	$630.40	$583.91	$585.88

probably be all right if you can show that it was resolved at least 2 years ago and that you've since established credit with somebody else. If you're party to a lawsuit, your lender will want proof that no future liability would prevent you from making your payments.

Provide the right credit references. What the lender wants to see: That you've paid your bills on time. Some bills, however, carry more weight than others. The electric company—which will turn off your lights should you neglect to pay its bill—is not as good a reference as, say, a student loan you paid off 2 years ago.

Ten Things Your Real Estate Broker Won't Tell You

1 My commission is negotiable.

When real estate agents tell you that the "customary" commission in your area is between 5 and 8 percent of the sale price, they expect you to fork it over without a fight. Don't. Before signing a listing contract, try to negotiate a lower fee with your broker. You'll be surprised at how easily you can knock off a percentage point or two if you hold your ground. (Your bargaining stance is measurably enhanced when you are both buying and selling a home. Then, a negotiated commission is an expected part of the deal.) "It's not something we like to tout," says a former Connecticut real estate agent, "but it does happen."

2 I'll chip in to make sure the deal goes through.

Agents not only will negotiate their commission up front but they may also take a cut later if it means saving a deal that is on the verge of breaking up over minor details. Who will pay for asbestos removal? Why shouldn't the seller have to replace the broken dishwasher? When these skirmishes arise, feel free to ask your agent to pitch in. Most will usually agree rather than see the sale—and their commission—disappear. As one former agent puts it, "It's not worth losing a $30,000 commission over a couple of thousand dollars."

3 You're the only bidder on this house.

When you express an interest in a house, the agent will often tell you that you'd better hurry because there are other bidders even when there aren't. If you suspect your agent is pressuring you to make an offer by exaggerating the activity on a certain house, ask to see the other bids. That information is supposed to be confidential, but if another offer really exists, in some cases the agent will show it to you.

4 *You should be using more than one agent.*

Agents will often pressure you to work exclusively with them. If they spend a lot of time getting to know what type of house you want and driving you around to see different properties, they figure you owe it to them to buy a house through them. But there's nothing to stop you from seeing homes with more than one agent. Checking in with a few of the best salespeople in each area is a good way to keep your finger on the pulse of the market. Many times an aggressive agent will show you a home before it appears on the multiple-listing service. And if you're looking in a large geographic area, you'll need more than one agent to make sure that you have access to all of the multiple-listing services in those places.

5 *These are all the things you need to know about this house.*

Because real estate agents are, in most cases, paid by the seller, they are supposed to protect any confidential information shared with them, like the seller's absolute lowest price, or the fact that the couple selling the house might be going through a divorce and thus may be looking for a quick deal. Furthermore, while brokers are required by federal law to tell prospective buyers about any structural problems in the house, they won't always tell you about other mitigating factors—for instance, that a murder was committed there. The subterfuge practiced by real estate brokers is often quite subtle. "When I was a seller's broker, in training class we learned to drive a certain route so buyers wouldn't see the bad houses near a listing," says Vienna Waale Besch, a buyer's broker in Seattle. "But now that I represent buyers, I drive right by the bad houses and point them out."

6 *I'll take whatever you tell me and use it against you.*

Again, because the brokers and agents are being paid by the seller, you have to remember that when you are buying a house, your interest in the deal is not the one being protected. So if you happen to mention to the agent the highest price you will actually pay on a house or that your company will pay closing costs as part of your transfer package, those are details that the agent must disclose to the person selling the house, thereby weakening your bargaining stance. Despite tougher laws in many states demanding that agents disclose their ties to sellers, many people still don't understand how the agent-buyer relationship works. Seventy percent of the consumers surveyed recently by the Consumer Federation of America said they didn't realize that most real estate professionals legally represented the seller only.

7   *This house is functionally obsolete.*

Agents have little phrases they share among themselves to classify houses that might be tough sales. This is one of them. Your agent may gush that the house you are looking at is a great deal—maybe even $10,000 under the market price—but what he or she probably won't volunteer is that a three-bedroom home with only one and one-half baths is an outdated dinosaur in an area where most comparable homes routinely include two full baths. Older homes with closed-off kitchens are also a drag on the market these days; going for much better prices are homes where the owner has knocked down a wall and added an island in the kitchen.

8   *I'm pushing my own listings.*

In most home sales, the listing agent splits his or her commission with another agent who saw the house in the multiple-listing service and brought it to the attention of a willing buyer. But an agent who finds a buyer for his or her own listing stands to rake in the full commission. With a windfall like that, you can see why some agents steer buyers toward their own listings, sometimes at the exclusion of more appropriate homes. If you're wasting a lot of time seeing homes that you don't like but that the agent is pushing, switch agents. If you are a seller, you'll want to make it clear up front that you expect the listing agent to accept less than the full commission if he or she finds the buyer. Agree on a discount before you sign the listing agreement, and make sure the amount is included in that document.

9 *This is the true value of your house.*

In order to get a listing, a broker will often give you a price that is well above the market. You put the For Sale sign up, expecting to make a killing, but the offers never materialize. A high price tag often means a house stays on the market for months, getting a reputation as a dud. This can be a particular burden in a troubled market where buyers are scarce under the best of circumstances.

10 *I'll do the footwork for you.*

It's mandatory that you thoroughly check out the neighborhoods and houses you like yourself so you know exactly what you're getting into. But there's no reason why your agent shouldn't help. Ask your agent for recent clippings from a local paper that talk about the neighborhood. Have there been any environmental studies of the area that he or she can get? What about SAT scores and other school district information? Any zoning skirmishes that may affect home values in the future? If an agent balks at these requests, find another, more aggressive one. When you do get this information from agents, however, keep in mind that they have their own agenda. It's not in their interest to tell you all the bad news about a place. But they can provide some leads that should make your own investigation easier.

Part 5

ALL ABOUT INSURANCE

Now you know why your mother worried. Why she knew to the *minute* what time you came home on those carousing teenage nights.

Parents are hostages to fate, prone to hysterical fear every time they think of something awful happening to their little one. What if the baby's fever gets worse? What if that elm tree, overburdened by your kid's new tree house, crashes onto the roof? What if something should happen to *you*—and you're suddenly unable to earn any income to support the family?

There are all kinds of insurance policies designed to ease your mind in times like these. But few parents have the time to research the major kinds of insurance they need—health, life, disability, home, and car. And even if you had the time, who wants to slog through the policy fine print, endless sales pitches, and reams of confusing figures?

Well, now you don't have to. In this section, we tell you everything you need to know to get the best insurance for your needs—and not one word more. Read it, do the worksheets, make some phone calls, and be done with it.

9

To Your Health

If Dickens wrote *Bleak House* today, it wouldn't be about the legal system. It would be about health care. Insurance companies and doctors are waging a seemingly endless war, and you are stuck in the middle. What used to be a reasonably simple system has devolved into several confusing options, none of them perfect.

Sure, if your employer still offers the old-fashioned indemnity (or "fee for service") insurance and you can afford it, most people will tell you to sign up and forget the managed care mess. But in 1997 only about a third of all employers still offered indemnity, down from half in 1996. And it's not cheap: Indemnity insurance costs the average family about $140 a month, plus a $500 deductible and 20 percent of all doctors' costs. Hence, most families are stuck with managed care.

Truth be told, this isn't all bad. Because there *are* good HMOs out there—HMOs that can offer your family quality medical care combined with very low costs and virtually no annoying paperwork for you to fill out. More good news: Your employer probably offers more health insurance options than even a year ago. Families with two working spouses can have as many as six plans to choose from. Chances are one of them is good enough. You just have to know what to look for in a plan. With the information in this chapter, you'll be able to pick the plan that works best for your family. We'll give you a crash course on the various types of insurance currently available, tell you what your plan should offer, and gird you for battle when you hear the dreaded words "claim denied."

Sizing Up Your Options

No question about it: If you're at all worried about medical nightmares befalling your children—and how many parents don't worry about that?—**indemnity** insurance will offer you the most peace of mind. This is the kind of insurance we all used to have before it got so expensive that most employers stopped offering it. With indemnity, most hospital costs are covered 100 percent. You see any doctor you want, and get reimbursed for 80 percent of the fee, after you've met your annual deductible. As a parent, what could be better than choosing any doctor under the sun?

Since indemnity policies are not an option for many of us, however, you need to know what the other alternatives are—and which is best for your family. Most insurance plans loosely fall into the following managed care categories.

Let's begin with the *least* attractive option: the plain old **HMO**, or health maintenance organization. Employers like to put the best possible spin on their HMO plans, giving them vaguely appealing names like Secure Horizon (PacifiCare) and PruCare (Prudential). That's their prerogative, of course. But what you've got to keep in mind is this: As a parent, you'll have to choose a primary care physician for yourself (internist, gynecologist, family doctor) and for your kids. Every time one of you needs medical attention, except in an emergency, you must see this "gatekeeper," who then

What you can expect to pay

Co-payments, deductibles, premiums . . . it's difficult to know what a particular plan could cost your family. None of them are cheap—even ordinary HMOs cost the average family $132 in monthly premiums—so it pays to do a little math before you make your final choice. Below are average out-of-pocket costs for a family in 1997 employed by a company with 500 employees or more. (FYI, the monthly premium you see here is usually about a third of the total cost of the insurance; your employer picks up the rest.)

	Monthly premium	Deductibles	Co-payments
Indemnity	$141	$500	20% of all doctor fees
PPO	$142	$500/$600*	10% of network doctor fees
			20% of non-network fees
POS	$141	$500/$700*	$10 per network doctor fee
			20% of non-network fees
HMO	$132	none**	$10 per doctor visit

*for seeing doctors out of network
**about a third of all HMOs require a $200 deductible for each hospital admission

decides whether to refer you on to a specialist. You pay a small co-payment (around $10) each time you visit the doctor, and most hospital and emergency room costs are covered 100 percent.

The original model for an HMO is called a **closed-end** HMO, and an example of one is the giant Kaiser Permanente—health care provider to Xerox and General Motors, among hundreds of others. The lab, the doctors, the physical therapists are all usually under one roof, all answering to one HMO. These clinics are often known as the prime culprits when it comes to long lines and impersonal care.

Alternatively, many HMOs contract out with a network of doctors, called an **independent practice association** or IPA, who practice in their own offices. The HMOs pay the IPA a flat fee based on the number of HMO patients they serve. (This is often called a capitated fee system). The IPA then has the freedom to determine how the money is spent. It's common for an HMO to have a contract with several IPAs at once.

Many insurance companies, including United Health Care, Kaiser Permanente, and Aetna US Healthcare, offer **point of service** HMOs. This option is better for most parents. As in a regular HMO, you're assigned a gatekeeper, and you owe only a small co-payment each time you use doctors in the network. The advantage over an HMO is that you also get reimbursed for seeing doctors *out* of the network; generally you'll pay 20 percent of a nonnetwork doctor's fee, after about a $700 family deductible. In other words, if your kid breaks his leg in three places, you can bring him to the best orthopedic surgeon in the country—regardless of whether the surgeon is affiliated with your insurance company—and the POS plan will cover most of the doctor's fee.

Finally, there's the **preferred provider organization**. This is a form of managed care that's so far removed from the old closed-end model that they don't even like to call themselves HMOs. (They prefer "PPO.") This is going to be the most palatable type of managed care health insurance for most parents, because it's basically the point of service model without the primary care doctor/gatekeeper. With Alliance PPO, part of BlueCross BlueShield in St. Louis, for instance, you can see any doctor in the network, though you pay anywhere from 10 to 30 percent of his fees, after a $500 family deductible. If you see a doctor out of the company's network, you pay 20 to 40 percent of the fees, after a $600 family deductible. Though they are the most expensive managed care plans, they are also the most flexible—because they both cut out that gatekeeper function and reimburse the lion's share of any doctor's fee.

Choosing the Right Plan

Never mind all those glossy health insurance brochures that your benefits department spews out every year. When choosing a health plan, the first thing you need to read is its certificate of coverage or the summary plan, which your company is required by law to make available to you. Granted, it's not the most exciting reading you'll ever encounter. But it's here you'll find out what's really covered— and what restrictions you may be under, such as whether the plan will cover congenital conditions, mental health problems, or pay for speech therapy or hearing tests. You'll learn whether your child will need approval from his or her primary care physician for every test, treatment, or visit to a specialist. You'll find out whether your plan demands preauthorization for local emergency room visits, and which ERs you are allowed to go to.

At a minimum, you should expect your health insurance to cover the following basics:

The right group of doctors. A few years ago, New York City mother Gail Landis signed up for a POS plan with Aetna, and at first she couldn't have been happier. Her pediatrician was on the list of doctors who accepted the insurance, which meant that she would have to fill out zero paperwork and her out-of-pocket costs for routine care would be next to nothing.

Until the next month, that is. Then her pediatrician dropped out. Like most employees, Landis was locked into her employer's plan for the next year. Yet she wasn't about to switch pediatricians. So she was stuck paying large fees every time her kid went to the doctor.

The moral: Don't just check the list of doctors your benefits department gives you; call the doctor's office directly and ask if he or she is happy with the program and intends to stay there.

Ideally you and the kids each get a doctor who stays with you

Choosing a doctor: Key questions to ask

What happens if my kid gets sick on a Saturday afternoon? In the middle of the night? Most doctors should offer at least some regular weekend office hours. It's all right to be told to call a referral number at night, but even then your doctor should have a clear system of backups, preferably with other nearby physicians.

How quickly can I schedule an appointment with you? For a routine exam, a week's wait is tolerable. For urgent care, a doctor should see you within an hour or two. Anything longer is a problem.

How many patients do you see in an hour? For a family practice doctor, four per hour is typical. Six or more suggests that the doctor may be rushing things.

Are you board certified in your specialty? Yes is the right answer. State medical boards set standards for each specialty, which nearly all doctors, including primary care physicians such as pediatricians or internists, try to meet. Doctors can still practice general medicine without being board certified. But board certification by now is regarded as a rite of passage for virtually every doctor.

What hospital or hospitals are you affiliated with? If you have privileges at more than one, do HMO patients have a choice? In some markets, HMO patients can get treatment at only certain hospitals. Often these are the less desirable ones.

How would you treat a rare disease that's beyond your knowledge? This is a dual-purpose question. It's a good way to find out how well-connected your doctor is to the leading specialists and teaching hospitals in your area. It's also a shrewd way to learn something about your doctor's personality. Is she or he the sort of confident, friendly person you'd feel comfortable with? Or is this doctor too curt and defensive for your tastes?

for years, monitoring your health. If you have to choose new doctors, find out what happens if you don't like your assigned pediatrician or gynecologist. Some HMOs allow you to transfer to a new doctor right away. Others may make you wait six months. Can you switch from one independent practice association to another if you decide one group better suits your family's needs? Also: How often does the HMO review the performance of its doctors? A well-run insurer should have annual reviews, allowing it to drop unreliable physicians quickly. *(Continued on page 157.)*

The real world: Will your HMO take care of your kids?

In November 1992 Katherine and Harry Christie's 9-year-old daughter, Carley, was experiencing severe stomach pains, fevers, and vomiting. After a battery of tests—including a CAT scan and a biopsy—the Christies' doctor delivered the bad news: Carley had Wilms' tumor, a potentially fatal disease in which cancer cells are found in certain parts of the kidney.

Several months later, on a Friday in late January, surgery was performed. After four hours in the operating room, Dr. Stephen Shochat, a pediatric surgeon and well-known expert in Wilms' tumor, removed Carley's tumor. That weekend the Christies camped out with Carley in the intensive care unit, helping their daughter recover from the surgery and trying to keep each other's spirits up.

On Sunday afternoon the telephone in the hospital room rang. Was it the doctor calling to check in? Was it perhaps the lab calling with the results of another series of tests? No. On the other end of the line was a man identifying himself as a "utilization review nurse" from the medical group contracted by TakeCare Health Plan in Concord, California, the Christies' health maintenance organization.

Coverage for Carley's surgery was denied. Because Dr. Shochat was not on the HMO's approved list of surgeons and the Christies had not gotten written preapproval to use an out-of-network doctor, TakeCare was no longer responsible for payment. The Christies would have to foot the $40,000 bill themselves.

Shock at getting the call turned to anger over its message. Relief over Carley's surgery was replaced by a stunning disbelief that the HMO was now refusing to pay for surgery that might have saved their daughter's life.

This isn't supposed to happen. Yes, HMOs have gotten a bad rap for supposedly squeezing doctors at the expense of patient care, for putting patients through hoops before approving their medical procedures, for turning health care into an unfeeling, strictly commercial enterprise.

But most of the criticisms are generally aimed at the way HMOs treat adults, particularly adults with chronic illnesses or life-threatening ailments—heart disease, breast cancer, prostate cancer—that require special care and expensive, long-term treatments.

Children are supposed to be the one group that is being well served by the HMO revolution. Join an HMO, and the endless routine visits to the pediatrician's office, late-night emergency room visits for the inevitable fevers and falls, and, just in case you need it, access to highly trained doctors if anything goes seriously wrong are all taken care of with low premiums and even lower co-payments. After all, HMOs were designed on the premise of preventative care—exactly the kind of care children, with their routine vaccinations and checkups, need.

It hasn't quite worked out that way.

In a rare look at how HMOs treat seriously ill children, Elizabeth Jameson, a senior analyst at the Institute for Health Policy Studies at the University of California at San Francisco School of Medicine, a leading health policy group, extensively surveyed 59 pediatricians, social workers, and nurses who treat large numbers of children with three serious childhood disorders: sickle-cell anemia, spina bifida, and craniofacial abnormalities. Jameson looked exclusively at HMOs that hold outside contracts with doctors, as opposed to closed-end plans, which require all doctors to be on staff.

The study, says Jameson, points to one overwhelming conclusion: Children in these managed care plans are far less likely to gain access to care consistent with recognized clinical guidelines than are children insured by Medi-Cal and California Children's Service, two state public health plans for low-income families. "The results of my study are incredibly dramatic," says Jameson. "Kids who are low income, who are qualified for state aid, are receiving better care than those in HMOs."

Kids with sickle-cell anemia, for instance, often avoid problems related to chronic lung disease by undergoing a series of pulmonary tests. But these tests are routinely denied by managed care plans, according to Jameson's survey results, despite their preventative nature and the fact that these procedures fall under accepted medical guidelines for treating sickle-cell anemia patients. Meanwhile, children with public insurance in California routinely receive these tests.

"Kids are ignored for simple economic reasons," explains David Lansky, president of a nonprofit group called Foundation for Accountability, which independently develops tools for evaluating HMOs. Children younger than 18 make up only about 20 to 25 percent of the general population. And the majority of them are basically healthy. Unlike heart attack patients or the elderly, who account for huge chunks of national spending on health care, only 5 percent of all children account for about 90 percent of all pediatric health care expenditures. Those who do fall ill tend to do so with rare and difficult-to-treat conditions such as cystic fibrosis, congenital heart problems, or spina bifida. These are the kinds of illnesses that require a battery of expensive specialists administering continuing care throughout a child's life—in other words, the kind of cases that are anathema to managed care's cost-conscious mandate.

While Jameson's study deals exclusively with treatment of chronically ill children, in general there are three specific ways in which HMOs work that tend to undermine their potential to give even healthy children the level of pediatric care your family expects.

HMOS DON'T WANT YOU TO SEE A SPECIALIST

First is HMOs' constant restraint in allowing primary care physicians to conduct costly tests and recommend specialists. This, of course, is a problem with adults too. But the situation is more acute with kids, because their ailments are often a mystery to doctors untrained in pediatrics or family care. "What sets children apart as patients," says Jameson, "is that they must be diagnosed and treated in the context of their rapid and continuous growth and development."

Consider 16-year-old Paige Lancaster from Stafford, Virginia. She started having severe headaches back when she was 11 years old. Paige was covered by her father's insurance with Kaiser Permanente of the Mid-Atlantic States. For more than a year Paige's mother, Barbara Lancaster, would take her daughter every few months to her Kaiser pediatrician, Dr. Corder Campbell, pleading with him to help find out what was causing Paige's headaches, nausea, and bloodshot eyes. But the doctor insisted that this was normal for some preteen girls and prescribed adult dosages of migraine medicine. Lancaster, concerned with her daughter's complaints of pain, short-term memory loss, and dramatically slipping grades, continued to lobby her doctor. "Should she see someone else? Have some tests?" she asked him. Each time, Lancaster says, he dismissed the problem as migraines.

By the time Paige was a freshman in high school, she was routinely vomiting from the headaches. Her learning problems were so extreme that Paige was placed in a special program at school. Her teachers, wanting to rule out any physical reasons for Paige's difficulties, kept asking Paige's mom what tests had been done. The school psychologist even wrote a letter to Campbell requesting an MRI and an EEG. According to Lancaster, Campbell's response was less than enthusiastic. "I'd like to report them for practicing medicine without a license," Lancaster remembers him saying. When he did finally order the tests, the MRI showed Paige had a cyst that emanated from a tumor covering 40 percent of her brain. It took two surgeries and severe radiation to get rid of most of it. And although she is recovering, Paige and her mom are still not sure to what extent Paige may be suffering permanent damage. "It just keeps hitting me in the face that Paige didn't have to go through the pain, the surgeries, the frustration with school, the humiliation, and the fact that the rest of her life may not be the quality it could have been," says Barbara Lancaster, who filed a lawsuit against Kaiser.

Lancaster sought the advice of Michael Miller, a local attorney. As he looked closer at the case, Miller consulted with Dr. Bruce Bertoff, an ear, nose and throat surgeon who is also an attorney in Miller's office. "Based on conversations I've had with other doctors," said Bertoff, "Kaiser will traditionally hold back 5 to 10 percent of the physicians' income and put it in a pool and pay it at the end of the year, depending on how close the physicians come to certain economic targets." One of the best ways primary care physicians can keep costs down, argued Bertoff, is to avoid expensive tests and specialist referrals. This incentive program, Miller and Bertoff charge, is what kept Paige's primary care physician from administering an MRI and referring her to a pediatric neurologist.

Neither Campbell nor his lawyer, Anthony Tringa, would comment on the Lancaster incident, and referred all calls to the HMO, which disputed the charges. Dr. Larry Oates, Kaiser's associate medical director, said that incentives are only a small part of a Kaiser physician's salary-based compensation, and that for the past several years the HMO has tied incentive programs for all physicians to broad goals such as quality of care and member satisfaction. Financial goals that deal with issues such as hospital stays or specialist referrals are applied to Kaiser's physician group as a whole. "We haven't driven that down to the individual physician level," says Oates, "because we are concerned about the impact on patient care." Nonetheless, the Lancasters won the case against Kaiser.

HMOS WANT YOU TO USE *THEIR* SPECIALIST, NOT THE *BEST* SPECIALIST

Even when an ailment is finally diagnosed, kids may be less likely than adults to get proper treatment. Why? Because most HMOs can recommend only plan-based specialists. And as Katherine and Harry Christie learned with their daughter, Carley, that's no guarantee that the doctor is the best, or even well regarded, in his field.

The Christies had learned, for example, that the National Cancer Institute recommends that pediatric surgeons with direct experience in Wilms' tumor perform the operation. But when the Christies met that week with the HMO oncologist who would be treating Carley, they found out her surgeon was neither a pediatric specialist nor an expert in Wilms' tumor. It was even more disconcerting when the Christies found out that Dr. Stephen Shochat, a pediatric surgeon with plenty of experience treating this rare cancer, practiced in the children's branch of the same hospital as their assigned doctor and was even contracted with the same HMO. Unfortunately for the Christies, however, Shochat was a member of a different independent practice association (IPA), or branch of the HMO, than the one the Christies had signed up with when they joined TakeCare. "What's going on?" Harry Christie asked Carley's primary care doctor. He says her only response was to defend the adult urologist assigned to the case. He's one of the specialists in the medical group they chose under contract with their HMO, he says she explained. Dr. Shochat simply wasn't on that list.

No way, thought Christie. "I can't risk my daughter's life by placing her in the care of someone not qualified." So Christie told the primary care physician he was going to make an appointment with Dr. Shochat. "You have to get us a referral," he told Carley's doctor.

When the HMO refused to pay, the Christies appealed several times, then ultimately took the case to arbitration. The committee ruled that TakeCare had to pay the bill. The Christies also filed a complaint with the California Department of Corporations, the state agency that oversees HMOs. The department fined TakeCare $500,000 three years after Carley's surgery, the largest fine ever imposed on a California managed care organization.

TakeCare is now part of PacifiCare, which won't comment on the case. But Mark Reagan, an attorney with Foley Lardner Weissburg & Aronson, who represented TakeCare in the case, stands by the plan's initial endorsement of the adult urologist. "There is evidence out there that you don't have to know Wilms' tumor to treat it," says Reagan, "but you do need experience in removing kidneys. The TakeCare doctor assigned to the case was an expert in these surgeries." But was he the most qualified? "Of course you want the most qualified doctors when it comes to your loved ones," says Reagan. "But the most qualified isn't always what you'll get. That's what goes along with lower costs."

HMOS DON'T PAY ATTENTION TO CHILD DEVELOPMENT

Another factor that leads HMOs to falter in their treatment of children is this: Most of their policies are based largely on adult care, which may not be appropriate for children. In Jameson's study, she found numerous examples of spina bifida patients who were denied a wheelchair or set of braces. HMO policies often provide for these devices only once or twice during a patient's lifetime. That may be fine for adults, but it doesn't take into account children's constant need for new devices as they grow.

Denise Tyriver knows what it's like to deal with plans that don't pay enough attention to child development. The Orlando mother of two switched her family to an HMO in June 1997, when her husband's employer started offering the option. Tyriver's 7-year-old daughter, Megan, has an autism-related disorder, and her constant care has meant plenty of medical bills. The HMO looked like the perfect, less expensive option.

Like a lot of children with this condition, Megan has trouble focusing her eyes. An optometrist using special exercises may be able to help train her vision. But the doctor group affiliated with the Tyrivers' HMO, Florida Hospital Healthcare System, turned down the request. Why? The HMO, American Medical Healthcare, will not cover what are called "developmental treatments."

Stunned by the refusal, Denise Tyriver pulled out her plan's certificate of group coverage and studied it carefully. She found out her health plan did not, indeed, cover treatments such as "learning-disabled testing . . . speech therapy for other than acute traumatic injury or physical functional defect incurred while covered under this certificate; vision therapy, including eye exercises . . ." Says Tyriver: "There it was in black and white. I couldn't believe I hadn't paid attention before."

"Most plans don't cover developmental programs," explains Dr. Edward Cabrera, chief executive of American Medical Healthcare, "because it falls in the vague category of 'not medically necessary.' It may help the individual, but it may not solve a medical problem. It's just not in her plan, so it's not something she bought. It's kind of like going to McDonald's and ordering a cheeseburger. If you want lettuce and tomato, you have to order the Big Mac."

WILL IT GET ANY BETTER?

Cases like the Tyrivers' are starting to put a long overdue spotlight on the problems with pediatrics and managed care. And at first glance, it looks like the industry is coming up with several encouraging initiatives, such as the Pediatric Asthma Clinic at Lovelace Health Systems in Albuquerque, New Mexico. Kids with asthma—one of the most common pediatric ailments—experienced a 60 percent decrease in hospital admissions and an 82 percent decrease in emergency room visits. The majority of HMOs, in fact, have introduced or are considering introducing asthma clinics. Meanwhile, a subsidiary of United Healthcare has recently started a nationwide pediatric transplant network, which includes access to specialists from all over the country in pediatric heart, lung, liver, kidney, and bone marrow transplants.

The American Association of Health Plans, an industry trade group, has stepped up its efforts to track medical outcomes in pediatric care, says President Karen Ignagni. And the nonprofit Foundation for Accountability is working on a 2-year project that will pinpoint a group of consistent pediatric measurements that companies can use to evaluate how well managed care treats children. Also, federal and state governments have stepped up efforts to regulate managed care companies.

Recognizing that more regulation is probably unavoidable, Kaiser Permanente, HIP Health Insurance Plans, and Group Health Cooperative of Puget Sound—three large nonprofit HMOs—have banded together with consumer organizations to come up with 18 guidelines for managed care. Among them: a full disclosure of how a health plan's compensation system is structured.

Is this enough? Maybe, but Elizabeth Jameson isn't holding her breath. "I'm less optimistic now than ever before on children and managed care," she says. "Kids who are sick are expensive, and managed care has a financial incentive to limit access to special care." Moreover, she points out, with the exception of illnesses like asthma, "kids who are sick are sick in small numbers." Far fewer children have leukemia than adults, for instance, so chances are slim that any particular HMO will have a pediatric leukemia specialist. And unless this HMO pays for out-of-network specialists, a child with leukemia may be stuck with a doctor who knows nothing about the latest advances. "No system is perfect," says Jameson, "but managed care won't work unless parents can be involved in challenging the system when it's wrong. HMOs want the cheapest providers and oftentimes these labs or brace-makers or orthopedic providers don't know a hill of beans about kids."

Pediatric specialists. Medicine has become far more specialized than any layperson could imagine, and pediatrics is no exception. "A tracheotomy on a two-year-old is a completely different procedure than a tracheotomy on an adult, I can assure you," says Dr. Vincent Riccardi, a pediatrician and head of American Medical Consumers, a for-profit group that helps patients deal with managed care plans.

Thus, your plan must include a:

- pediatric orthopedist
- pediatric neurologist
- pediatric cardiologist
- pediatric gastroenterologist and a
- pediatric ear, nose and throat doctor

If your health plan doesn't have the pediatric specialists you need, your primary care physician may balk at referring you to a more costly doctor outside the plan. And in that case, there's no telling whom you'll get. A recent study of HMOs by the University of California at San Francisco, for example, describes a pediatrician who referred a lupus patient to an adult urologist for a kidney biopsy. Treating the kid like any other patient, the urologist performed an open-back biopsy. But this type of biopsy is inappropriate for children, and a pediatric urologist would have performed a less invasive procedure. The open-back wound resulted in serious complications from the anesthetic required for the procedure.

Affiliation with a hospital that offers pediatric emergency room care. Ideally you'll get a local *children's* hospital with pediatric emergency room care. Your employee benefits department should be able to give you a list of the hospitals affiliated with your plan; call those hospitals and ask if they have pediatric specialists (not just pediatricians) on call in the ER 24 hours a day. Ask if it's a children's hospital, which means that it is a teaching hospital in pediatrics, where specialists who teach and conduct research are aware of cutting-edge treatments. Once you've found a good hospital, check with your pediatrician to make sure she has admitting privileges to that hospital and routinely makes referrals there.

The right credentials. The plan should be accredited by the National Committee for Quality Assurance *(www.ncqa.org;* 1350 New York Ave. N.W., Suite 700, Washington, D.C. 20005; 888-275-7585), which has accredited about half of all HMOs. In addition, ask your employee benefits department or the insurance company's marketing department directly what percentage of its doctors are board certified. For each specialty, state medical boards set standards that must be met for a doctor to be a certified specialist in a particular area. It's standard for doctors to be board certified, says Lois Gaeta, spokesperson for the American Medical Association; certification involves taking courses and meeting criteria to ensure that the doctor is up-to-date in her area of expertise. Typically, 80 percent of an HMO's doctors have passed their board exams. The remainder aren't necessarily weaker doctors; if they are beginning their careers, they may be midway through board review. It's worth asking about.

Good emergency room coverage. There are two policies managed care companies use to determine whether they'll pay an ER fee. Diagnostic coverage means the HMO will pay the bill only if you got prior approval or if, after the fact, the plan determines the situation was truly an emergency. In other words, if your child has an extremely high fever and it turns out to be nothing, you'll be stuck with the bill. Preferable is the prudent layperson policy, enforced by any plan accredited by NCQA, which means that if it's reasonable for an average person to think it's an emergency, it's covered. For example, it's reasonable to assume that a young child with an extremely high fever could have meningitis, so even if the child turns out to be fine, the cost of the ER visit is covered.

DON'T BE SURPRISED IF YOUR FAMILY HEALTH INSURANCE WON'T COVER . . .

Mental health. Some HMOs pay 100 percent of the costs for as many as 30 outpatient sessions a year. Others require you to start paying part of the bill as early as the second session. Similarly, HMOs vary widely in what sort of drug- and alcohol-abuse counseling they will cover.

Ancillary services. Aetna US Healthcare's marketing material assures that members can count on "a full spectrum of health management, preventive care and wellness programs that address unique needs at various ages." Later on is a list of 14 services for which it won't pay the bill. These include hearing aids, custodial care, long-term rehabilitation therapy, and immunizations for travel or work.

Your money's worth

I s that mole cancerous? What do lice look like? What are the symptoms of meningitis? Sometimes you're too antsy to wait for the doctor to return your call; you need to know *now.* A quick glance at a good family medical guide goes a long way toward restoring your peace of mind. Problem is, which one? Nearly every prestigious medical school—including Johns Hopkins and Yale—has its contender. Which one will tell you what's wrong in language you can understand?

Worth it: Mayo Clinic Family Health Book (Morrow, 1996): $42.50
In plain language, the Mayo Clinic's guide is the best reference to gird you for the doctor's confusing pronouncements and instructions. Instead of just listing the various treatments for ear infections, for example, it includes an essay on the pros and cons of surgery to prevent recurrence. It has plenty of photographs of various skin ailments (brace yourself), so you can compare your blemish with a cancerous "bi-colored" mole in the picture. The *Family Health Book* is broken into consumer-friendly sections—"Ages one through five," for example—so that you can spend some time browsing through a section to get a sense of what's ahead. Best of all, when you finally get to the doctor, you'll have a running start and won't spend his harried 10 minutes on the basics.

Not worth it: The Columbia University College of Physicians and Surgeons Complete Home Medical Guide (Crown, 1995): $50
First of all, with its hospital-tile-blue boxes and dreary prose, it will bring to mind those brochures you got in high school about "health" topics that teachers were too embarrassed to talk about. More important, the authors of the *Home Medical Guide* don't seem to know why you bought this book. For instance, let's say you want to know if Mom's painful cramps could mean an ovarian cyst. Whereas the Mayo Clinic book explains what cysts and their warning signs are, how doctors can diagnose them, and how they may ultimately be treated—in its own Women's Health section—the Columbia guide only explains *what* the cysts are, never bothering to describe diagnostic techniques or possible treatments. Chances are, that's precisely the information Mom wants.

Inquire whether a prospective plan covers prescription drugs, eye care, dental care, foot care, or chiropractors.

Maternity "extras." If you're planning more children, check into the plan's maternity coverage. Most HMOs cover regular doctor visits during pregnancy, as well as 100 percent of delivery costs. But not all will cover sonograms, maternity vitamins, amniocentesis or other genetic testing, midwives, or birthing coaches. Moreover, you could be out of the hospital well before you're back on your legs: Some plans, for instance, limit C-section hospital stays to 48 hours.

Experimental procedures. Nearly every health plan has an "experimental exclusion" clause, which means your insurer won't cover any procedures it considers to be an unproven method of treatment. It also may not cover drugs that are prescribed "off-label"— that is, for a condition other than its FDA-approved usage. Ask which, if any, experimental procedures your plan covers (such as a bone marrow transplant for leukemia). If you think experimental therapy coverage could become an issue, ask colleagues and benefit managers which HMOs are more lenient in this area.

WHAT YOU WON'T FIND IN THE COMPANY BROCHURE

Most HMOs have no idea how good (or bad) their pediatric care really is. Adult health issues in managed care have been the subject of countless studies. But ask about studies on children and HMOs, and most researchers draw a blank. For instance, the NCQA collects information on 71 data points to analyze and evaluate HMO performance. But only 12 of those points have anything to do with children. And of those, 3 deal with prenatal or obstetrical care, and 2 deal with adolescents. By comparison, no such dearth of information exists on adult treatments. Looking for the latest numbers on beta blockers? The NCQA will tell you that an average of 62 percent of heart attack victims receive this drug from their HMO to ward off a second attack. Interested in similar data on treatment for chicken pox or ear infections? Sorry. Not available.

The terms "medically necessary" and "not medically reimbursable" are favorite HMO loopholes. Plans constantly use this wording to deny care. In Missouri, state regulators became so concerned by the number of consumer complaints about HMOs' denials that they set up an independent panel of doctors to review them. "We kept running into this situation where an HMO would say, 'This procedure wasn't medically necessary,' and the patient or their doctor would say, 'Yes, it was medically necessary,' " says Tom Bixby, director of the consumer affairs division for the state insurance department. In two years, the panel found that nearly 50 percent of the people who complained about their claims had been unfairly denied.

Nearly everyone you see in a managed care network has a financial incentive to keep you out of his or her office. Many managed care plans now pay their primary care doctors through some sort of capitation system. That is, rather than simply pay any bill presented to them by your doctor, most HMOs pay their physicians a set amount every month for each of their patients.

That sounds like an incentive to keep you healthy: Even if you don't need your doctor, he or she gets paid. But what you need to look out for are additional financial incentives that come with some capitation systems. Some HMOs have "withhold" systems, in which a percentage of doctors' monthly fees are withheld and then reimbursed if they keep their referral rates to specialists low enough. Others pay bonuses for low referral rates. And still others have so called risk pools, whereby primary doctors get a lump sum on top of their capitation rate to pay for any patient tests or specialist referrals. Anything left over is their bonus. The result: You'll have primary care physicians either doing procedures for which they're not adequately trained or, more commonly, just cutting corners. They'll aggressively prescribe antibiotics for chronic ear infections instead of sending your child to a specialist, for example. What can you do? Speak up. If you don't pester your primary care physician for specialist referrals, you may never get them.

Treatment guidelines are set by number crunchers. Actuaries collect data on historical care and perform outcome studies on different procedures and lengths of stay. Then they provide the information to HMOs to be used as industry standards. And these standards are written in stone. Lee Wesner, an electronics manufacturing manager, needed back surgery for a pinched nerve. The condition was so bad that he was losing the use of his foot and actually dragging it. Yet despite the fact that his orthopedist said delaying an operation could cause serious damage, Wesner's health plan wouldn't approve immediate surgery. Why? The condition had only persisted for 4 weeks, 2 shy of the recommended 6.

You can fight the "usual and customary fee" problem. Indemnity, PPO, and POS insurers say they'll reimburse a percentage of doctor's fees—anywhere from 60 to 90 percent. Don't be surprised, though, if your insurer pays less from time to time. Its excuse? Your doctor charges more than the "usual and customary" fees for the area. What to do when your insurer says it won't pay the full bill? Your best bet is to go after the insurance company and convince it that you're not being gouged. The easiest way to do this is to call your doctor's office and ask the billing manager how much other insurers have paid for the procedure you're getting. (Of course, you're

---

The going rate: The cost of keeping baby healthy

An ounce of prevention is worth a pound of cure, right? When it comes to creating a firewall between illness and baby, for many parents, money is no object.

	Philadelphia, Pa.	Denver, Colo.	Atlanta, Ga.	San Francisco, Calif.	Dallas, Tex.
Natural Baby organic cotton crib blanket	$ 42.95	$ 42.95	$ 42.95	$ 42.95	$ 42.95
Organic apples (1 lb.)	$ 1.99	$ 1.99	$ 2.39	$ 1.99	$ 1.99
Tom's of Maine all-natural toothpaste, Silly Strawberry (3.5 ounces)	$ 2.39	$ 3.05	$ 2.89	$ 3.69	$ 2.79
Cod liver oil (90 tablets)	$ 5.99	$ 5.90	$ 6.75	$ 5.89	$ 3.99
Reduced fat Oreos (20-ounce package)	$ 3.29	$ 2.99	$ 3.59	$ 2.59	$ 1.99
Flintstone's vitamins (60 tablets)	$ 5.97	$ 6.25	$ 5.49	$ 6.69	$ 6.99
"Mr. Babyproofer" home video	$ 19.98	$ 19.98	$ 19.98	$ 19.98	$ 19.98
Purell hand sanitizer	$ 2.79	$ 3.99	$ 2.71	$ 3.49	$ 3.79
Aranizer air filter	$225.00	$225.00	$225.00	$225.00	$225.00
Baby-sized sunglasses	$ 3.99	$ 10.00	$ 6.00	$ 3.00	$ 3.99
Munchkin's White Hot Baby safety spoon	$ 2.99	$ 2.99	$ 2.99	$ 3.29	$ 2.99
Playskool Microban 1-2-3 high chair	$ 74.99	$ 79.99	$ 74.99	$ 74.99	$ 74.99
Carewatch video monitoring system	$299.95	$299.95	$299.95	$299.95	$299.95
Total cost	$692.27	$705.03	$695.68	$693.50	$691.39

out of luck if your doctor really is overcharging you. Then it's time to consider switching doctors, not carriers.)

What to Do When Your Insurer Won't Pay

The words "claim denied" are so common that you would think people are routinely submitting claims for colonic irrigation and laser hair removal. The reality is that some insurance companies automatically deny a certain number of procedures each month. Why? They don't really pay attention to the specifics of each case. They also figure most people won't fight. But when people do fight, they often win: Some plans have reversal rates as high as 76 percent on denials.

Managed care companies are required to have a grievance or appeals process in place. If you've been denied coverage, or if you forgot to get preapproval, start with a letter briefly describing your complaint. Include letters from professionals outside the plan, such as teachers or counselors that support your position, copies of your child's medical records that pertain to your complaint, and any other supporting documentation you might have. Does your primary physician agree with your complaint? Ask him or her to include a letter saying so. And get your company's employee benefits department on board. The last thing an HMO wants to do is anger the person paying the bills.

Send all of this to the HMO's medical director, head of customer service marketing department, and top executives. Send copies to your state insurance department or agency that oversees HMOs. It's never too early to get your grievance on file with the government.

If you get no response, don't sit and wait. You may find you have to fill out a formal grievance form that your HMO requires. More importantly, there may be a deadline for the filing, such as no later than 30 or 60 days after treatment. This filing formalizes your appeal and sets it apart from a routine complaint. It also forces someone at the HMO who was not involved directly in your case to review your complaint. Get on the phone, get names, take notes, and don't give up.

If the answer is no, insist on appearing before a grievance committee. Granted, these companies are full of HMO employees and are likely to be far from objective. But when a grievance goes this far, the HMO knows you're likely to take further action. And, in most states, it is mandatory that you follow every step of an HMO's grievance procedure before you can pursue a lawsuit.

How to Cut Your Family's Medical Costs

For most families, there's only one way: a flexible spending account. Many employers offer these accounts as an employee benefit. At the beginning of each year, you get to set aside a portion of your salary, tax-free, for anticipated medical expenses. Say you set aside $1,000 (usually taken out of your salary in monthly increments). As soon as you reach $1,000 in expenses—through deductibles, your share of doctors' fees, etc.—you get the money back. Your savings for the year? If you are in the 28 percent tax bracket, about $300 dollars. The best way to gauge how much money to set aside in a medical flexible spending account is to look at out-of-pocket medical costs from last year. Then set aside slightly less. Why? Any money left over in the account is forfeited.

10

Protecting Your Family

You're barely home from the hospital before the insurance sales-people start calling. They know that you need to have some life and disability insurance—so that your kids will be taken care of financially if you die or get injured.

Precisely because buying insurance is such a deadly chore, few of us ever approach it with the zeal of the impassioned bargain hunter, armed with fact books and worksheets, ready to beat the saleman down on every last dollar. Instead, we often wait passively for someone else—usually an insurance agent—to bring up the subject and then let that person dictate the course of the conversation. Perhaps that's why the Consumer Federation of America, a non-profit organization of consumer groups, estimates that Americans waste $6 billion every year on unnecessary life insurance premiums alone.

Why waste money on coverage that you don't need, or even understand? With just a little bit of attention, you can track down the exact right life and disability insurance policy for your family. You can set up a plan that will pretty much go on autopilot so you only have to tinker with it every few years. And you can get it at the right price.

The Best Life Insurance Strategy

Just about the last thing an insurance agent wants to sell you is term life insurance. In fact, in a 14-page "special advertising section" in a recent issue of *Newsweek* magazine, term insurance is barely mentioned. Whole life and its various "cash value" cousins take up most of the space. Why? There's a lot less money to be made selling term policies.

Of course, that's not what a sales agent will tell you. Rather, his pitch will go something like this: If you buy term, you are covered for a specific span of time, say 5 or 20 years. Whether you buy level term (premiums stay constant) or annual renewable (premiums gradually increase), you get only one thing: the death benefit, or a lump sum payment to your beneficiaries if you die during the life of your policy. If you don't die, you get nothing, nada, bupkus.

Whole life insurance, on the other hand, combines a death benefit with a savings component. You pay the same premium every year (which, by the way, is usually 5 to 10 times higher than premiums for term—at least until you're 50 or so). Part of that premium accumulates in a tax-deferred "cash value" reserve that earns interest. In addition to interest, many companies credit the reserve with an annual dividend, depending on the company's performance. The reserve can be borrowed against and can eventually be used to pay for your kid's college or for your retirement. It's not just insurance, it's an *investment*. You can't go wrong!

Well, yes you can. For the vast majority of parents, the best life insurance policy can be summed up in a word: term. There are two reasons why: (1) Many families on a tight budget won't be able to afford the amount of coverage they need if they buy whole life insurance; (2) Whole life is, for most people, a bad investment. The policy's advertised rate of return, which are a set of hypothetical numbers that your salesman will call the "policy illustration," can have little or no relation to reality. In fact, the policy's returns will usually significantly trail returns available from other investments. If you are in your twenties or thirties, you'd be better off buying term and putting the rest of the money in a portfolio of well-managed mutual funds. (See Chapter 14, "The Big Picture.")

Moreover, if you're looking at whole life as a savings account, bear in mind that in general, it takes about 10 to 15 years for the cash value of your policy—the amount you get if you cash it in—to equal the amount you've paid in annual premiums.

Finally, by the time term premiums cost as much as premiums for whole life—for most people, sometime in their fifties or sixties—your children will be supporting themselves (one hopes) and you won't need life insurance, period.

Watch Out for Variable and Universal Life

Two other kinds of cash value, or permanent insurance, seem, at first glance, to be a better version of whole life. Universal, like whole life, combines insurance with savings. The savings component, called an accumulation fund, earns interest monthly and is used to pay the mortality charge (the operating costs of the policy). The sales pitch for universal is that premiums are flexible—as long as you pay enough to maintain the mortality charge, you can skip adding to the accumulation fund if money is tight. And if you contribute enough to the accumulation fund in the policy's early years, it can throw off enough income to pay your premium in later years.

How to find the best insurance company

Will your insurer be there to come through on its promises? Picking a company with high marks from the independent ratings agencies is no guarantee, but it is your best bet. A. M. Best assigns letter ratings to almost 2,500 insurers. Check your local library for the latest annual edition of *Best's Insurance Reports*. You can also get Best's ratings by checking out *www.ambest.com* (each service has a nominal fee). For whole life insurance, look for 10- and 20-year performance data on how well the insurer has treated people who bought in the past.

But don't leave it entirely to Best. Because life and disability insurance are such long-term commitments, rating agencies have a difficult time evaluating insurance companies. Call the three big bond-rating firms: Standard & Poor's (212-208-1527, *www.ratings.com*), Moody's Investors Service (212-553-0300, *www.moodys.com*), and Duff & Phelps (312-368-3157, *www.dcrco.com*). Look out for insurers that have any ratings well below the top three ratings at each firm.

As for agents, don't rely on state licenses—nearly anyone can pass the state licensing exam—or streams of acronyms on a business card. The most meaningful industry credential—chartered life underwriter—means that the agent has passed 10 exams in such areas as law, personal-risk management, and insurance contract analysis. Your next best step is to choose someone who has at least one or two clients whom you know. If that's not an option, at least ask for some references and find out how long the agent has been in business.

A captive agent sells products for one company only; an independent agent sells for many. Many of the biggest companies, such as Nationwide, Northwestern, and State Farm have captive agents. Captive agents may be able to get you a better deal on term, because the company picks up some of the overhead. Although independent agents may charge slightly higher commissions, they may be a better bet for permanent insurance.

But there are significant drawbacks to universal policies. Again, a good investing plan will generally outperform any accumulation fund. And just because the premiums are flexible doesn't mean they're smaller. If you skimp on premiums in the policy's early years, you can be socked for higher charges later on, when you originally planned on paying little or nothing. The alternative is to drop the policy and withdraw savings you may have built up. If you drop the policy in the first few years, you may have to pay a hefty surrender charge.

With variable life insurance, your savings component is invested in one of several portfolios that are offered by the insurance company. On average, most companies offer 10 different portfolios, including stock, bond, and money-market funds. The insurers often manage these funds themselves, collecting fees for both administering the insurance and managing the portfolios.

There are two basic types of variable life. One demands a fixed-premium payment. The other, variable-universal life, has a flexible premium like universal life. Remember, though, that variable returns can fluctuate along with the financial markets. If the stock market takes a hefty dive, you may find the cash value portion of your policy in the tank. You have little control over where those investments go or how they are managed. Again, you'd be better off with a mutual fund, which you can simply sell when the going gets rough.

What Happens If You Cancel the Policy

There are three things you can do when your term policy is up: drop it, renew it, or convert it to a permanent-insurance product like whole life—at a higher premium, of course. Some policies are guaranteed renewable—that is, you do not need to submit to another physical examination to renew your policy when the term is expired. Almost all have a conversion feature that allows you to convert the policy to a permanent product later without having to submit to a medical exam. You can also just stop making payments before the term is up, and the policy will automatically be canceled. Just be aware that if you want another policy in the future, it may cost more than what you're paying now.

Term vs. whole life: A comparison

W ho cares if whole life insurance isn't such a good savings strategy?" you say. "At least I'll be saving *something*—which is more than I'm doing now." Perhaps the following example will persuade you to think otherwise.

We did the math on two types of policies for a 30-year-old nonsmoking male. One policy is $100,000 in whole life coverage from Northwestern Mutual Life, while the other is $100,000 of term coverage from John Hancock. After paying premiums for 20 years, here is what he gets.

The annual premium on the $100,000 whole life policy is $1,124. The dividends that he'll be earning on the policy—which are linked to the company's performance—are automatically invested into more insurance; by year 20 our policyholder will, in Northwestern's best-case scenario, have an additional $42,905 in insurance.

The cost of annual premiums for 20 years: $22,480 (in today's dollars). How much would he get if he wanted to cash in his policy at this time? If he hadn't borrowed against the policy and had paid his premiums regularly, the cash value would equal $44,175, according to Northwestern's best estimate. After taxes, assuming he's in the 28 percent tax bracket, he'll end up with a check for $38,100.

Sounds pretty good, until you consider the alternative. Let's say our same young father buys a 20-year $100,000 term policy from John Hancock, which has an initial premium of $155 and annual premiums of $172 after that. He will spend $3,423 over 20 years to keep this coverage. More important, though, is what he does with the savings: Each year, if he invests the difference between the cost of the annual term premium and the annual whole life premium ($952 per year) in a mutual fund that returns an average of 12 percent—about what the stock market has done, historically—he will have, after taxes, $51,045. Case closed.

Whole life, on the other hand, is a long-term commitment. If your cash flow is shaky, you could end up being among the nearly 30 percent of whole life policy holders who drop the coverage in the first 3 years. You will have had life insurance—but you would have paid dearly for it, as the policy is too new to have any cash value.

To cancel after 5 years, for example, a 35-year-old male with a $250,000 whole life policy would receive the $7,500 cash value of his policy, according to one company's policy illustration. But he would have paid $14,490 in annual premiums—not exactly a state-of-the-art investment. Only after holding the policy for 17 years

How much life insurance do you need?

The worksheet below will help you estimate how much life insurance you need. Each income-earning adult in your family should fill it out.

Step 1: Your income shortfall

Current monthly living expenses (enter figure from Chapter 1)   A _____

Survivors' future monthly living expenses (about 75 percent of current   B _____
expenses)

Survivors' expected monthly income (include spouse's income,   C _____
pensions, and Social Security)

Expected monthly shortfall (B-C)   D _____

Annual shortfall (D times 12)   E _____

Lifetime shortfall (Line E times the number of years your income   F _____
will be needed—usually until the youngest child finishes college)

Step 2: Figuring one-time expenses at your death

Your final expenses

    Funeral costs   _____

    Burial vault or cemetery plot   _____

    Taxes (most people will not incur federal or state taxes, but check   _____
      with your accountant to make sure)

    Probate court costs   _____

    Medical costs (if your health plan is less than comprehensive,   _____
      budget at least $10,000 for uninsured medical expenses)

Total final expenses   G _____

Your survivors' extra expenses

    Emergency fund (3 times Line A)   _____

    Tuition ($100,000 per child for private, half for public)   _____

    Any outstanding debts (bear in mind that if you include your
      mortgage, you should deduct this from your monthly expenses
      on Line A)   _____

    Child care   _____

Total survivors' extra expenses   H _____

Total one-time expenses (add G and H)   I _____

Step 3: How much you need

Add Line F and Line I (total needed)   J _____

Total assets you're willing to dip into (i.e., excluding your home)   K _____

Total insurance you need (J minus K)   L _____

would the policyholder come close to breaking even, having paid premiums totaling $49,266 and receiving the policy's cash value of $48,750. It's only after 20 years that the investment begins to pay off, when premiums would total $57,960, while the cash value would be $61,000 and growing fast.

Where to Get the Cheapest Term Insurance

Several insurance companies, such as **USAA Life** (800-531-8000) and **Ameritas Life Insurance** (800-745-6665), bypass agents and sell to the consumer directly. Others, notably **John Alden** (800-435-7969), sell "low-load" term, with discounted sales charges.

That's not to say that agent-sold term policies are always more expensive. Term insurance costs insurers very little, since they rarely have to pay out. As a result, insurers that are willing to pay skimpy commissions to their agents or accept low profit margins can beat the direct sellers' best premiums. For example, agent-sold Valley Forge Life/CNA charges $83 annually for a $100,000, 10-year level-premium term insurance policy for a 35-year-old non-smoking male. USAA Life charges $178 annually for a similar policy.

Wherever you get your quote for a term policy, you should compare it to one of the following computerized databases that specialize in giving term life quotes for free: **Quotesmith** (800-556-9393, *www.quotesmith.com*) has a database of 159 companies that sell low-load and agent-sold policies. If you specify the type of policy you're looking for, Quotesmith will send you or let you download, free of charge, a list of the cheapest policies that meet your criteria. San Francisco–based **SelectQuote** (800-343-1985) performs essentially the same service, working off a much smaller database—19 companies. **TermQuote** (800-444-8376) of Dayton, Ohio, covers over 100 companies and will furnish 16 agent-sold quotes free of charge. **Wholesale Insurance Network** (800-808-5810) markets products from 7 companies. Bear in mind that most of these services offer no hand-holding, no advice. If advice is what you want, you'll probably get bounced to financial planners or agents themselves.

Nine Ways to Cut Your Life Insurance Premium

1. *Forget corporate loyalty.* Life insurance through your employer is convenient, but it may not be the best deal. Under group policies, everyone, no matter what their health situation, has to be accepted, which drives up the cost of group insurance. Compare your employer's policy to at least one of the computerized quote services. (Obviously, if your employer is giving you the insurance as part of your compensation, there's no reason to decline it. You may just want to look elsewhere for *supplemental* insurance.)

2. *Surrender and win.* There are no surrender charges or penalties for discontinuing your term policy, so there's no harm in shopping for a new policy every 3 years or so. Selling term insurance is a competitive business, and chances are good that you'll find a better deal than the one you have. If you don't want to change policies, you may even be able to convince your insurance company to give you a better deal. Arm yourself with quotes from other companies, threaten to take your business elsewhere, and they may cave in.

3. *Don't assume your insurer's decision is final.* Kevin Campbell thought he was just being honest when he told a medical examiner for John Alden that he'd smoked 6 cigars in the past five years. The Ohio physician, who gets out and jogs twice a week, had no history of medical problems and figured that the insurer would understand that for him, cigars were a way to mark special occasions.

No such luck. As far as John Alden was concerned, there was no difference between Campbell and a 2-pack-a-day man. The company quoted him a $2,150 annual premium for a $1.3 million, 10-year term policy. That was $1,150 more than the nonsmoker's rate.

But Campbell wasn't having it. He wrote a letter to John Alden demanding a nonsmoker's rate. After 3 weeks of negotiating, the company cut his initial quote by 50 percent. (If you do smoke, 'fess up. If you die of a smoking-related illness, your insurer can choose not to pay your death benefit.)

4. *Beware false positives.* Prudential agent Steve Richter knew his client wasn't a pothead or a pill freak. There was no way that this man, a 35-year-old father of four who co-owned a construction company, would jeopardize his business or his pilot's license.

Yet as part of the medical exam that Prudential requires before issuing a policy, Richter's client had tested positive for an illegal drug.

At Richter's urging, the client decided to challenge the test results. He submitted to 3 random, unannounced urine tests administered by a Prudential-hired paramedic whose preferred testing time was 5:00 in the morning. The client also offered to submit hair samples that Prudential could test for the presence of other illegal drugs. When the additional tests showed no traces of marijuana or other illicit substances, the client got his $250,000 policy.

5. *Buy in bulk.* Just like with Cheerios, if you buy more, you get a better deal. If, for example, a 35-year-old male nonsmoker buys a $100,000 10-year term policy from USAA, it could cost him $178 annually. If he buys a $250,000 policy, it would cost him $260 annually. Moreover, if you pay your policy in one lump sum each year, you may save about 5 percent of what it would cost if you paid in 12 monthly payments.

6. *Buy back your old policy.* Trying to get a policy back after you've dropped it can be a tough task. Jeffrey West, a Massachusetts financial adviser, has one client who was short on cash and had to drop his $150,000 whole life policy a few years ago. He had no way of recouping his premiums. But when he got some extra money, instead of buying a new policy, the 37-year-old developer went back to the company and asked it to consider reinstating his old one. The company agreed, on the condition that he pass a physical and pay his outstanding $2,300 premium. His savings? About $2,000 in premiums.

7. *Don't get taken for a rider.* Insurance companies have come up with a host of extras that sound good but aren't worth the dough. Consider the accidental death rider, more commonly called double indemnity. For about $50 more a year, an insurance company promises to pay your survivors double the face amount of a policy if you die in an accident. But it's foolish to speculate on the manner of your demise, especially since accidental death is relatively rare.

The waiver-of-premium rider is another one you should skip. Under this rider, which can cost as much as 10 percent of your annual premium, your insurer will continue your coverage in case you're disabled and unable to pay the annual rate. But you should

---

How much does peace of mind cost?

W hat does it cost to make sure your family will be taken care of if you die or become unable to work? We looked for the lowest annual rates available for term life and disability insurance, as of spring 1998, for a 30-year-old female and a 30-year-old male, both healthy nonsmokers, each with an annual income of $85,000. Here's what we found.

Female

Term life insurance	$270
(BR 20 Premier Plus N/S $500,000 policy, for 20 years, from North American Company for Life and Health, Chicago)	
Disability insurance	$645
(Provident Cornerstone 400 N/C policy, which would pay $17,000 a year, equal to 20 percent of $85,000, up to age 65, 90-day elimination period, from Provident Life and Accident)	
Total, per year	**$915**

Male

Term life insurance	$340
(Star 98 20 Preferred Plus N/S $500,000 policy, for 20 years, from Old Republic Life, Chicago)	
Disability insurance	$415
(Provident Cornerstone 400 N/C policy, which would pay $17,000 a year, equal to 20 percent of $85,000, up to age 65, 90-day elimination period, from Provident Life and Accident)	
Total, per year	**$755**

---

already have enough disability insurance (see page 182) to cover your premiums. If you do, you don't need a waiver of premium.

8. *Clean up your act.* You may know that you can cut your insurance premium if you stop smoking and lose weight, but you may not know just how much you can save. Well, how does 50 percent sound? That's right, most insurance companies charge twice as much to insure a smoker. The rewards for getting back down to the right weight for your height can be just as great. That's what Quotesmith president Robert Bland learned. When Bland went shopping for $3 million in term, he was five feet, 11 inches and 245 pounds. He got premium quotes ranging from $4,000 to $7,000 a year. When he balked at those prices, he was told that his premium would be more like $3,000 if he were 35 pounds lighter.

9. *Don't buy insurance for your family members.* First, unless

your kid is supporting the family, there is simply no reason to insure him. Second, before you go out and buy insurance for a stay-at-home spouse who takes care of the kids, make sure you do the math. The insurance industry claims that, when stay-at-home spouses die, surviving spouses get hit with major domestic help costs. But are you sure you intend to employ full-time help if your wife dies, or will a grandmother or aunt step in to help? More important, money that is currently spent on feeding, clothing, and entertaining Mom, not to mention saving for her retirement, will no doubt cover some of the costs of child care should she die.

The Best Disability Insurance Strategy

Disability insurance is a slippery business. Unlike with life insurance, where no one can dispute that you're dead, the question of whether or not you deserve the benefits all too often ends up the subject of a bitter debate. For example:

Your money's worth

For the first time, as you speed through the airport, a flight-insurance kiosk pops into the corner of your eye. The least you can do for the little ones at home, you start to think, is buy some travel insurance. Or should you?

Worth it: A simple term life insurance policy. Let's say you're a 30-year-old nonsmoking female. You can buy $400,000 of insurance from Pacific Life Insurance for roughly $160 a year. True, that's a lot more than you'd pay for an airline policy. But here's what you need to keep in mind: This one covers you every single day of the year, including those days when you're doing something *really* dangerous, like standing outside in the rain (a 1 in 28,500 chance of getting struck by lightning). Your per-day cost: less than 50 cents.

Not worth it: It certainly looks like a good deal: For a mere $17, Universal Travel Protection will pay your family $400,000 should you die on your flight. But think about it for a second. This policy will only cover you *today*—a day that you happen to be doing something that's actually quite safe. Your chances of dying on that flight are 1 in 8 million, according to Prof. Arnie Barnett of the Massachusetts Institute of Technology, who bases his estimate on data from 1990 to the present. Put another way, if you chose one random flight per day, you would, on average, go for 21,000 years before catching a fatal one.

- Nick Avtonomoff, a San Francisco lawyer who suffered a severe head injury that affected his short-term memory and made him unable to practice law, was denied coverage by Paul Revere Life Insurance because he spent a few hours each day in his office fielding phone calls.
- Thomas Broatch, the owner of a Honolulu dental lab, was denied coverage after an illness because his insurer, Connecticut Mutual, claimed Broatch had overstated his income.
- George Montgomery, a California lawyer, was denied coverage when he had a heart attack. His company, the Mutual of Omaha, did a sweep of his medical records and discovered that he had had bypass surgery 15 years earlier and that he was taking an anti-anxiety medication. (They never asked for a medical history when they signed him up.)

These are hardly isolated examples. While there are no national statistics tracking the number of times disability claims have been challenged by insurance companies, evidence suggests that it is happening more and more. In Texas alone, 405 consumers complained about problems with their disability insurers in 1997, up from 208 in 1993. Why are insurers fighting so hard? Selling disability insurance is not always profitable. Some carriers have fled the business entirely. Only a handful of major companies continue to offer individuals disability policies with premiums that are guaranteed to stay level until age 65, says Allan Checkoway, who runs Disability Services Group, an employee-benefits consulting firm in Newton, Massachusetts. These include Mass Mutual (call 413-788-8411 or your local agent), The Guardian (800-662-1006), Berkshire (call your local agent), Provident (800-924-3684), and Northwestern (888-228-9665 or 414-271-1444).

So why buy it at all? It's simple: According to Disability Services Group, 3 out of 10 working people between the ages of 35 and 65 are disabled for 90 days or longer. That's a financial hit that few families can take. Your life—and your children's lives—depend on a decent salary, one that continues even if you can't work. It's expensive, but the chance to pull in $50,000, $75,000, even $125,000 annually, if you're unable to work, is the reason many people are willing to shell out premiums of $3,000 or more a year.

And don't necessarily count on your employer's policy: Most only offer disability insurance for 60 percent of your salary.

Armed with the following information, you can go out and find yourself a (virtually) loophole-free disability policy.

FIND OUT WHAT YOUR EMPLOYER'S POLICY COVERS

Up to now, probably the only time you even think about disability insurance is when you get a new job, or during the annual benefits review at your company. Most employers offer basic disability as part of your compensation package—which you will want—but employer-provided coverage has loopholes all its own. Ask the following questions about your company's policy before you shop for coverage to supplement it.

How much long-term disability coverage do I have? Most employers offer 60 percent coverage for long-term disability benefits. If you make $50,000 a year, you'd get $2,500 a month. But if the company pays the premium, those benefits are taxable. You'd actually collect $1,800 if you're in the 28 percent tax bracket.

Is there a cap on my coverage? Some companies cap monthly disability benefits, though often the cap is as high as $15,000 a month.

What is the definition of disability? For the first 2 years of your disability, your company will likely pay benefits if you can't perform the duties that fall under your job description. But after 2 years, group policies may keep paying only if you can't work at any job commensurate with your education and previous salary level.

Are there partial payments? Many group policies will reward your efforts to return to work gradually by supplementing the hours you work with disability insurance, so that you can collect as much of your full salary as possible.

Are my payments adjusted for Social Security? Group policies routinely subtract what they expect Social Security to pay you, even though Social Security's definition of what constitutes a disability is so strict that 50 percent of the people who apply are denied the first time around. The average Social Security benefit: about $700 a month; the maximum is around $1,500.

WHICH ADD-ONS DO YOU NEED?

While you usually can't add policy add-ons, or "riders," to your employer-sponsored disability policy, you will be offered several from your agent selling you a supplementary policy. While many of these riders make sense, some clearly do not. Your best strategy is to ignore them all—at first. Only once you've figured out how much basic coverage you need should you begin evaluating the bells and whistles. Here are some of the more popular disability riders, and what you should know about them.

Residual disability. Most basic policies provide you with some income if a disability keeps you from doing any reasonable job for which you're qualified. But what if you eventually can go back to work, only at a lower-paying or part-time job? Well, you'll lose your coverage. That's when residual disability kicks in. It's there to make up the difference between what you're earning on your new job and what you would be getting from an ordinary disability policy. This is one of the few options that is almost always worth the price. If your policy doesn't have residual disability built in, pay the extra 25 percent or so and have it added as a rider.

Own occupation. This is an add-on favored by many professionals such as doctors and lawyers. It assures that your policy will continue to pay in full when you can't go back to the exact job you had when you were injured—a surgeon who lost a finger and can no longer operate, for instance, would be covered. If the surgeon only had an "any occupation" policy, his disability insurance company might require that he go back to work as a professor or other kind of physician. This rider generally adds 10 percent to the cost of a policy, though not all professions get the same rates.

Guaranteed increase option. All first-time disability buyers have to pass medical muster. Though increases in your income may make you want additional coverage in the future, you probably won't want to undergo a second physical—especially if you've acquired an ulcer or a bad back since you bought your policy. A guaranteed increase option, sometimes called a guarantee of insurability rider or future-increase option, will help you avoid this hassle. These riders prohibit the insurer from demanding additional medical information when you increase your coverage. Some insurers offer the guaranteed increase option for free. Other insurers tack on 3 to 10 percent to the policy's price.

Cost-of-living adjustment. Disability policies adjust for inflation in two ways. The first is a sort of mini-adjustment, which many underwriters build into their policies and allow policyholders to either take or forgo. Takers will find that both their premium and benefits automatically go up each year by the change in the consumer price index. Typically, insurers will continue this automatic adjustment for 5 years before making you prove that you're making more money.

The going rate: The cost of living forever

You would think, looking at all the health remedies out there, that there was some way to win this game and live forever. Here's what true believers buy in the hopes of staving off the inevitable:

	Ann Arbor, Mich.	Berkeley, Calif.	Key West, Fla.	Santa Fe, N.M.	Worcester, Mass.
Now devil's claw tablets (100)	$ 4.95	$ 5.00	$ 4.95	$ 6.99	$ 5.00
Celestial Seasonings herb tea sampler	2.99	2.89	2.79	2.79	2.59
Consultation with licensed homeopath	150.00	165.00	175.00	225.00	150.00
Deepak Chopra's *Ageless Body, Timeless Mind*	14.00	14.00	14.00	12.68	14.00
Nature's Way echinacea tablets (100)	9.39	10.49	10.49	8.99	14.50
Garlinese 4000 garlic tablets (100)	37.50	37.50	37.50	37.50	37.50
Bunch of parsley*	0.69	0.59	0.99	0.50	0.79
Box of Altoids**	1.99	2.19	0.99	1.99	1.29
Blue-green algae tablets (90)	23.95	15.95	19.95	20.99	20.00
Flax-seed eye pillow	10.00	14.50	10.00	10.00	7.99
Acupuncture session	65.00	75.00	60.00	130.00	65.00
Introductory yoga session	12.00	12.00	10.00	12.00	12.00
Feldenkrais method bodywork session	70.00	10.00	75.00	80.00	60.00
Pain journal	4.95	7.00	3.99	3.99	3.00
Vulcan's *Child Healing* CD	15.00	15.00	15.00	15.00	15.00
Eclectic valerian tincture (1 ounce)	7.00	7.15	7.00	7.99	10.39
Patchouli oil (1/2 ounce)	9.50	4.75	9.89	16.99	9.95
Tray of wheatgrass	9.99	5.99	10.00	5.00	11.69
Crate of tofu	19.08	16.68	21.48	20.28	17.88
Beano antigas supplement	6.65	5.00	4.29	5.99	4.97
TOTAL COST	$474.63	$426.68	$493.31	$624.67	$463.54

*For halitosis. **For when parsley fails.

The second option is a cost-of-living rider, which kicks in with additional benefits after a full year of disability. You can choose to increase your benefit check either by a set percentage or a flat rate. Approach this one carefully, because it can be very expensive. Adding a cost-of-living rider to a policy can increase premiums by up to 40 percent.

Return of premium. Watch out for this one, too. These riders, among the most controversial disability products going, are basically a ploy to make disability more like cash value life insurance. The idea is that you get back some of the premiums you put into the policy. For example, you might set it up so that 10 years after purchasing your policy, you get 80 percent of your premium back, including the cost of the rider minus any claims. For the privilege, you'll pay another 50 to 100 percent on top of your premium. Some insurance company brochures advertise an annual return on your premium of 12 percent. But that's only if you have no disability claims. If you have a claim, it shoots your whole investment.

Lifetime benefit. Here's a way to guarantee that your disability payments will continue beyond age 65, when most policies cease payment and Social Security takes over. In your twenties, it will cost you an additional 2 to 5 percent a year. But when you get to 40 and older, expect to pay around 25 percent more. Basically, you want to be sure you'll have enough money to retire on—whether you're disabled or not. Unless you lock into this kind of policy while it's cheap, you're better off stashing the money in your retirement account and letting it grow. That way, you'll be certain to make use of it.

HOW TO CUT YOUR DISABILITY POLICY'S COST

There's a good chance that you could end up paying too high a premium for benefits you may never get to collect. Before you sign up for any policy, consider two ways to cut the premium:

Increase the elimination period. This is the number of days from when you become disabled to when the first benefit check appears in your mailbox. Years ago, the industry average was a reasonable 7 days, then it jumped to 30, and now the industry standard is 90 days.

It's no wonder: Lengthening your disability period from 30 days to 90, or from 90 to 180, can cut the cost of your premium by up to 50 percent.

Take an exemption. Brian Desrosier thought he'd never qualify for a disability policy because of the herniated disk in his back. But the owner of Computer SuperCenter in Greenwich, Connecticut, knew he needed to supplement his group coverage. So Desrosier opted for a rider excluding his back condition from the disability coverage. With premiums costing him $112 a month, the exclusion saved him as much as 20 percent. According to Arthur Goldstein, an agent with The Guardian, people with recurring medical troubles such as knee problems, tennis elbow, and even some cancers also can take the exclusion rather than pay a higher premium.

IF YOU GET HURT, READ THIS FIRST . . .

Say you suffer an injury that jeopardizes your ability to do your job, and you decide to file for disability. Whatever you do, *don't go back to the office.* This may seem like drastic advice, but it's crucial if you ever want to collect full benefits on your policy. Lawyers say even going to the office for a few hours to clean off your desk after an illness or accident could get you into trouble. (Get someone else to do it for you.) Insurers can—and will—use that information as proof that you're not too sick to work and then deny you the benefits you think you have coming to you.

Next, have your lawyer look over your claim form, disability policy, and original application before you submit anything to your company. Filling out a claim seems straightforward, but keep in mind that your insurer may well challenge you on anything, whether it's information you volunteered on your application, the date you say you became disabled, or the way your doctor writes his report. And if an insurer says you've filed a claim improperly, or without adequate documentation, it can delay your payments for months.

How much disability insurance do you need?

E ven if you get disability coverage from your employer, it's unlikely that you could live on 50 or 60 percent of your current salary, the coverage provided by most employers. Here's an easy way to figure out how much disability insurance you need, whether your employer supplies you with coverage or not.

Add up your monthly expenses. Use the figure from page 9 in Chapter 1, though you should probably add monthly payments for tuition, retirement, and debt repayment if any. Then figure out what monthly income you can count on, including spouse's income, investment income, Social Security benefits, and any long-term disability payments you expect to get from your employer.

Subtract income from expenses: This is how much additional monthly coverage you should get for yourself.

Monthly expenses   A _____

Expected monthly income   B _____

Monthly disability needed (A–B)   C _____

Next, you should figure out how many months you can afford to live without your salary. This will help you choose the ideal elimination period—the amount of time before your disability payments kick in.

If result is negative, set elimination period at the point when your   1 _____
short-term benefits expire.

Line A minus short-term benefits from your company.

Enter amount of savings you'd be comfortable spending   2 _____

Divide Line 2 by Line 1: This is the number of months you can get by   _____
without long-term disability coverage

11

Safeguarding Your Assets

You played hardball over the price of your home. You haggled over your car. You courted and flattered that unappealing bank officer on both accounts. Now can't you just relax? No. Now you need to get the best deal possible on auto and property insurance—after you make sure your policy covers what you think it does. Here's what to do.

Your Best Home Insurance Strategy

Jack Rotman knew he should do something about his homeowners insurance. For more than 10 years he was shelling out annual premiums of $1,844 to Aetna, and he was pretty sure he was paying too much. "Insurance was killing me," he says. But he just never got around to shopping for a new policy. It was a costly mistake: Armed with information about his Westport, Connecticut, residence, we went in search of cheaper coverage for him. Within an hour, after calling a half-dozen carriers, we had a policy that was $300 cheaper.

That's a lot of baby formula.

Just about the cheapest quote that anyone can get on a homeowners insurance policy will come from one of the direct writers, such as **Amica** (800-242-6422) or **USAA** (800-531-8100), which eliminate the agent by selling over the phone. There's just one catch: The direct writers are extremely selective. Amica gets most of its new business via referrals from existing customers. USAA limits its pool of potential customers to people with an armed-forces connection. Forget it if your home is in a dangerous neighborhood, with an unleashed or unfriendly dog, an unfenced swimming pool or a pool with a slide or diving board, or any structure with a wood-burning stove. These hard-liners like to insure people who live near

When your home insurer won't pay

Y es, you can fight back. Here's what to do when you hear the following responses to
your claims:

"That's not covered." Claiming that something isn't covered is very often a property
insurer's first response—an opening gambit that, with any luck, you won't contest. "They'll
test you," says Dallas roofing contractor Robert Younger. "They'll have a trial-balloon stage
where they'll say, 'That's just an old worn-out roof.' And they'll see if you come back at
them. That works maybe half the time." Instead, write to the insurer and make your case
on paper, copying your state's insurance department. Sound too time-consuming? Try turning to a public adjuster—a person who makes his living fighting claims for policyholders,
generally for a cut of the payout.

"No receipts? Sorry, no coverage." Do *you* keep all your receipts? Do *you* have a
videotape of everything you own? We didn't think so. Most people don't. But hope is not
lost—as Joan and George Cocuzzo found out. After burglars broke into their Vermont ski
house in February 1995, making off with some $7,000 worth of ski equipment, the Cocuzzos
spent several months trying to track down receipts and canceled checks so they could get
reimbursed. Although they were able to muster about $2,000 worth of receipts, the Cocuz-
zos' insurer, New England Guaranty, wouldn't cover the remainder, writing that the claim
"substantially lacks supporting documentation."

It's a common problem. But it's also one of the most common myths of homeowners
insurance—and one that insurers aren't eager to dispel. Go ahead: Look at your policy.
There's no provision that says you must have receipts. You just have to show some proof
of what you owned. At the suggestion of a public adjuster, the Cocuzzos gathered photos
that included images of the equipment. They also got sworn statements from friends and
relatives about the gear that was stolen. They then sent the photos and the statements to
their adjuster at New England Guaranty, and the company quickly paid the claim.

"Damage? What damage?" Though insurance adjusters will often hold forth with great
authority on the condition of, say, your roof or your walls, you shouldn't assume that they
know what they're talking about, especially when a large-scale disaster strikes. In that
case, insurers often ship in hundreds of adjusters from out of state to handle your claims;
keep an eye on them, because what they don't know may hurt you. After Hurricane Andrew
struck in 1992, says Miami attorney Brian Pariser, many of the claims adjusters who were
flown in "weren't particularly familiar with construction practices and prices in Florida."
The result: Claims were being paid out at all sorts of rates. The moral: Always consult with
a contractor before accepting an insurance company's payout.

"Your home was hurt before you made this claim." If your insurance company can
establish that your home was already damaged in any way before you made your claim,
you have what's called a preexisting condition—which your insurance company may use
as an excuse not to pay.

You might be startled by what passes for a preexisting condition. Mike and Cathy

Harrell certainly were. Their roof took a real drubbing in a hailstorm that hit the Dallas area back in April 1994. The shingles were battered and gouged, and the central air conditioner unit was covered with golf ball–sized pockmarks. But when their State Farm adjuster arrived, Cathy Harrell says, she took one look and declared, "It was an old roof but it had no hail damage." The result: Claim denied.

At their wits' end, the Harrells turned to their roofing contractor, Robert Younger. He had a suggestion that worked out beautifully: The couple should canvass their neighborhood, asking other residents if they had State Farm coverage and, if so, whether State Farm had paid for new roofs.

They found three neighbors whose roofs had been covered. Armed with that information, the Harrells contacted another State Farm agent—theirs had retired—and asked him to come by and have a look. When the second agent climbed up on the roof, he agreed it should be covered by the claim, which was paid to the Harrells in full within months. (A State Farm spokesman declined to comment on individual claims.)

fire stations in brand-new houses in historically low-risk areas such as New York State.

Most galling, they won't insure people with a history of small claims—a roof leak here, a storm-damaged deck there. One of the most maddening aspects of the insurance business is that companies don't like to sell insurance to people who have a tendency to make use of it.

If the direct writers won't have you, you'll need to move on to one of the big companies such as State Farm, Allstate, Aetna, ITT Hartford, and Chubb.

Only as a last resort should you work with an independent insurance agent, who usually represents 6 or 7 companies. While a good agent is a storehouse of valuable information and advice, most simply aren't going to be price competitive: They need to build in their commissions as well as pay all of their own overhead.

The one time an independent agent comes in handy is if you're having trouble getting insurance at all—say you live within striking distance of water or, for instance, in a state that has been hit by hurricanes or earthquakes. But coverage from these sources doesn't come cheap. A policy on a $200,000 home in southern California, which would have cost about $700 from a firm like Twentieth Century before the Northridge earthquake, now costs upwards of $2,400 when purchased from a specialty carrier.

If you live in a flood-prone area and are having trouble finding any insurance at all, call the Federal Insurance Administration (800-427-4661) and ask about the National Flood Insurance Program.

How Much Insurance Should You Buy?

Forget what you paid for your house. What you need to insure is the cost to rebuild it, and often that's a wildly different sum. To figure rebuilding costs, multiply your square footage by the building cost per square foot in your area. Then add on how much it would cost to replace any extras like central air or a Jacuzzi. How do you know? Check with a few contractors in your area. They'll have the numbers at their fingertips.

Once you have your figure, your best bet is to buy insurance to cover all of it. If you're tempted to get coverage for only 80 percent of the house's rebuilding cost, beware. Your insurer will foot the entire bill if, say, you have a kitchen fire. But if the whole house is destroyed, you get only 80 percent of what it would cost to rebuild. If you're less than 80 percent insured, your carrier will only pay for that percentage of any damages. A better alternative is to up the insurance to 100 percent and increase your deductible.

Now you need to choose among the 3 main types of homeowner policies: **cash value, replacement cost,** and **guaranteed replacement cost.** Cash value insurance is the cheapest, but as its name implies, it will pay you only the cash value of any asset you lose. If your 10-year-old furnace goes bust in a basement flood, a cash value policy will pay only what it's worth, not the cost to buy a new one. Replacement cost will cover what it takes to buy a new one, but with a price cap. Guaranteed replacement is best: It usually has no cap. The only thing it won't cover is the cost of upgrading your home to meet building codes that have changed since the house was built.

The hitch: As a result of the last decade of disasters, fewer and fewer insurance companies offer guaranteed replacement cost policies. Instead, State Farm's new Option ID, which is available in over 30 states, and Allstate's building structure reimbursement extended limits endorsement provide extra coverage of up to 120 percent of the policy limit—and not a penny more. Farmers Insurance, the country's third-largest insurer, now offers extended replacement coverage, capped at 125 percent of the policy limit. Most other insurers limit coverage to anywhere from 120 to 200 percent of the policy limit. Unfortunately, this puts the onus on you to make sure that your home is adequately insured; this means paying higher premiums to cover the real cost of rebuilding your home.

If you're determined to get guaranteed replacement, Chubb, CNA, and the Andover Cos. still sell it in some states, though they each have restrictions.

How much does peace of mind cost?

W hat's it going to cost you to insure two of your biggest assets, your car and your home? Every case is different, but we asked Amica Mutual Insurance Co., a direct underwriter based in Lincoln, Rhode Island, to come up with rates for a hypothetical couple living in Cleveland Heights, Ohio. Their home, which they recently bought for $300,000, was built in 1954, is made of brick, and is within 5 miles of a fire department. It has a basement, a 5-year-old furnace, 15-year-old fuse boxes, 15-year-old plumbing, and a 10-year-old roof. They've got smoke detectors and fire extinguishers. Our young couple's cars? A 1997 Chevy Suburban 1500 4 × 4 (which Mr. Couple was driving when he got a speeding ticket 3 years ago) and a 1990 Volvo 240 Sedan. Both cars are being driven 15 miles or less to work, along with the usual family outings. Here is what Amica would charge our young couple each year to insure their biggest assets:

Special Form Plus homeowner's policy   **$499**
Includes $352,000 replacement cost limit on house and garage, which should be enough to rebuild the house to code; $240,000 replacement cost limit on property; $64,000 limit on loss of use, $300,000 limit on personal liability, $1,000 limit on medical payment to others. Includes a 10 percent discount for smoke detectors and fire extinguishers. Deductible is $1,000 per claim.

Auto insurance policy   **$1,084**
Includes $300,000 liability per accident (for both property damage and bodily injury); $300,000 for uninsured motorist coverage per accident; $5,000 medical for each person in their car per accident; $7,500 for property damage to the Volvo per accident with an uninsured motorist; collision on the Suburban for actual cash damages. Includes a $1,000 collision deductible on the Suburban, a $250 deductible per car for other than collision loss, and a $250 deductible per car on property damage for uninsured motorists.

Personal Umbrella Policy   **$120**
For up to $1 million of liability coverage.

Total   **$1,703**

If you have cash value coverage on your structure, you probably have it on the contents, too. This means you'll likely get garage sale prices if your 10-year-old sofa is ruined. Replacement cost coverage on the contents, which will give you enough to buy a new couch, is usually preferable. At an extra 10 percent to 20 percent, it's worth it.

Certain items have limited coverage regardless of the total cap. Jewelry is usually capped at $1,000 (total, not per piece) and firearms at $2,500. If your individual valuables are worth more, you may want to buy additional coverage by tacking riders onto your policy (see below).

The last piece of your homeowners policy is liability coverage, in case someone breaks his leg on your wobbly porch steps and decides to sue. Most policies come with $100,000 of liability, but unless you have less than that in assets, including your home, it's nowhere near enough. If you have $200,000 to $500,000 in assets, experts agree, you need $1 million in liability. It doesn't cost a lot, and in this litigious society, getting sued for $1 million isn't rare.

The cost-efficient way to buy liability insurance is to raise the liability coverage you have on your homeowners policy to $300,000. Buy the same amount of liability on your auto policy. You can then buy an "umbrella" policy to cover you for liability in both your home and car from $300,000 and up. Umbrella policies come fairly cheap because the risk the underwriter is taking—that a liability claim against you will exceed $300,000—is slim. Coverage from $300,000 to $1 million—for home and auto combined—will cost you $100 to $300 a year. Adding another million will cost roughly $60 to $100.

Renters don't have to worry about covering the building they live in, but they should be concerned about what's inside, as well as accidents for which they could be held liable. Thus, a renter's policy is just like a homeowner's, except there's no coverage for the structure itself. If you rent, you'll have to come up with an estimated value for your contents. For liability, use the same guidelines as above.

Which Add-ons Do You Need?

You may also want to consider some riders to your policy, which can prevent nasty surprises on top of catastrophes.

Building-code upgrade rider. Also called a codes-and-ordinances rider. If you live in an old house that doesn't meet your current municipality's building code, and it burns down, most insurance companies will only pay to replace that house in its original condition—not a house up to code, which is much more expensive. Some companies, such as Safeco (800-332-3226), include code coverage in the terms of their basic policy. Otherwise, the coverage will add 10 percent to your base premium.

Protection from zoning changes. Some policies make it difficult to rebuild on your original site. Many homeowners learned this after the fires that tore through southern California in 1993. When the smoke had cleared, many residents learned that they couldn't rebuild on their original site because their neighborhoods had been rezoned as hazardous areas. If the cost of rebuilding on a new site was more than the face amount of the coverage, tough luck. Most policies paid only up to the policy's face amount. To protect yourself, make sure your policy states that you can build your exact house, no matter what the cost, on a different lot.

Protection from foundation damage. You may also need a policy that covers the cost of replacing your foundation. Some insurers argue that foundations don't burn. Maybe not, but in a fierce fire, a foundation can melt. Foundations are also susceptible to earthquake damage. If you live in a vulnerable area, check your policy to make sure your insurance will pay the cost of rebuilding your home from the ground up, including the foundation.

Luxury goods coverage. Basic insurance policies usually limit coverage of expensive items such as jewelry, silver, oriental rugs, computers, or antiques to a maximum payout of $1,000. You can get separate coverage in riders known as personal-articles policies. At State Farm, for instance, a jewelry rider would cost $11.70 per $1,000 of extra coverage per year (up to $10,000) for someone living in White Plains, New York. Any personal-articles policy should itemize each insured piece, including its appraised value. That way, if a piece is lost or stolen, you and your insurance company have already agreed on its worth. Another advantage of a jewelry rider, or any rider for that matter, is that it covers you for a loss that occurs off your property. So if you lose your wedding ring playing touch

The real world: Anatomy of an insurance claim

I t's a given, really. When you file an insurance claim, you pretty much assume that your insurer's not going to fork over the maximum amount of money you'll need to make things right.

But how does your insurance company actually come up with a dollar figure? And how can it be so radically different from what you think you need? George Kehrer, a contractor who heads Community Assisting Recovery, a Northridge, California, advocacy group (818-888-6338), walked us through a hypothetical case.

Say there's a storm. A big storm, with lightning and fierce winds. All of a sudden there's a huge crash as a 100-year-old oak tree lands on your roof, splintering a small part of it. That in turn sends wood, dirt, and glass into your family's entertainment room. What a mess: The roof now has a hole in it, your furniture is shattered, and your carpet is soiled and covered with glass.

Your insurer responds immediately. Within days you get its estimate: You're covered for $10,365. That will take care of roof repairs, patching and repainting your walls, cleaning your carpets, and replacing your furniture, TV, and stereo. Sounds fair enough. You're tempted to accept. But because you're ever the diligent consumer, you bring contractors in to get your own estimate. And that's when the trouble begins: They say everything will cost you $30,700—almost 3 times as much.

Now wait a minute. You have a guaranteed replacement cost policy, which supposedly assures that your insurer will make you whole. How, you ask, could the two estimates be so far apart? Here's a few examples of how it happens.

First, your insurer wants you to *restore* your roof, not replace it. Though it will pay for a few new tiles in the damaged section, the company refuses to pay for the wood rafters and sheathing beneath the tiles, using the argument that some rot was already present in the wood. Thus, the adjuster tells you, the wood damage is not covered, because of the clause that prohibits payment for "preexisting damage." Your contractor, meanwhile, says you've got to replace the entire roof because it won't match otherwise. That includes shingles for the roof ($7,745), new rafters and sheathing ($640 combined), and a new gutter ($140), among other items.

What your insurance company will pay to fix the roof: $1,235. What it will really cost: $8,780.

The same issue arises inside the house. Your insurance company will pay for you to steam-clean your carpet. Your contractor, on the other hand, observes that the glass and dirt will never fully come out. You need a new carpet, he says, and you'll have to get it for the whole floor, to make it all match.

What your insurance company will pay to clean up the entertainment room: $120. What it will really cost: $1,130.

Your adjuster also tells you that the company won't cover the water damage to the wood floor underneath the carpeting because you weren't technically "using" the floor. But your contractor points out that it's badly damaged and needs replacing.

What your insurance company will pay to replace your hardwood floor: $0. What it will really cost: $3,895.

How about the walls in your entertainment room? Your adjuster will argue for patching Sheetrock on the wall rather than replacing the whole thing. He skips an asbestos test—which you'll probably want in an older house—as well as an electricity test.

When it comes to paint, your adjuster is cutting corners all over the place. He won't factor in a coat of primer paint, for instance. And he may even round down on the measurements of your room. Let's say the dimensions are 20 feet 3 inches by 16 feet 2 inches by 8 feet 3 inches. By rounding down, he can calculate the wall and ceiling area as 896 square feet rather than the actual 929 square feet. That allows him to shave a little off the paint costs.

What your insurance company will pay to fix and paint the walls: $670. What it will really cost: $1,705.

Your adjuster also "forgot" to mention that cleanup, both for the damage and the work, is covered. That could add another $1,355, according to Kehrer. (He points out that consumers are entitled to payment for *their own time* spent working on the cleanup—a fact many people don't know.)

What about the ruined furniture and electronic equipment? Your adjuster will challenge you to produce receipts for that pricey amplifier you bought a few years back. Assuming you're willing to work hard and produce detailed evidence of all your possessions, you may agree on, say, $7,000 for the property.

You should know, though, that the adjuster's estimate doesn't mean you'll actually get a check for that amount. Even on replacement policies, your insurer will probably subtract depreciation charges when it writes you a check. Each individual piece of furniture and equipment will be discounted based on its age and wear and tear (that discount is negotiable, Kehrer notes). Then, when you go out and buy the replacement items, the company will reimburse the difference as long as you purchase the new items within a year.

So even if your insurer agrees you'll need $7,000 for the furniture and equipment, it might write a check for just $4,500. The company also can subtract depreciation on your roof claim, deducting another $200.

There's more. Some insurers hold back an additional 20 percent for the contractor's overhead and profit. (As with the depreciation charges, State Farm will reimburse you for that amount when the work is finished.) That cuts out another $400. Subtract your $500 deductible and what are you left with? An initial check for $6,765 from your insurer.

That, clearly, is unacceptable. So what are you going to do about it? Take all your contractor's numbers and confront your adjuster with them, advises Kehrer. If you keep pushing—and providing documentation—you'll eventually get something closer to what's fair, he says. "They may not pay the guy next door or the guy down the road," he says, "but they'll pay you."

football at the local high school, your jewelry rider covers its replacement. Another advantage to having a rider to cover luxury goods is that a loss claim won't count against your total contents coverage.

Trimming Your Home Insurance Costs

Once you've settled on your carrier and decided how much coverage you need, it's time to cut the best possible deal. You can shave hundreds of dollars off your annual premium by taking advantage of the many discounts that nearly every insurer offers. If you already have a policy, it'll list what discounts you currently have. Don't assume that those are the only discounts you can get. You may already know that a burglar alarm will garner you a discount. But did you know that if you have a live-in housekeeper, Chubb will give you a 2 percent credit, since the presence of that live-in employee can reduce the chance of break-ins?

What follows is a guide to the discounts that may be available to you. Bear in mind that some companies cap the total discounts available to any one policyholder; others, such as Allstate, just let the discounts pile up. It's possible, if you're the right age and own the right house, to knock 65 percent off the basic Allstate premium.

Just like new. So what if your house is old? Have you upgraded electrical, heating, and plumbing systems? You're in luck: You may qualify for a discount. By the same token, just about every insurer gives a discount for new homes. And a few give discounts for homes that are merely newish; Allstate gives a discount for homes built within the past 9 years.

Join the "in" crowd. In almost any market, one company wants your business more than its rivals do. For example, a couple of years ago you were highly desirable to American Express if you owned a home in New York, Minnesota, Arizona, Illinois, or Connecticut, where historical loss rates are low. For a home in suburban Connecticut with $230,000 guaranteed replacement coverage and $300,000 liability, AmEx was undercutting Allstate by almost 20 percent, or $128.

Other insurers go after groups of customers they judge to be affluent and responsible. Zurich Insurance (800-323-7592) is going after university alumni and employees across the country with premium discounts of up to 20 percent for a comprehensive package of home, auto, and life insurance.

How do you find these deals? Call your alumni association or business club to see if it has a deal with an insurance company. If all else fails, check with a local agent.

It pays to be safe. When Wayne and Leslie Becker moved into their new home in Darien, Connecticut, they had no idea that their central alarm system would save them money on their homeowners policy. In fact, they didn't learn about it until several weeks after their move, when a representative of the alarm company came out to inspect the system and casually mentioned the potential savings. The next day, Wayne called his insurer and, sure enough, knocked $200 off his premium.

That's typical. Allstate will give you 15 percent off for a basic security package including smoke detectors and a burglar alarm. Amica gives a 10 percent discount for a similar system. USAA gives 8 percent off for having a sprinkler in every room. And in some states, Chubb and other companies give 5 percent discounts on homes equipped with closed-circuit TV cameras or outside motion detectors.

Make the car connection. Many companies give discounts of up to 15 percent off your homeowners policy if you combine it with your auto policy. The only time it may be cheaper to keep them separate is if your auto policy has a recent blemish on it.

Again, the Beckers are a handy example. They bought a homeowners policy from the same company that insures their car, but they didn't link the policies. The reason: They had had a recent minor fender bender. "My agent advised using the same company for both as an incentive for them not to cancel the auto," Wayne says, "but not combining them until the accident is off our record."

Brilliant deduction. If you already have homeowners insurance, you probably have the standard deductible of $250, though some deductibles go as low as $100. But if you're willing to take a higher deductible, the savings can be substantial. When Roy and Reenie Makowsky insured their new home in Nantucket, Massachusetts, they opted for a $2,500 deductible. Their savings: $640, or about 30 percent off the base premium of $2,149.

The going rate: The cost of home security

America may well be a safer place these days. But we've got a hunch: It's not that the bad guys have all been locked up. They've just been outspent.

	Chicago, Ill.	Detroit, Mich.	New York, N.Y.	San Diego, Calif.	Valdosta, Ga.
Brink's standard home security system	$ 997.30	$ 997.30	$ 997.30	$ 997.30	$ 947.30
Intermatic outdoor light timer	14.40	14.99	10.00	29.00	19.50
Jogging weights with pepper spray	24.95	24.95	24.95	24.95	24.95
Chain-link fence (100 feet) with razor wire	480.00	645.00	1,250.00	650.00	700.00
Radar Watchdog alarm (with electronic barking)	99.95	99.95	99.95	99.95	99.95
Doberman pinscher (with authentic barking)	699.00	400.00	950.00	595.00	400.00
Self-defense class	300.00	250.00	260.00	298.00	178.50
Armed personal bodyguard (per hour)	38.00	40.00	50.00	110.00	45.00
Easton Redline baseball bat	249.95	219.95	199.99	249.99	249.00
Colt .45-caliber pistol	556.00	550.00	550.00	569.99	459.00
Home Alone video*	8.00	17.00	19.00	14.99	12.99
TOTAL	$3,467.55	$3,259.14	$4,411.19	$3,639.17	$3,136.19

*For new ideas, when all else fails.

Water works. If you live out in the boonies, be prepared to pay higher rates than folks who live in town. That's because it's harder for the local fire brigade to reach your home in an emergency.

In most cases, you'll be bumped to a higher rate class if you live more than 5 miles from the nearest firehouse or more than 1,000 feet from the nearest fire hydrant. But rural insurance specialists such as Old Guard Insurance of Lancaster, Pennsylvania, give a discount up to 30 percent if the local fire department has access to a large nearby water source such as a lake.

If you're determined to live in the country, don't count on finding a policy with a direct writer. Instead, work with a local insurance agent to price-shop among small mutual insurers, such as Old Guard Insurance, that specialize in insuring dairy farms and rural homes.

Do a slow burn. If your house is constructed of fire-resistant materials such as brick or concrete, you may have money in your walls. Both Chubb and Allstate may give you as much as a 15 percent break.

The Best Car Insurance Strategy

When Paul Manus, a 32-year-old resident of suburban Chicago, set out to get a policy for his Honda Accord and Jeep Grand Cherokee, his mission was to get the lowest price possible. Nearly 2 hours later, after being on the phone an average of 25 minutes with 4 different suppliers, and being grilled on everything from the length of his daily commute to the age of his daughter, he was the proud recipient of a Geico policy with an annual premium of $1,359. That's $180 lower than the next-lowest quote he got, from State Farm.

Then there's the experience of a Connecticut couple in their thirties. Around the same time, they, too, worked the phone lines to get the best policy for their 4-door Saab sedan. And they, too, were the very model of a good risk: Newly married, living in the

---

Your money's worth

The minute an antitheft device comes on the market, some thief is already figuring out how to get past it and steal the car anyway. But some devices give thieves more pause than others—and convince them to skulk along to the next car.

Worth it: Immobiliser Inc.'s Classic ($349, includes installation). It may seem pricey, but the Classic is your best defense against filing a stolen-car claim. Passive immobilizing systems are the most effective antitheft products on the market; this keylike device plugs into a port (usually near the dashboard) and sends signals to the engine. Without the Classic, the car won't budge. Hot-wiring won't help, and tampering with the port will do little but blow the circuits, which still leaves your car right where you parked it.

Not worth it: The Club ($39.99). Protecting your car with the Club is like guarding your house with a Chihuahua. Both are easy to sidestep. A handsaw can go through the metal in seconds, and cutting the much softer steering wheel takes even less time. Here's another tidbit: L.A. gangs used to steal cars with the Club in ritualistic mockery, leaving the useless device where the car used to be.

suburbs, good driving records, and a car that has a reputation for being safe and sturdy.

A few hours after their initial call, they had been quoted policies from 4 different carriers, with the price tags ranging from $1,180 to $1,417. The highest? It came from Geico. As far as Geico was concerned, everything was fine about this couple except for one thing: Their car comes equipped with a turbocharger. Geico doesn't like to see turbos on pre-1990 Saab 9000s; they make it too easy to exceed the speed limit. Drivers with cars so equipped get an extra 15 percent tacked on to their annual premium.

Welcome to the world of auto insurance, where confusion reigns, where the best deals aren't the most obvious ones, and where one wrong answer to a probing salesperson can cost you hundreds of dollars—or disqualify you for coverage.

But take heart: For many car owners, auto insurance rates are falling. Industry leader State Farm Mutual Automobile Insurance, which insures 2 out of every 5 drivers in the United States, lowered overall rates last year for the first time in over 20 years. Moreover, despite the confusion and multiplicity of choices, you can probably cut your car insurance bill by as much as 25 percent. You just have to know where to call, what discounts you qualify for, and how to respond when the questions start flying at you.

As with other kinds of insurance, you should start with the direct selling companies that offer the best prices, such as **Geico** (800-841-3000), **Amica** (800-242-6422), **USAA** (800-531-8100), and **20th Century** (800-443-3100; from New York, 818-989-3265). The 800-number carriers, however, are very picky.

If you have had more than one accident or one moving violation in the past 3 years (or if you have a teenager in the house—every car insurer's nightmare), a Geico policy is likely to be 20 percent more expensive than a policy from Allstate or State Farm. And if even a single blemish mars your driving record over the past 3 years, Amica probably won't offer you a policy.

However, if you've had two or three accidents or three or more speeding tickets over the past 3 years, your best bet is to get a quote from **Allstate** (888-860-3226) or **State Farm** (call your local agent), which cover a much broader range of drivers. Once you get that quote, ask an independent agent to try to beat it. Most agents regularly work with 6 or 7 companies, and about half the time can beat your best quote.

When your auto insurer won't pay

J ohn Crowe will never forget the holiday season at State Farm. It was when the office switched into high gear every year. The reason: the annual "pending drive," when his office would make an all-out effort to settle as many open, or pending, claims as possible.

Competing for prizes ranging from golf balls and Windbreakers emblazoned with the company logo to a free dinner or even a paid day off, claims adjusters would battle to see who could close the most claims for the least amount of money.

"Christmastime is great for closing claims," explains Crowe, a former adjuster who has since left the company. "People needed the money for gifts, so we'd have a big push. People were susceptible then, and we knew it." (The company's legal counsel says that if there were "pending drives," they were not "company-driven.")

But don't get the idea that these methods are unique to Crowe's old office. In fact, they're common at insurance companies both big and small, as are the following things your auto insurer is likely to tell you.

"This part doesn't need to be replaced." It is perhaps the most common of all scenarios after a crash: Your car is damaged, but at least it's fixable. The question is, how will it be fixed? Will your broken parts be replaced, or will your insurer only pay for them to be "banged back into shape"?

Jerome Cummings has a pretty good idea which answer it will be. After his son's Jeep Cherokee was in a crash a couple of years ago, Cummings's Tallahassee, Florida, mechanic told him the air conditioner and radiator were bent out of shape and needed to be replaced. But the other driver's insurer, Progressive, wouldn't pay the $800 to replace them, he says. Cummings complained that failure to replace the broken section of the car would violate the terms of his warranty, but he says Progressive wouldn't budge—until Cummings called its adjuster to say he was going to hire a lawyer to file a civil suit against the company. Only then did Progressive break down and pay for a new air conditioner and radiator, he says. "Once I mentioned the lawsuit, their whole attitude changed," says Cummings. "The adjuster agreed to [pay for] the repair by the end of the day." (Without a case number, which Cummings did not make available, Progressive spokeswoman Leslie Heinrich couldn't comment. But, she insists, "in every case, we work toward a resolution that is mutually satisfying.")

Why would a threatened lawsuit work against a big, well-funded insurance company? In many property damage cases, the dollars in question simply don't justify a protracted court battle.

"We'll decide which parts you use—and you can be sure they'll be cheap." Whenever possible, an adjuster's estimate of your damages includes the use of so-called aftermarket parts. These components aren't made by your car's manufacturer. Instead, they're imitations modeled on the parts they're replacing. There is considerable debate over the quality of these parts. Some body shop owners say they're fine; others say they're terribly inferior. But it's not hard to see why insurance companies like them: They're cheap. A Honda Accord fender made by the original manufacturer costs $199.16. Its aftermarket clone costs $105.

Your first move: Complain. Then check your policy to see if it even allows aftermarket parts; some policies are written specifically to exclude them—a fact your adjuster may have "overlooked." If that doesn't work, call your state insurance department to see where it stands on aftermarket parts. In West Virginia, for example, manufacturers' original parts must be used in cars that are less than 3 years old. Texas law requires replacement components that are identical in "like, kind and quality."

"Your car was worth less than you say. A lot less." Your car is totaled. So how much will you get to replace it? Possibly less than you expect, as there's a chance your insurer will cite the lowest possible blue book value when appraising it.

Kansas City lawyer Allen Speck found out firsthand when his wife's Toyota Camry was totaled a couple of years back. The other driver's insurer, USAA, offered the Specks only $12,500 for the car, but Speck looked up its value in the *NADA Official Used-Car Guide* at a local used-car dealer and saw that the adjuster had chosen the value of a very low-end Camry; the couple's higher-end version was worth at least $15,000.

Speck says he called the claims rep and complained, pointing out that his wife's car had all kinds of options not in the bare-bones standard model, including a cell phone, a CD player, a sunroof, and a premium, V-6 engine. The insurance company professed ignorance of this, Speck says, and it quickly came up with $1,500 more.

"We'll pay you when we're good and ready." Why should your insurer rush to pay you off? When a claims dispute gets strung out over several months, it's money in the bank for the insurance company.

If you get the feeling you're being strung along, consider a lawsuit—or at least threatening one. San Francisco consumer advocate Bill Ahern went that route, to great effect. The insurance company handling his daughter's claim was sitting on its hands, balking at covering more than $1,500 in medical bills or reimbursing her for her totaled car. The insurer claimed the hospital visit wasn't necessary and even hinted that the accident was her fault. "I called the adjuster myself because [my daughter] was practically in tears," Ahearn recalls. "I said, 'We've got witnesses who say this accident wasn't her fault. And it was the paramedics who brought her to the hospital. She didn't just decide to go.'" The adjuster was still reluctant. "Finally, I said, 'What do I have to do, hire a lawyer?'"

Faced with the threat of a lawsuit, Ahern says, the adjuster finally gave in, and the company paid for the car and the medical bills—and $1,000 for pain and suffering.

How Much Auto Insurance Should You Buy?

Most auto policies have 6 primary parts: bodily injury liability (for treating injuries to people in the other car), property damage liability (for fixing up the other car after a wreck), medical (for treating people in your car), collision (for fixing up your car), comprehensive (to cover fires, theft, etc.), and uninsured/underinsured motorists (in case you get injured by someone who lacks insurance).

Liability insurance is the most important. Most states require drivers to take $20,000 or $30,000 of bodily injury liability per person, with a maximum payout of $40,000 or $60,000 per accident. For property damage, the minimum required by law is usually $10,000 per accident. But this coverage falls way short for most people. Unless you have very little in the way of assets, you should raise your liability to a minimum of $100,000 per person and $300,000 per accident, with an additional $100,000 for property damage per accident. As with homeowners, if you have over $200,000 in assets, you need a personal umbrella policy that provides up to $1 million in additional liability coverage (you only need one to cover both your house and your car). This umbrella policy will cost $100 to $300 a year.

Uninsured/underinsured motorist coverage is not mandatory in every state, but these days it's crucial. In some states more than half of all drivers are uninsured. If one of them hits you, you'll have to pay for anything your medical insurance doesn't cover, plus other expenses resulting from the accident. Insurance advisers recommend at least $100,000 worth, which will run less than $100 a year.

How to Cut Your Car Insurance Bill

The good news: Now that you're a parent, you're considered responsible, and your premiums should drop. Here are 10 more things you can do now to save hundreds of dollars.

Drive safely. And slowly. Allstate offers up to a 20 percent discount if all drivers on a policy have been licensed for 3 years and have had no accidents or violations in the past 5 years.

Stop smoking. Insurers often consider smoking a dangerous activity when it comes to driving. First off, it's an indication that you have a penchant for high-risk activity. But there's another reason. If an ash falls in a driver's lap, they'll be looking at their lap instead of the road.

Buy a conservative car. Infinitis, BMWs, Mercedes, Porsches are considered by insurance companies to be expensive to repair, and therefore are going to cost more to insure—as much as 15 percent more. And for some companies, some cars are too racy to insure at any price. State Farm and Allstate both publish rankings of cars by their risk category. In both listings, the best cars, for lower-than-standard collision and comprehensive premiums, include the Chevrolet Suburban and the GMC Safari van, among others.

Load up on safety features. Insurance companies bestow big discounts on drivers of cars with some or all of the latest safety features. Some states require discounts for cars equipped with antilock brakes. Geico offers 40 percent off the injury coverage premium for 2 air bags, and 15 percent for people who sign a safety belt usage pledge.

Raise your deductible. Raising deductibles is one of the easiest ways to cut your bill substantially. In general, increasing your deductible from $200 to $500 reduces your premium by 15 percent to 30 percent.

Take a defensive driving course. Some insurance companies offer up to a 10 percent discount for drivers who volunteer to take a state-approved defensive driving course.

Drop some coverage. If your car is more than 5 years old and/or you're paying more than 20 percent of its blue book value for collision and comprehensive, you may want to consider junking those coverages altogether. After all, the insurer will reimburse you only for the blue book value of the car, which may now be negligible. (The *Kelley Blue Book* is typically available at your local library or online at *www.kbb.com*).

Insure your home and car through the same company. Most insurers offer discounts to customers who combine their home and auto policies.

Stop driving. If you've recently switched jobs, for instance, and your new workplace is significantly closer, call up your insurance company for a low-mileage discount. Some insurers will slash your premium by 10 percent if you drive, say, fewer than 5 miles to work (or fewer than 7,500 miles a year).

Teenagers and car insurance: Making the best of a bad situation

A h, the memories of parenthood. Your child's first tooth. The first day of school. His first day behind the wheel of a car.

Well, that last memory won't be quite as pleasant as the others. Not even the calmest parent can keep from worrying whether Junior will smash up the car and do the same to himself in the process. Then there's the not-so-minor matter of money.

A teenage driver will jack up your car insurance payments faster than a Porsche will cover a quarter mile—double or even more the amount that you paid before. And this increase happens automatically the minute he gets his license, whether he drives your car or not. Not only that, he will be assigned as an "occasional driver" to the most expensive car in the house.

While teenagers with a B average will garner a discount from some insurance companies, truth is, there's no way to make teenage drivers easy on your pocketbook. We're talking lessening the pain here. And the best way to do that is to remember this: With a teenage driver in the house, it can be just as cheap—and a lot more convenient—to insure 3 cars as it is to insure 2.

Here's the trick: The cost of insuring your child on the late-model upscale cars that you and your spouse are driving can be astronomical. But if the kid gets a good old-fashioned clunker, you can insure all 3 cars for virtually the same amount that it will cost to insure your child on your own 2 cars.

Say, for example, that you live in Carrollton, Texas, a suburb of Dallas, and that you drive a Chrysler Town & Country minivan while your spouse drives an Oldsmobile Aurora. Assuming, of course, that you both have good driving records, you're paying $2,280 a year for insurance, according to State Farm agent David Daniel.

Suddenly, though, Junior turns 16 and gets his driver's license. He's now automatically included in the coverage of both cars as an "occasional" driver, which shoots your car insurance bill up to $3,884 a year. That's an annual increase of $1,604, or nearly 70 percent. (A daughter would be cheaper to insure, but, at least initially, not much so.) A month or two later you're tired of sharing your car with your son, so you pick up a 10-year-old Toyota Corolla. It's got 90,000 miles on it but is in pretty good shape. You pay $2,300 for it. Now your son doesn't have to be classified as an "occasional" driver on your cars—although he can still drive them in a pinch and be fully covered. So the annual insurance bill on your Chrysler and Oldsmobile drops back to $2,280.

But you still have to insure your son's Toyota. The trick here is to forgo collision and comprehensive coverage on the car, which at $624 a year (on a $250 deductible) hardly seems worth it for a car that cost a mere $2,300. Just think of the Toyota as a disposable car. Without collision, it can be insured for $1,648 a year. Add that to the $2,280 you're paying on your car and your spouse's, and the family's total annual car inusrance bill comes to $3,928. That's just $44 a year more than if you didn't have the clunker and your son had to be specified as a driver of your cars.

Three Things that Will Raise Your Car Insurance Costs

1. *Having bad credit.* Many insurers consider credit history "more revealing than a guy's driving record," says Ron Sundermann, an agent with Skogman, Ralston, Carlson of Cedar Rapids, Iowa. "What's really important is what this guy does with all his money." If you have a bad credit history, you can expect your annual premium to increase by as much as $100.

2. *Making claims not related to an accident.* Insurers are increasingly wary of people who frequently make claims for glass breakage or other small bits of vandalism to their car. And they know about every claim. Most insurance companies report to Equifax's CLUE (Comprehensive Loss Underwriting Exchange) service, which keeps a database of all claims. When you apply for a new policy, a company will order a CLUE report to see what kind of claims record you have.

3. *Having a teenager in the house.* Short of being convicted for drunk driving, this is perhaps the easiest way to jack up your premium. If you add a 16-year-old girl to your policy, State Farm, for instance, will up your premium *90 percent*. If it's a boy? 180 percent. If it's a boy who drives the car regularly? 290 percent. You'll get a bit of a break if your child is a good student in high school (and is thus, insurers surmise, more responsible). You may find that you're better off just buying your teenager an old clunker, paying for minimal coverage on it, and not even insuring him on your car (see page 201).

Ten Things Your Property Insurer Won't Tell You

1 *We have our own caste system.*

Many insurance firms slot their policies into different categories, such as preferred, standard, and substandard, depending on your risk profile. Sam Mayer, a physician in suburban Chicago, had insured his home, car, and life with Metropolitan for 10 years without filing a single claim. But after a damaged roof and a burglary led to two legitimate claims totaling $3,000, the company dropped Mayer from its preferred coverage, citing his "claims history," and instead offered him a higher rate—even though his risk profile hadn't really changed. If you're not in the preferred category, ask why. Your agent—or even the insurance company itself—may be able to move you into a more favorable slot.

2 *Anything out of 'the ordinary' gives us the creeps.*

What do a couple going through a divorce and someone living in a downscale part of town have in common? The answer: Insurance companies hate them. Some insurers use illegal underwriting guidelines to "red-line"—the industry term for discriminate against—certain groups or areas. Independent agents say they often get memos from insurance companies identifying undesirable zip codes or reminding them to stay away from couples who are having problems in their marriage. If you think you've been discriminated against, raise a fuss by contacting your lawyer or even the American Civil Liberties Union.

3 *One wrong move and we'll drop you . . .*

As insurance companies tighten their belts, they're getting to be even more particular about who they'll cover and who they won't. Some insurers will drop you if you start an at-home business. Others will even label you too risky if you've missed a credit-card payment or two. And once you've been dropped, very few insurers will want to touch you. That's what Mike Martin discovered when his

Labrador took a nip at an appliance repairman and his insurance company paid out a claim. When his policy came up for renewal, he was shocked to learn that he was being dropped. Martin, a Maryland financial planner, spent the next couple of weeks frantically calling up insurance agents to get a new policy. But since dog bites are a red flag for insurers, he was shunned by all. It wasn't until he filed a complaint with Maryland's department of insurance that he got his original policy reinstated.

4 . . . especially now that Big Brother is watching.

Privacy? You're asking for too much in the information age. Insurance companies now have access to their own version of a credit report that reveals all sorts of information, from the number of claims filed with other firms to past behavioral patterns. The most pervasive is called the CLUE report, short for Comprehensive Loss Underwriting Exchange. Others such as Patrol and Property Loss Score are risk-scoring models that use an individual's credit history to determine his riskiness as a homeowner.

5 We're more secretive than the CIA.

Here's a little test: Call your insurer and ask how many claims it would take for the company to drop you or deem you "risky." Chances are you won't get much of an answer, for even if your insurer has written guidelines, it's under no obligation to share them with you. Ron Sundermann, an independent agent in Cedar Rapids, Iowa, learned the hard way: Over three years, a customer with a stellar record filed four small, perfectly legitimate claims totaling less than $5,000 and was dropped by his insurance company. When Sundermann pleaded his customer's case, he was reminded that it was the frequency of his customer's losses, not the severity, that made all the difference. The lesson? Filing one big claim may well land you in less trouble than four small ones.

6 You're paying too much for your policy.

When it comes to your home, the last thing you want to be is underinsured. But could you actually be overinsured? It happens a lot, regulators contend. Often, it's the mortgage lender's fault. For instance, a bank may require that your insurance cover almost the entire value of your home, including the land. That doesn't make a lot of sense, because land doesn't burn down. What you really want to cover is the house itself.

If you're like most homeowners, your policy's rate gets raised every so often to account for inflation. But read the numbers carefully: Your rates may be quite a bit higher than the actual inflated value of your home.

7 *You're covered for a lot less than you think.*

Rick and Anne Morrissey of Indian Hills, Colo., were sitting quietly in their living room one day when they heard a tremendous crash in the backyard. Rushing outside, Anne was shocked to see that two giant elk had come along and demolished their children's swing set.

They were even more shocked when their Allstate adjuster called. Her verdict: not covered. Damage by animals, it turns out, is not covered by most insurance—and it's only one of the many surprises you may find by reading the fine print on your policy. Among the most commonly misunderstood parts of any policy are the ways it handles missing objects, says David Thompson, an independent agent in Vero Beach, Fla. If you drop a piece of jewelry down the drain, it's generally not covered. But if you merely leave it by the sink in a public place and it's not there when you return, most policies will treat this as a theft and reimburse you for the loss.

8 *We like some agents more than others.*

Insurance companies will tell you that any authorized agent is a good agent. But in fact they do have their favorites—the ones who generate the most business, have customers with the fewest claims or both. State Farm, for instance, celebrates its heaviest hitters as members of the President's Club.

Buying through one of these agents can pay big dividends to consumers. The chosen few tend to have increased flexibility on pricing and, more important, greater leeway on underwriting guidelines. Other advantages to preferred agents: They may have an easier time retaining someone who has had claims and would otherwise be canceled; and they often can get their clients moved from a company's standard carrier to its preferred one.

9 *We are biased against older homes.*

You have your eyes set on a beautiful prewar colonial, with the original slate roof and parquet floors. Now try getting insurance. Insurers are increasingly clamping down on more "mature" homes, even when they're only 30 or 40 years old. "In Texas, a 1953 house is considered ancient," says Yvonne Darrah of Austin, who called at least 10 insurance companies before she could find one that would insure her 32-year-old home at a reasonable rate. "We were desperate," she recalls.

Even if you do get insurance for your older home, you may not get the best kind. Some companies won't sell "guaranteed replacement cost" policies—coverage that will pay whatever it takes to restore your home exactly as it was. You could end up with coverage that is limited to only a few risks. Or you might be offered "cash value" coverage. These policies will only cover the cost of replacing what's damaged, minus depreciation. "If you had a kitchen that was built 20 years ago and it is destroyed, the cash value is no help," says Mary Griffin, insurance counsel at Consumers Union.

10 *You need to check up on us—and it's easy.*

Insurers may not be the most forthcoming companies in the world, but thankfully, you can find out a lot about them. Your first stop ought to be your local library, where you'll find ratings reports from agencies such as A.M. Best, Moody's, and Standard & Poor's. At least 200 insurers have gone belly up over the past several years, making high ratings more important than ever. For Moody's and S&P, the top three ratings are AAA, AA, and A. At A.M. Best, the top three are A + +, A +, and A.

You might be surprised at what you can get from your state's insurance department as well. Some, for instance, have websites with information on the latest rates in different areas and tips on how to file a complaint. If nothing else, a phone call to the state will let you know how many complaints have been filed against your insurance company.

Part 6

TEACHING YOUR KIDS ABOUT MONEY

Back when you were a kid, money was simple. You got a lollypop while your mom cashed Dad's paycheck at the bank. Groceries were paid for with dollar bills straight from Mom's wallet. Your allowance was strictly for comics, candy, or—when you got older—albums. Your parents didn't teach you how to handle money until you headed out the door to college—if they bothered at all.

Today couldn't be more different. Your salary gets zapped electronically to the bank. ATM dispenses cash as if it grew on trees. You wield a dizzying array of plastic cards for your purchases—when you're not making them through catalogs or cyberspace. The old-fashioned passbook has given way to a financial software program. Which means your kid doesn't have a clue where money comes from or where it goes.

At the same time, an entire universe of kid-oriented products has sprung up in just the last decade, vying for those allowance dollars.

So how do you teach your kids how to handle money? In this chapter, we'll show you the way. We've got age-by-age information on kids as consumers, along with a worksheet to help you dole out a reasonable allowance. We've also provided guidelines for teaching older kids about saving and investing. Our aim throughout this chapter is to help your kids develop good skills and habits, to master the basic mechanics of money management.

Look at it this way: *someone* in the house has to be responsible about money.

12

Dollars and Sense

It's Saturday morning, and you take your kids out to run a couple of errands. You stop at an appliance store, where you plan to buy a new cordless phone for the kitchen. Did you bring along an ad from the local newspaper showing competitors' prices? Do you grill the salesman on which model offers the best features for the least money? Or do you just grab the sleekest one, regardless of cost?

You might not think your kids are paying attention to your shopping strategy (or lack thereof), but they are. More than any other influence, your actions and attitudes toward money will shape your children's financial behavior. How you make decisions on big purchases, whether you pay with cash or credit, when you sit down to battle the monthly bills—all of this affects how your children will handle money when they grow up.

How do you make sure they don't turn out to be financial deadbeats? It's easier than you think. Give them an appropriate allowance, teach them how to budget, show them how to spend wisely, and encourage them to save regularly. Though your daughter will start clamoring for a bag of candy or a small toy as early as 2 years old, it will be another 12 years or so before she starts shopping for herself through the J. Crew catalog. So you've got plenty of time to help build good habits.

When Do Kids Become Consumers?

Even by age 3, kids have picked up a few basics about money. They know you need it to buy stuff. They know that to have money, Mommy and Daddy work; that ATM machines hand out cash and that credit cards can pay for things, too. And they know that if they ask for something, they just might get it.

Up to age 8 or so, kids are hardly sophisticated shoppers. Sure, a 6- or 7-year-old can name each coin and tell you how many pennies there are in a nickel or a dime. But she's not hunting for bargains when she goes shopping—and she has a dim understanding of what things cost or what they might be worth.

Between 4 and 7, however, kids take several major steps as consumers. At this age, kids can recognize brand names, especially for cold cereals. If you give them a dollar or two, they can pick out and pay for a product for the first time, with parents nearby. They have caught on to what their parents will buy, will not buy, or are reluctant to buy. In other words, they've begun to perfect the art of pleading.

You've surely noticed, to your great annoyance, that stores always put candy racks down somewhere low, like beneath the cash register. Now you know why: That's eye level, for kids. And these days, there are a lot more products geared toward kids than ever before. There's Dial for Kids, Pert Plus for Kids, and Sesame Street Band-Aids, among countless other products. A recent issue of *Time for Kids* was sponsored solely by Ford Motor Company, to jump-start brand loyalty, no doubt. There's even a trade magazine called *Selling to Kids*.

Clearly, if there was ever a time to start teaching your kids about money, it's now.

When Should You Start Doling Out an Allowance?

Not every child develops at the same pace, so while some 6-year-olds may be ready to handle and understand an allowance, some 7-year-olds may not. You'll get a few hints that it's time to start an allowance. It might happen on a family vacation when your 7-year-old son decides he must have, indeed *needs,* a $16 baseball cap from the Hard Rock cafe. Or you're at the toy store picking out a birthday gift for his best friend and he has asked for the fifth time that you buy the $150 deluxe Sony Playstation.

Helene Silverman, a Chicago mother, decided to give her daughter Lauren an allowance because "I was buying her whatever she wanted and she would lose interest in it after an hour," she says. "I wanted her to learn that she has to think about how much she really wants it."

Starting pay: Chores vs. allowance

S hould your kid have to earn his allowance? Or should he receive it free and clear? Should everyone in the house be expected to pick up his own room, wash dishes, set the table, and unload grocery bags—regardless of whether an allowance is involved? Or should he only get the allowance if he helps out?

These are questions you should discuss with your child before you fork over the first allowance payment. But we think the two should be kept as separate as possible. Regular activities such as folding laundry and cleaning up after dinner are part of being a family member. You do your fair share around the house, period.

The allowance, you can explain, is simply your child's fair share of the pot. Let him know that his allowance is part of the family money and he gets it because he's part of the family. You are *allowing* your child to have that money. That's why it's called an allowance. Whether you want to withhold it when the room is a rat's nest for weeks on end is your choice. You just might point out that someone who can't do his fair share isn't entitled to his fair share.

Conversely, you may want to pay your child extra for some jobs that occur only once in a while, such as cleaning out the garage or refrigerator, or weeding out a flower bed. You can settle on an hourly wage or a set fee. Paying kids for odd jobs around the house might teach them a thing or two about what it takes to earn money.

Where kids get their money

W hen you're figuring out how much to give your kid each week, bear in mind that allowance is only a portion of their income. Here's where James U. McNeal, marketing professor at Texas A&M University, estimates kids aged 4 through 12 get their money:

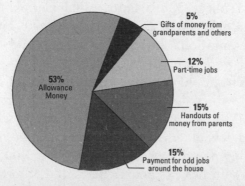

5%
Gifts of money from
grandparents and others

12%
Part-time jobs

53%
Allowance
Money

15%
Handouts of
money from parents

15%
Payment for odd jobs
around the house

Bear in mind that the biggest reason—indeed maybe the only reason—to give your child an allowance is to teach him how to handle money. It's not about *having* money, it's about *managing* it, no matter how small the amount.

A few ways to tell if your child is ready:

- She can tell the difference between a dime and a nickel and understands what each coin is worth.
- She can count ones up to 50 and tens up to 100.
- She needs to carry money for lunches, snacks, maybe even transportation.
- She needs new sneakers, and while you want the $25 pair, she's insisting on the $40 pair with stars embroidered on them.

How Much Is Enough—but Not Too Much?

Chances are the $2 or $3 your parents gave you each week for taking out the trash would be scoffed at by today's teens. Just ask Tom McFarland, a father of two in suburban Boston. "C'mon upstairs, Dad," said his daughter, Kristin, then 11, leading him by the hand to the family's office/loft. There he was flabbergasted to find that Kristin and her 13-year-old sister, Heather, had used the family's personal computer to document their need for an allowance hike. Their presentation, complete with Excel spreadsheets and slides, showed how prices for movies, CDs, and clothes had gone up and how—if they got a 25 percent increase in their $10 and $20 allowances, respectively—they could actually save some of their own money for college. McFarland, a financial planner, was so impressed that he gave them each a 100 percent raise. "They had quite a nice presentation," he says, shrugging. "I'd seen professionals do jobs that weren't nearly as good."

So how much should you give your kids? A lot of parents, particularly those with younger children, use the simplest equation: When your child is 7 you give him $7 a week; when he's 8, $8. But as your kid gets older, we recommend using a more systematic approach: Sit down and figure out, with your child, what expenses are associated with her extracurriculars and entertainment. Then, estimate how much you should pay for each item—you may decide, for instance, that she shouldn't have to pay for lunch with her allowance money—and add it up. What's left over is her allowance.

	TOTAL	Parents' Share	Allowance
1. Birthday gifts for friends *(per month)*	$_____	$_____	$_____
2. Lunch money	$_____	$_____	$_____
3. School supplies	$_____	$_____	$_____
4. Snacks	$_____	$_____	$_____
5. Books, magazines, comics	$_____	$_____	$_____
6. Toys	$_____	$_____	$_____
7. Sporting equipment	$_____	$_____	$_____
8. Clothes	$_____	$_____	$_____
9. Club dues and uniforms	$_____	$_____	$_____
10. CDs, tapes, records	$_____	$_____	$_____
11. Video rentals	$_____	$_____	$_____
12. Movies	$_____	$_____	$_____
13. Souvenirs and postcards	$_____	$_____	$_____
14. Transportation	$_____	$_____	$_____
15. Savings	$_____	$_____	$_____
16. Church and/or charity	$_____	$_____	$_____
17. Total	$_____	$_____	$_____

How Do You Fork It Over?

Instead of just handing your kid a few bucks every once in a while, make sure your payment is as reliable as a paycheck.

- **Make it a routine.** Choose a relatively relaxed day—maybe Saturday or Sunday—for handing out allowances. The worst thing you can do is forget one week and then fork over two weeks' worth of allowance. Like thirsty stragglers, they'll probably blow it all too quickly because they haven't had the luxury of the allowance for a long time.
- **Use a see-through piggy bank.** To a child, a traditional ceramic piggy bank can seem like a black hole: The money goes in, and it's lost forever. A see-through container, like a jar, might work better so your kids can watch the money accumulate.
- **Don't bail them out.** Initially, your kids will spend the allowance too fast and bemoan the fact that there isn't any left. Offer sympathy, but don't give them an advance on a future allowance. Limits are a part of life. Spending within limits is your goal, but children will not reach that goal until they've

made mistakes. If you bail them out, you'll defeat the whole purpose of limiting them with an allowance.

How Do You Teach Them to Spend?

It's better not to put too many limits on what your child can do with his money—it's his money after all, and the joys and sorrows of spending will be learned much quicker if he makes all the decisions. But you can set a few guidelines. He can't spend the money on toy guns, for instance, but other toys he wants to buy are okay.

How Do You Teach Them to Save?

Forget about lecturing your 7-year-old on the benefits of saving: Those stories about how you saved for three years to buy a car, or how you helped pay for college will seem preposterous to a second-grader. It's not so important that your child understand why she's saving—that will come later. Just get her started now, so it feels like a natural thing to do any time she receives any money, whether it be an allowance, a paycheck, or a gift from her grandmother.

Your money's worth

Piggy banks don't hold much these days—a couple weeks' of allowance and then it's full, with the money burning a hole in your kid's Old Navy jeans. Better to get one that literally lets your child see his savings grow.

Worth it: The Parking Meter Bank (Fantazia Marketing Corp, 413-534-7323, $35) looks just like a parking meter, except that the pole is clear plastic. The kids put change (or folded bills) in a slot in the side, then twist off the head to dump the money out. The 55" bank holds $1,000. One final plus: The kids will get a civics lesson in how local towns nickel-and-dime their residents.

Not worth it: The Mickey Mouse Statue of Liberty piggy bank (The Disney Store, $8). The kids can't see through the soft plastic to watch their allowance add up. It only holds about $50 and it's difficult to insert dollar bills. Perhaps most egregious, the bank is Mickey Mouse dressed as the Statue of Liberty. Now that's a civics lesson they can do without.

The going rate: The cost of being cool

Peer pressure has its benefits. Finally, your daughter won't insist on wearing her Cinderella crown before every outing. Your son will leave his entire Buzz Lightyear set at home. But peer pressure also has its dark side, not the least of which is that it's expensive. Here's what your kid will spend in four cities to be part of the "in" crowd.

	Anaheim, Calif.	Hershey, Pa.	Sugar Land, Tex.	Youngstown, Ohio
Cost of Spice Girls latest CD	$ 14.99	$ 14.99	$ 16.99	$ 14.99
Kid's ticket to the movies	$ 4.50	$ 4.50	$ 4.00	$ 4.25
Nintendo 64 system	$129.99	$129.99	$129.99	$129.99
Nintendo Pocket Gameboy	$ 49.99	$ 49.96	$ 54.99	$ 49.99
Full outfit of Rollerblades	$111.96	$159.96	$ 79.80	$122.93
Kid's miniature golf game fee	$ 5.00	$ 4.25	$ 3.00	$ 5.00
One dozen Goosebumps series books	$ 47.88	$ 47.88	$ 47.88	$ 39.00
One dozen Babysitters' Club series books	$ 47.88	$ 42.00	$ 47.88	$ 35.40
Kid's bowling fee	$ 3.75	$ 3.00	$ 4.25	$ 2.75
Family day pass at nearest amusement park	$132.00	$ 93.80	$118.86	$ 73.96
One day family cost of local parks & recreation swimming pool	$ 3.00	$ 16.00	$ 4.00	$ 3.00
Entrance fee to nearest Discovery Zone kids' indoor play center	$ 5.99	$ 7.99	$ 7.99	$ 7.99
Go-cart speedway ride	$ 4.25	$ 5.00	$ 3.00	$ 4.00
McDonald's Happy Meal	$ 2.14	$ 2.11	$ 2.15	$ 2.23
Bag of Blow-Pops	$ 1.37	$ 1.29	$ 1.20	$ 1.07
Total	$564.69	$582.72	$526.07	$497.35

It will be easier for your child to save a little of his allowance every week if you dole it out in small denominations. A $10 bill is impossible to divide. But give him one $5 bill and five $1 bills, and he can easily slip two of those $1 bills into a piggy bank—you can even buy two banks, one for a regular savings pot, the other for charity.

The minute he wants something he can't afford, you should pounce. This is how he can learn the why of savings. Maybe he's been clamoring for a new video game? Or she's dying for a new soccer ball? Help your child devise a short-term strategy: How much money will she have to save—over what period of time—to buy the ball herself? Make the time frame short, one or two weeks at the most, so it will seem feasible to your child.

You can pitch in a little to make time go faster. Think of it as a payroll deduction plan and a 401(k) matching plan rolled into one.

The real world: Money lessons your kids don't need

Remember your first lesson in the value of a dollar? Maybe it was when you got an allowance, or that day in the toy store when you asked for a gift your parents said was "just too expensive." However your education about money began, we'll venture it didn't include:

- *Piggy Banks to Money Markets,* a $21.98, 30-minute video that instructs elementary school–age kids about business basics, using a lemonade stand as a model.
- A $30 **World of Money Allowance Kit,** which includes, along with a three-chambered plastic piggy bank, a motivational cassette tape. ("If you do learn how to save money," the tape advises, "you might just end up filthy, stinking rich.")
- **Acquire,** a board game where players compete to create the biggest hotel chain through Boesky-style raids on one another's companies.
- A four-week **$2,800 summer camp** that teaches teenagers everything from accounting to futures to franchising. It also offers lessons in "businessperson's sports" such as golf, squash, and tennis, as well as field trips to such popular teenage hangouts as the New York Stock Exchange.

As bizarre as these offerings may seem, they're real—and really popular in certain affluent communities. Eager parents have snapped up more than 150,000 Allowance Kits since they were introduced in 1996 by Summit Financial Products of Englewood, Colorado. In fact, sales are so strong that six months later Summit released a junior version aimed at children ages 3 to 7. Still, those kinds of homespun lessons just aren't good enough for some parents. Every summer, about 30 teenagers pay $3,000 a week to attend JKSC business camp in Haverford, Pennsylvania.

Even mutual fund companies are getting in on the act. At the Stein Roe Young Investor fund—which offers a quarterly newsletter for kids and a portfolio full of such stocks as Disney and Coca-Cola—assets surged to $725 million by mid-1998.

What's behind the proliferation of books and games, software programs, and camps aimed at teaching kids about money? To a large degree, it's fear. Baby boomers are frightened that their kids will grow up to be financially irresponsible. Judith Shine, a Denver financial planner, is petrified by that notion. "There is no heartache," she contends, "like the fear of your kids not understanding the basics of money."

OK, so maybe that's an overstatement. But even if we assume that no one wants a child who's dumb about money, are the products being peddled these days the best way to get the message across? Probably not.

Most grown-ups, for instance, will agree that stocks are the best investments over the long haul. That's especially true for children and other young savers, who can weather bad markets and wait a few decades before tapping their capital. But you wouldn't learn it from reading the Allowance Kit handbook. According to the handbook, Wall Street is only a step above a trip to Las Vegas as a way to earn high returns, and the handbook gives stocks a resounding "maybe" as a worthwhile investment. Why? Because "buying stocks involves risk." There's no mention of mutual funds as a way to balance that risk or any sense that stocks are anything more than a gamble. Only banks get an unreserved thumbs-up as a place for kids to stash their cash.

The Money Book, another popular guide for elementary schoolers, doesn't discuss stocks or funds either. What investments does the book recommend, besides the passbook savings account? Comic books. In the video _Piggy Banks to Money Markets,_ meanwhile, your kids will learn that "baseball cards are a great investment." As one fresh-faced kid explains, "You buy them, keep them for a while, and then they're worth more than what you paid." Well, some of them anyhow—if you're lucky.

The game Stocks & Bonds will teach your kids some, um, interesting lessons as well. Among them: Bond prices don't move up or down. And the board game Acquire never makes it clear just where or how the acquirers get the money they use to create their huge hotel chains. Every player just starts with $6,000.

The fact is, trying to teach kids about money with books, videos, and games is just ridiculous, contends Paul Prunier, a Chevy Chase, Maryland, child psychiatrist with two teenage sons. "It's a matter of common sense, just simply talking with your children and explaining how money or the markets work," he says. He invested in McDonald's, Disney, and Coca-Cola with his two boys, and the kids watch the stocks' every move in the paper. "They've really learned about finance and the markets just from seeing how these stocks work," says Prunier.

What about younger children? Elissa Buie knew her 6-year-old daughter, Lauren, wasn't ready to start tracking the stock market. But Buie, a financial planner in Falls Church, Virginia, still wanted Lauren to start learning. So she went out and bought a miniature version of the Filofax-type organizer she uses at work. Working together at the kitchen table, mother and daughter drew a ledger where each week's allowance of $6 could be recorded. They devised three goals to save money for: personal treats, gifts for other people, and daily spending money.

As your kids get older, you could take a lesson from Anne Badanes. At the end of each year, the Cincinnati mom pays her eldest child, David, to enter all of the family's checks into Quicken. "It was wonderful for him to realize what it costs for camp, for his sports, for travel," she says. "When he saw what it costs to raise a family, he was just blown away."

For every dollar he saves, throw in 10 to 25 cents—that's a lot better than the interest rate he'll find anywhere else.

How Should You Teach Them about Investing?

Kids love piggy banks. They love to shake them and peer inside them and dump their coins out all over the floor. But by the time most kids reach age 10 or so, they're ready for a **basic savings account** at a bank. This accomplishes a couple of things. They'll learn about interest and bank fees. And they won't be able to toss their savings all over your floor anymore.

The minimum required to open an account varies from bank to bank. When we called a handful of Chicago banks, we heard everything from $100 (most banks) to $500 (Citibank).

Once your child has opened a bank account, you can explain that the **stock market** is a way to earn better returns—but it comes with much larger risks. One good way to demonstrate: Give your 10-, 11-, or 12-year-old a fictional amount of money to spend on the stock exchange, then reward her gains. For instance, your kid could take an amount equivalent to the savings portion of his allowance and invest it in two or three stocks and see the difference in value between the savings account in her bank and her stock portfolio over 6 months. When your kid decides to cash in his stocks, you could reward the gains with either a nickel for every dollar or a hot fudge sundae.

While you should encourage your kid to pick winners, picking a loser isn't so bad; then he learns the real meaning of the word risk. You might even have him put together his own "mutual fund," a group of stocks that he favors, so he can see how these funds spread risk: Sure, some stocks may go down, but others go up so much that the fund itself increases in value. The key at this point is to convey to your child that the better you manage money, the more you get.

Taking the Plunge: Checks and Credit Cards

Older teenagers—say, 16 and up—should learn how to handle checks and ATM cards, at a minimum. For one thing, it's safer. If your teen works part-time, he may be buying bigger-ticket items, and you don't want him running around with a wad of cash in his pocket.

Unfortunately, it's not going to be easy finding a bank that will take your kid. Most big banks won't open accounts for anyone under 18 these days, figuring that the teenage crowd is more trouble than it's worth. You'll likely have better luck at smaller banks, like Colorado East Bank and Trust in Lamar, Colorado. It still allows teens to open accounts and write checks in their name, though an adult needs to co-sign on the account.

Think your kid is mature enough to handle a credit card? You can ease her into it by issuing an extra card on your account. Once she's over 18, she can apply for a secured card, like the one offered by Chase USA (800-482-4273). She'll have to deposit a sum of money with the bank, say $300, and she'll get a $300 line of credit. If she runs up a big balance on the credit card bill and can't pay, the bank takes what she owes from the $300 and cancels the credit card.

However you choose to put plastic in your kid's wallet, here are four tips for making the most of the experience:

- Do a math exercise to illustrate how expensive credit cards can be. For example: If you charge $500 dollars and pay the minimum balance each month, with an interest rate of 15 percent, it will take 30 months to pay it off. The interest itself will cost $86.90.

- Limit the amount of money your child can charge per month. Tie the amount of money to his allowance—50 percent or less, for instance.

- Set some guidelines, or make suggestions, as to when it would be appropriate to carry the card (for instance, when they're going on a ski trip with friends or they're going to get the car fixed and don't have cash to pay the bill, etc.), and when it should be left home (the weekly trip to the mall).

- Ask for something in return. Clients of Judy Barber, a family business consultant in San Francisco, gave their teenage daughter a $100 monthly allowance, a checkbook, and a credit card when she entered high school—all of it on one condition: That she use a Quicken program to balance her checkbook and keep a record of all her purchases. "If the checkbook didn't balance one month, that was the end of it," says Barber. Did she stick to it? You bet. Soon thereafter, she was working on weekends as a waitress in a restaurant and saving money to pay for her car insurance bill.

Ten Things Your Kids Won't Tell You About Money

1 *I spend way more than you think.*

Remember when you were a teenager and you saved your allowance and baby-sitting money for weeks, just to buy a record or a new pair of jeans? Well, moderation is no longer in style, and neither are $8 LPs. In 1997, teenagers spent $122 billion on themselves, according to James U. McNeal, a marketing professor at Texas A&M University who has studied kids and money. Based on the population of 12–19-year-olds in 1997—30.2 million—that means that the average teenager spent over *$4,000* on stuff that year.

Four thousand dollars a year! If that doesn't convince you to teach your kids about the value of money, we don't know what will.

2 *I'm clueless—and it's your fault.*

Are your kids having difficulty hanging on to their allowance longer than it takes them to reach the nearest toy store? Maybe it's because you've never allowed them to experience life without ready cash. You may think that you're giving them everything you never had, but you may also be giving them the idea that money is an infinite resource. "I find that those [most generous] parents are often bailing their kids out," says Robert Hendren, director of child and adolescent psychiatry at Robert Wood Johnson Medical School in New Jersey. "The kid says, 'I spent all my money' and if he nags long enough, the parents say, 'Oh all right.' Parents are having a hard time setting limits."

So what can you do? First of all, consider your own spending habits. "Children learn what they live," says Hendren. If the problem doesn't lie with you and your spouse, then take action in a constructive way. "If a child consistently misspends, parents can offer to help monitor money with the child, help them make a budget and keep it." But remember that moderation is key. "Sometimes parents can go too far from one extreme to the other," says

Hendren. In other words, don't suddenly decide that your child shouldn't have any money at all—help him learn what to do with it instead.

3 *I'll do anything for money . . .*

The minute kids understand the concept of money and what it can get them, they'll be willing to take on any number of onerous tasks you could never get them to do before. The upside: You've begun teaching them the value of money. But watch out. Once you start paying your kids to empty the recycling bins and shovel the walk, they may never do anything else you ask them to do without holding their hand out for some cash. "I think kids should have an allowance. It's a way for them to learn about money," says Hendren. "I don't think they should be paid to do what they're expected to do, like take their dishes to the sink, clean their rooms, or do well in school . . . Otherwise it teaches them to only do things they get paid for, and that's not a good value."

4 *. . . but you should pay me what I'm worth.*

Paying kids for "extra" work around the home is a good way to teach them about what a job is and how to save money to buy something they want. "Those are basic value judgments that one has to learn," says Bennet Leventhal, a child psychiatrist at the University of Chicago. "It's never too soon to start teaching those." But you have to be reasonable about the salary you offer. Parents, says Robert Hendren, "should probably pay a fair market value" for something like mowing the lawn on a weekly basis. The point is, if you overpay your kids, they'll never learn that having a job doesn't automatically mean you have as much money as you want or need. If you underpay them, they'll have a hard time understanding the true value of money (e.g., that two lawn mowings equals enough cash to buy a new CD).

5 *No matter how much allowance you give me, I still like to shoplift . . .*

Kids, particularly teenagers, have shoplifted from time immemorial. Why? Peer pressure, rebellion, wanting something they can't afford, or just the thrill of getting something for free. According to Shoplifters Alternative, a unit of Shoplifters Anonymous, 89 percent of kids say they know other kids who shoplift, and 33 percent of kids who shoplift say that it's difficult for them to stop, even after they get nabbed. Another study found 36 percent of high school students admitted to stealing from a store in the previous 12 months.

What happens if you find a new trinket at home that your child couldn't possibly have afforded? March the kid right back to the store, have her pay for it (out of her allowance), and confess to the shopkeeper. Whatever you do, don't ignore the problem and don't bail your kids out, no matter how long it takes them to pay the money back. Shoplifters think they're not hurting anyone, so many times they don't ponder the consequences or the seriousness of their acts. Insisting that your kid pays will certainly make an impact.

6 *. . . and I steal from you, too.*

You pull out your wallet to pay for something and . . . *Hey, wait a minute. Didn't I have an extra $20 in here yesterday?*

Sneaking money from a parent's pocketbook is more common than you might think. Twenty-eight percent of high school students say they've stolen from a parent or relative in the last year, according to a survey by the Josephson Institute of Ethics.

Many kids opt to steal from their parents because they think it's a safe way to "experiment" with theft, says Hendren. "Kids at some point or another may try taking something that isn't theirs. One hopes that they have an internal monitor that says, 'I shouldn't have done that and I won't do it again.' "

As with shoplifting, the best way to prevent repeat offenses is to catch your child in the act and tell him or her that it's wrong. Otherwise, kids forget that what they're doing is wrong and worry only about getting caught, Hendren says. That's certainly not the message you want them to get.

7 *I supplement my allowance by selling drugs at recess.*

Every year for the past two decades, at least 82 percent of high school seniors have said they find marijuana "fairly easy" or "very easy" to obtain, reports Common Sense for Drug Policy Foundation, a Washington D.C. nonprofit. Care to guess who's making it so easy? That's right: other kids, hanging out in a corner of the playground selling pot.

If you think it could never be your star athlete doing the selling, think again, says Kevin Zeese, president of Common Sense for Drug Policy. "Kids definitely have access to drugs and I think they get it from other kids. That's why alcohol is harder to purchase: Pot is sold by kids while alcohol is sold by state licensed adults. The most effective thing a parent can do [to stop a kid from selling drugs] is be involved in a kid's life."

8 *I give your money to other kids.*

Sure, you want to teach your kid to be generous and share with his friends, but what if he doesn't understand the limits and you find yourself buying a new lunch box every three or four weeks because he's gleefully handed his off to an admirer? This kind of rampant giving can be the result of two things. If your child is young and just doesn't understand the concept of how much it costs to replace things, you need to take immediate action by demonstrating that every lunchbox isn't replaceable. But there may be a larger problem at the root of such behavior. Some kids start to equate money with love and friendship, so you want to make sure your child knows that money is money, and nothing else. "With our society increasingly focused on what money can buy comes the misunderstanding that money is the deeper value," says Hendren.

9 *Every dollar you give me means $100 for the dentist.*

Kids tend to spend about one-third of their money on food and drink, according to McNeal's research. Put that together with a recent report from the Center for Science in the Public Interest, which found children's consumption of sugary soft drinks has skyrocketed in the last two decades, and it's not too hard to figure out where most of that money is going.

The numbers are scary. Teenage boys drank 7 ounces of soda a day in the late '70s, while girls drank 6 ounces. By the mid-1990s, those numbers had risen to 19 ounces for boys and 12 ounces for girls.

Since refined sugar is a major promoter of tooth decay, it's no surprise that the biggest jump in cavities corresponds to the age when kids are starting to build up their allowances and make extra money: Only 5.6 percent of nine-year-olds have fillings, according to the American Dental Association, but by 11, a staggering 81 percent have met with the dentist's drill.

10   *I'll decide how you spend your money.*

Think you're the one in control when you cruise the supermarket aisles? Think again. "Children's influence of their parents' spending has grown at least as robustly as spending of their own money," says McNeal. About 90 percent of product requests children make to their parents come with a brand name attached, and in 1997, children's direct influence on their parents' spending habits peaked at around $188 billion, according to his research.

Even if you don't have your kids with you, jumping up and down and begging for this cookie or that cereal, they're making their presence felt through what McNeal calls "indirect influence." In effect they've brainwashed you to buy the brands and products they want. You know Susie likes Frosted Cheerios better than Special K, and so you buy Frosted Cheerios. In 1997, this kind of indirect influence accounted for about $300 billion of the $500 billion of household spending determined by children, according to McNeal.

Part 7

INVESTING FOR THE FUTURE

Forget baseball. These days, it seems like investing has become the new national pastime. You can scarcely turn on the TV, go to a cocktail party, or even take the kids to the park without hearing somebody talk about their broker or their financial planner or their favorite mutual fund.

Until now you could always happily ignore all that chatter. But not anymore. As a parent, you can't afford to tune it out. You've got to learn, at least on a basic level, how to be an investor. Because when the costs of parenthood start mounting, you're going to find that the puny returns paid out by savings accounts just won't cut it. You're going to need your money to work harder than that. A *lot* harder.

The following two chapters will get you started. In the first, we'll help you begin investing for that most daunting of expenses—college tuition. (The good news is, much more money is available for financial aid than ever before—even to parents who can't demonstrate a financial "need." We'll help you get a leg up on the process.) In the second, we'll lay out a simple, low-maintenance asset-allocation plan that will ensure you've got money available when you need it for life's other necessities. Like braces. And a bigger house. Oh yeah, and your retirement.

13

The Tuition Fund

With a four-year bill at a state school now exceeding $43,000 and an Ivy League school tab easily topping out at around $130,000, it's tempting to just throw up your hands and decide it can't be done.

Bad move.

Yes, you will have to save. Yes, you have to invest wisely. Yes, it's going to be a struggle. But it's not the impossible dream that it might appear. The fact is, despite a decade of doomsday pronouncements about rising tuition costs, millions of kids do troop off to college each fall. And there's hope that things will actually improve. In the last couple of years, colleges have begun to reduce the astronomical rate of growth in tuition increases.

Most parents—even those who get a late start on their savings—can probably put together a combination of savings, loans, and financial aid to cover the cost of a college education. In this chapter, we'll lay out for you a simple, three-step program that will help you pay for college when the time comes.

One other thing to keep in mind: Life is rarely as simple as financial planners and tuition guides make it out to be. While it would be nice to set aside $200 or so a month starting at birth, and then gradually build a nest egg over the years, we know that isn't how things usually work. Far more likely is that tuition savings will go in waves. Years where summer camp and piano lessons take priority may render saving for college nonexistent. Other years that bring a financial windfall will translate into a bonus for the college account.

While it's impossible to calculate the specifics of each situation, for most parents this kind of fits-and-starts saving can be just as productive as dogged month-by-month planning. Say you save $100 a month from the time your child is born, for a total of

$21,600 by the time he goes off to college. Assuming you earn the projected returns in the *SmartMoney* portfolios we'll describe in this chapter, you'll have $38,500 after taxes by the time the tuition bills come due. But let's say your savings habits are slightly less routine. If you manage to stash away $5,000 by the time your child is 3 (think gifts from grandparents), add $3,000 when your child turns 5, invest $5,000 about the time your child turns 8, add $6,000 more when your child hits 13, then add $2,600 two years before your child starts college, you'll end up with $38,300 after taxes—almost the exact same amount as the once-a-month saver.

Step One: Doing the Math

Take a few minutes right now and fill out the worksheet on page 232. It will help you gauge how much you can afford to save for

---

Afraid to ask: Four terms you should know before getting started

Bond. A bond is like an IOU, made to a company or a government. The issuer gets the money and promises to pay it back, with interest. This is why bonds are known as fixed-income securities. Typically they are less volatile investments than stocks.

Stock. Shares of stock represent ownership in a company. They're sold first by the company—in an initial public offering, or IPO—and then traded by individuals. People who buy stock expect to profit when the company profits. Dividends, usually paid out in cash once a quarter, are investors' share of the profits.

Mutual fund. A fund is a collection of stocks or bonds, or sometimes both, owned by a group of individuals and managed by professional investors. There are thousands of funds to choose from, some with specialties so arcane they'll make you dizzy. (What exactly are you supposed to do with a multiasset global fund, anyway? Don't ask us.) For most investors, a few basic funds like the kind we describe in this chapter are more than enough.

Large cap, mid cap, small cap. A company's capitalization, or "cap," is really just a six-syllable way of saying "value." It's the value that the market puts on the shares of a company. So if you've got a company whose shares trade for $10 apiece, and there are 10 million shares, its market cap is $100 million. Market values of $1 billion and under qualify as small caps, $1 to $4 billion are mid caps, and $4 billion and up are large caps. Why should you care? Because they all behave differently at different times, so it's important you have some of each in your portfolio.

college right now—and how much you'll *need* to save, after financial aid.

What if it shows that you need to save more than you currently have available? Well, you've got a couple of options: You can adjust your spending patterns to make more money available for saving, or you can simply do the best you can—hoping that you'll have more money available at a later date.

You'll notice in the worksheet that we expect you to contribute the maximum amount to your retirement account *before* saving for Junior's college fund. That may seem like a selfish attitude, but there are some good reasons for it. First of all, when figuring financial aid eligibility, schools don't consider money placed in IRS-sanctioned retirement savings accounts part of your overall assets (that may change, however, now that the IRS allows penalty-free IRA withdrawals for some college expenses). For now, your IRA or 401(k) money is not counted when it comes time to figure out how much you should be expected to contribute to the cost of tuition. (Some schools, however, may look closely at the amount of money you contribute during the years your kids are in school, expecting you to forgo that amount for the college years.)

The second reason you should keep saving for retirement: You're going to need that money. You may find that if you rob your retirement account now to pay for your children's education, they'll have to turn around and support you when you hit sixty-five—a prospect no parent relishes (and no child can guarantee). For more on retirement savings, see page 266.

Step Two: Investing the Money

In most parents' tight budgets, finding the money to set aside for college is hard enough. But once you've done that, where are you supposed to invest it?

We've done the legwork for you, assembling five sample investment portfolios. In these five portfolios, you'll see a mix of mutual funds that we've determined best suits the needs of parents who are investing for college—whether that first tuition bill is 18 years away or just around the corner. We did so using an exclusive risk-rating system developed by *SmartMoney.com*. This system assigns a letter grade, from "A" to "F," to every mutual fund, based

Whose name should you save the money in?

H ere's a one-question quiz that you should definitely take before opening a college savings account: Is it better to save the money in your kid's name or keep it in your own account?

OK, you can put your pencils down. The correct answer, as it happens, depends largely on your income, your tax bracket, and your assets. But most people should keep their children's college savings in the parents' names.

That's because the amount of financial aid you can qualify for hinges on what's known as your "expected family contribution." There's a formula to arrive at this number, and it works like this: Your kid's portion of the expected family contribution is 35 percent of his savings and half his income above $1,750, after taxes; you, the parent, are supposed to supply up to 47 percent of your income and up to 5.6 percent of your assets, not including your home or retirement savings. Only once you've hit these thresholds are you eligible for financial aid.

So it's simple: A student with very little in the way of assets will hit the 35 percent threshold more quickly than a student with a big savings account will. The "wealthier" student qualifies for less in aid. This is a lesson that Mick and Judy Von Bergen recently learned, to their chagrin. The Madison, Wisconsin, couple dutifully saved $40,000 in their triplets' names only to find that the money wiped out their eligibility for aid. They don't regret saving the money, but they certainly wish they'd done it in their names. "If we had spent the money, we might have gotten some aid," Judy says with a sigh. Their kids are helping to pay their expenses by holding down jobs while attending school and during the summer.

Families in the top tax bracket, however, ought to do just what the Von Bergens did— and keep the money in their kids' names. Two reasons: If you've got, say, $100,000 in income and $200,000 in savings, you're probably not going to qualify for financial aid anyway. Meanwhile, the tax break you get from keeping the money in your kids' names could be huge. Young children—those under 14—don't pay any tax on their first $700 in annual income and only 15 percent on the second $700. (Once they're over 14, they pay at their own rate—usually 15 percent.) That's quite a difference from the 39.6 percent you're paying on your income. In addition, the 1997 tax law changes cut the long-term capital gains tax on children's investments to a mere 8 percent starting in the year 2001, compared with 20 percent if the money is in your account.

Unsure of what your finances will look like when your kid starts to prepare for college? Who isn't? Many financial planners suggest that you wait until your child is 14 before deciding whether to save in his name. At that point you'll have a better sense of your own financial situation, as well as whether the child is mature enough to use the money for college rather than buying a Ferrari. (When the money's in your child's name, it's legally your child's to spend as he or she sees fit. A pair of solutions: You can put the money in a trust or a custodial account, both of which let you limit your kid's access to the money until he or she is older. See page 308 for more details about how they work.)

If you've made a mistake and realize that your kid shouldn't own so much of his or her college savings, don't despair. There are some ways to work around the problem. No, you can't simply change the name on the account; money you set aside for your kid in an account with his or her Social Security number is an irrevocable gift, according to the IRS. However, you may be able to "spend down" the account before you apply for college aid by using it to pay for items outside the scope of basic parental responsibilities, such as a computer or summer camp. (To be sure you're spending the money on items the IRS deems acceptable, check with a tax adviser first.)

In some cases, you may find that you can even negotiate with the college of your choice over financial aid. Marlton, New Jersey, college planner Ray Loewe has a client who had dutifully saved $35,000 for his two daughters. When it became clear that the savings would wipe out any chance at financial aid from the top eastern college they both wanted to attend, he got the college to recalculate the ratios as if the money were in his name. "The standard answer at most colleges is that they don't bend rules," says Loewe. "What we find is that when [colleges] are up against the wall and they're not getting enough enrollment, colleges do make changes and bend the rules."

on the returns it has earned relative to its volatility (i.e., its ups and downs).

Looking only at funds receiving "A" grades, we then broke these winners into three main groups High , Medium-, and Low-Volatility—each with specific investing goals. High-Volatility funds, for example, are appropriate for long-term investors who don't need to cash in their accounts for many years. Medium-Volatility funds are best suited for a five- to 10-year investment horizon, while Low-Volatility funds fit well with three-to-five-year investment goals. Our choices for the 11 best funds in each of these categories appear in the table on page 235. Though some of them show minimum initial investments of several thousand dollars, don't be alarmed. Most of them will waive or reduce those minimums if you agree to invest a certain amount every month. (Also note, we included two funds—Investment Company of America and American Balanced—that are available only through brokers or financial planners, in case you choose to go that route.)

The first two portfolios, geared to parents whose children range in age from birth to 8 years old, are heavily weighted toward aggressive investments because this is when you can afford to take the most risk. By the time your child reaches high school age, and during the 4 years he or she is in college, safety will be your No. 1

Tuition worksheet

I. HOW MUCH YOU CAN EXPECT IN TOTAL COLLEGE BILLS

1. Expected cost for 4 years: Check Table A (on page 234) for an estimate of 4-year college costs, including tuition, room and board, books, and other expenses. Separate projections are provided for public, private, and elite colleges. For more than one child, add the appropriate amount for each child. $_____

II. HOW MUCH YOU CAN AFFORD TO SAVE

2. Enter your current monthly income after taxes. $_____
3. Retirement account savings per month. This should be the maximum allowed by the IRS, not necessarily the amount you are currently saving. For each adult in the household using Individual Retirement Accounts only, enter $166. For each adult with a 401(k), enter 7 percent of the amount on line 2 or $554, whichever is less. Those with Keogh, SEP, or other retirement plans should enter only the after-tax cost of their maximum possible contributions. (To estimate after-tax cost, multiply the maximum by 0.7). $_____
4. Subtract line 3 from line 2. $_____
5. Household expenses on a monthly basis (you can bring this number over from the worksheet in Chapter 1). $_____
6. Subtract line 5 from line 4. This is the maximum you can save for tuition per month. $_____

III. HOW MUCH YOUR SAVINGS WILL GROW

7. Multiply the amount on line 6 by the Monthly Savings Factor in Table B (on page 234) that corresponds to your child. This is how much your future tuition savings, plus the after-tax investment returns, will be worth when your child reaches college age. Table B assumes that you invest your savings according to our investment plan and that you increase the amount of your monthly savings by 5 percent per year. If you are saving for more than one child, divide line 6 by your number of children. Then multiply each portion by the appropriate figure from Table B. Keep the results for each child separate. (If you want to see how much in monthly savings is necessary to cover all your tuition goals, divide line 1 by the corresponding Monthly Savings Factor). $_____
8. Existing tuition savings. Reduce what you've set aside by whatever taxes you would owe if you sold the investments today. Enter the result here. $_____
9. Multiply the amount on line 8 by the appropriate figure in the second column of Table B. This estimates how much your existing savings will compound, on an after-tax basis, by the time your child reaches college, assuming you follow our investment plan.

If you have more than one child, divide the amount on line 8 by your number of children and multiply each portion by the appropriate factor from Table B. Keep the results separate. $_____

10. Total estimated tuition savings. Add line 7 and line 9. Keep each child's figures separate. $_____

IV. HOW MUCH YOU CAN EXPECT IN FINANCIAL AID

11. Enter the value of your current assets—cash, stocks, bonds, mutual funds, and real estate—excluding your home equity and retirement account savings. (If you plan to send your child to a private or elite college, add your home equity back in.) $_____

12. Divide line 7 by the amount in the Present-Value Divisor column of Table B that corresponds to your child. For more than one child, use the appropriate divisor for each child. Then add the results for all children. This calculation will put your future savings in today's dollars. $_____

13. Total assets available for tuition. Add the amounts on line 11 and line 12. $_____

14. Percent paid by financial aid. Refer to Table C (on page 235) using the information on line 13 and your family's current pretax income. _____%

15. Multiply line 14 by 0.01. _____

16. Estimated amount of financial aid you can expect based on today's aid standards. (This figure may include government-guaranteed student and parent loans, depending on the type of aid awarded by individual schools.) Multiply line 1 by line 15. $_____

If you will have two children in college at once:

a. Subtract the amount on line 15 from 1.0. _____

b. Multiply line a by 0.5. _____

c. Add line b and line 15. _____

d. If the children will be in college together all 4 years, repeat the entry from line c. If they will be together for 1 year, multiply line c by 0.25; for 2 years, by 0.5; for 3 years, by 0.75. _____

e. If the children will be in college together all 4 years, enter zero. If they will be together 1 year, multiply line 15 by 0.75; for 2 years, by 0.5; for 3 years, by 0.25. _____

f. Add line d and line e. _____

g. Multiply line 1 by line f. Replace line 16, above, with this amount. $_____

V. HOW MUCH YOU MAY NEED TO BORROW

17. Add the amounts on line 16 and line 10 (combine any separate figures from line 10). $_____

18. Subtract line 17 from line 1. This is the estimated amount you may have to borrow (in addition to any loans in your aid package) to pay for 4 years of college for your children. If the number is negative, it means you're in the clear. $_____

Table A: Four-year college costs

Four-year average costs for tuition, fees, books, supplies, room, board, and expenses.

Years until college	Public Colleges & Universities*	Private Colleges & Universities**	Elite Colleges & Universities**
1	$42,324	$ 93,382	$133,189
2	$44,185	$ 97,595	$139,327
3	$46,134	$102,004	$145,756
4	$48,175	$106,620	$152,489
5	$50,313	$111,451	$159,542
6	$52,553	$116,509	$166,929
7	$54,899	$121,803	$174,667
8	$57,356	$127,345	$182,773
9	$59,931	$133,147	$191,264
10	$62,628	$139,222	$200,159
11	$65,454	$145,582	$209,477
12	$68,416	$152,241	$219,239
13	$71,519	$159,213	$229,467
14	$74,771	$166,514	$240,182
15	$78,180	$174,158	$251,409
16	$81,752	$182,163	$263,171
17	$85,496	$190,546	$275,496
18	$89,420	$199,324	$288,409

*Projections based on 5 percent annual increase in tuition & fees; 5 percent annual increase in room & board; 2 percent annual increase in books, supplies, and expenses.
**Projections based on 4 percent annual increase in tuition & fees; 5 percent annual increase in room & board; 2 percent annual increase in books, supplies, and expenses.

Table B: How your savings will grow

Years Until College	Monthly Savings Factor*	Existing-Savings Multiplier	Present-Value Divisor	Years Until College	Monthly Savings Factor*	Existing-Savings Multiplier	Present-Value Divisor
1	12.47	1.04	1.04	10	193.44	1.61	1.48
2	26.02	1.08	1.04	11	225.20	1.73	1.54
3	40.77	1.13	1.12	12	260.04	1.85	1.60
4	56.89	1.17	1.17	13	298.67	1.97	1.67
5	74.47	1.22	1.22	14	341.37	2.11	1.73
6	93.78	1.27	1.27	15	388.45	2.26	1.80
7	115.09	1.33	1.32	16	440.64	2.42	1.87
8	138.68	1.41	1.37	17	498.20	2.59	1.95
9	164.74	1.51	1.42	13	562.23	2.77	2.03

*Assumes you increase your savings by 5 percent a year.

Table C: How much will financial aid cover

| | Family's Annual Pretax Income | | | | | | | |
| | $30,000 | | $50,000 | | $70,000 | | $90,000 | |
Total Family Assets*	Public	Private	Public	Private	Public	Private	Public	Private
$ 20,000	80%	91%	53%	78%	0%	47%	0%	20%
40,000	80	91	53	78	0	47	0	20
60,000	75	88	33	69	0	40	0	15
80,000	70	86	24	64	0	37	0	9
100,000	69	85	12	58	0	31	0	4

*Does not include equity in home

Data: T. Rowe Price

11 great mutual funds for college savers

Fund Name	Phone Number	Average Annual Total Return*	Minimum Investment
High Volatility			
Legg Mason Value Trust	800-577-8589	27.3%	$ 1,000
Ariel Growth	800-292-7435	15.6%	$ 1,000
Baron Asset	800-992-2766	15.3%	$ 2,000
T. Rowe Price Small-Cap Stock	800-225-5132	12.6%	$ 2,500
Medium Volatility			
Safeco Equity No-Load	800-624-5711	20.0%	$ 1,000
T. Rowe Price Dividend Growth	800-225-5132	19.2%	$ 2,500
Investment Company of America	800-421-4120	17.6%	$ 250
Fidelity Equity Income II	800-544-3902	16.8%	$ 2,500
Low Volatility			
American Balanced	800-421-4120	13.6%	$ 500
T. Rowe Price Capital Appreciation	800-225-5132	12.7%	$ 2,500
Hotchkis & Wiley Balanced	800-346-7301	10.9%	$10,000

*For the five years ended Oct. 30, 1998

Data: Lipper Analytical Services

concern. So we've included two portfolios encompassing those years as well. In both we selected a mix of short-term investments that are almost as safe as cash but whose returns far exceed what you would receive from a money market account or a certificate of deposit.

The Model Portfolios

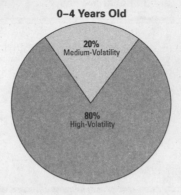

0–4 Years Old

20%
Medium-Volatility

80%
High-Volatility

As any new parent will tell you, scraping up money for tuition savings during these early years is tough. When you're trying to deal with the costs of raising a small child, both expected (medical bills and child care) and not (who would have thought you'd shell out $1,000 for a swing set?), the last thing you want to think about is a college bill 15 years off in the distance.

That's why whatever savings you can cobble together—whether it's just $100 a month or maybe that $1,700 tax refund check—should be invested at least 80 percent in High-Volatility funds. It may seem like you're taking a nerve-racking amount of risk with money you know you are going to need in the future, but this is the time to do it. Any dips in the market (and there are bound to be several over the next decade) will almost certainly be made up for by the long-term growth of your portfolio.

We suggest diversifying in at least 3 funds. With a longer time frame, it's true that you suffer far less market risk than someone with a horizon of less than 10 years. But any time you buy a fund, you're taking a chance that the manager will lose his touch, make a disastrous mistake, or leave the fund in lesser hands. Choosing 3 funds helps cushion the risks.

5–8 Years Old

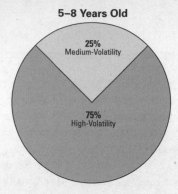

25%
Medium-Volatility

75%
High-Volatility

If you've already started saving before your child reaches age 6 and you've chosen an aggressive mix of investments (see age 0–4), then there's no reason to shift any of your portfolio around just yet. The age 0–4 strategy works just as well during these next few years. But if you're starting your college savings program now, you don't have quite as much time to make up for market downturns. That's why we suggest starting with 75 percent of your college savings in High-Volatility funds and putting the other 25 percent in our steady picks. (Parents who have already started saving should simply direct any new money toward these Medium-Volatility funds.)

Because the fund managers in this Medium-Volatility group often use what's known as a value style of investing, these funds tend to have the most consistent returns through all types of markets while still achieving above-average returns.

9–13 Years Old

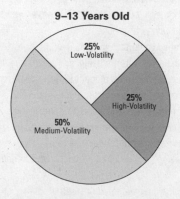

25%
Low-Volatility

25%
High-Volatility

50%
Medium-Volatility

These are the awakening years. Graduation from grade school and junior high dances are all too constant reminders that your kids are

Playing catch-up

F eeling panicked because your child is almost ready for high school and you haven't even begun to amass the amount of money you'll need? You're not alone. According to a recent survey by Fidelity Investments, about 10 percent of parents who said they have earmarked a special savings account for college have less than $5,000 set aside so far.

Starting late for any financial goal puts you in a real quandary. Because you're behind, you need to make a killing when you invest your savings. But you can't afford to take a chance on volatile high-return investments because you don't have the time to make up for potential short-term losses.

Saving for tuition is one of the few exceptions to this rule. That's because if the stock market is in a steep decline just when you need to pay tuition bills, you can borrow from the government-sponsored PLUS loan program until the market rebounds. Under this program, creditworthy parents can borrow up to the full cost of their child's tuition at attractive rates. (If you took out a loan today, you'd pay 8.98%, compared with the 12% or so a bank would charge for a consumer loan.) True, you'll have to start repaying your principal and interest almost immediately. But it's better than taking a bath on your investments and still having to borrow.

Unlike in the recent past, the government will now allow a tax deduction for the first 60 months of repayment on all private and government-backed student loans, including PLUS. The maximum deduction was $1,000 for 1998 and will climb to $2,500 by 2001. It is phased out for singles with incomes between $40,000 and $50,000 and joint-filers with incomes between $60,000 and $75,000. For more information, call 800-4-FEDAID.

Even with this backup plan, however, we don't recommend that late starters invest in the very riskiest investments. The chance of losses is just too great. Instead, we suggest parents invest their college savings in our Medium-Volatility funds. With a projected 10 percent return (8.9 percent after tax), a family with a 14-year-old that can scrape together $5,000 to start, and add another $300 a month for the next 4 years, and will have $24,253 by the time their child heads away to school.

True, this won't cover the whole tab. In fact, it will pay for only about half of the 4-year costs at a public school. But parents using this approach will be more than $2,000 ahead than if they had invested the same amount in a run-of-the-mill money-market fund.

Because it's impossible for late starters to completely make up for lost time, you'll probably have to rely on financial aid and loans to some extent. This is where the PLUS loans come in. But if you have a whole life insurance policy, check with your insurer first. You may be able to borrow against that policy at rates lower than those offered by the PLUS program. And, if you don't mind depleting your death benefit, you need never repay the loan.

If your child is awarded a government-sponsored student loan and the school doesn't use the direct-loan program run by the Department of Education, be sure to check the terms carefully. Most commercial lenders charge a guarantee fee of up to 4 percent and deduct it from the amount of the loan. With a little hunting you can find banks with the lowest fees and best repayment terms. For more specific loan information, check out the website run by financial aid expert Mark Kantrowitz *(www.finaid.org).* In addition, local libraries often have books that print the same lists used online, as well as information you might not find on the Web.

The real world: The single mother

D arlene Easterwood felt a surge of pride when she first heard the news in April of 1994: Her son, Seth, had been accepted into Cornell University—just what he had worked so hard for during high school. Then came the surge of panic: How could she possibly pay for it?

She and Seth's father had been divorced for 15 years, and neither of them had much money (Darlene's salary was less than $30,000 a year). They had begun setting aside funds for Seth's college education after he turned 12, but they could never afford more than sporadic contributions—every now and then Darlene would pull a $20 bill out of her wallet and put it in an envelope. Seth himself chipped in what he earned from his summer jobs. But the family only squirreled away $10,000.

That would have been enough, Darlene thought, if Seth were a little less ambitious. Most of his friends were headed to the University of Kentucky, situated just a few blocks from where Seth and Darlene lived in Lexington. Tuition there ran only a few grand a year. Cornell, of course, was another thing. Annual expenses were estimated at $25,000, well beyond the family's financial means.

Yet Darlene didn't want to deny her child an Ivy League education. So she and Seth started scrambling. She spent two months working on their financial aid application to Cornell—back and forth to her accountant almost daily, trying to make sense of everything the school wanted, badgering her ex-husband for information on his finances, doing whatever she could to illustrate that the family's circumstances were dire. For his part, Seth set himself to researching the other, independent scholarship possibilities out there. He put in a bid for every one he could find—nearly 40 in all.

Their efforts paid dividends, but not nearly enough. Cornell offered a package of loans, grants, and work-study for Seth's freshman year that came to $5,400. He won outside scholarships for another $1,900. But even after they loaded up on another $5,000 in loans, that still left them way short of what they needed.

Cornell offered them one way out: a payment plan. All they had to do was come up with $1,455 a month. But that was easier said than done. Darlene and Seth's father sat down and worked out the math. They would each contribute $485 a month out of their current income. Another $485 a month would be supplied out of the $10,000 in savings. Those payments, plus Seth's aid package, loans, and scholarships, would just meet the bill.

Since then the financial sacrifices have been constant—no new clothes, no trips home for Seth during midyear vacations, extra hours at work. But to Darlene, it's all been worth it: "You learn to make do," she says.

growing up. Fast. If you haven't saved until now, this is the time you'll probably start worrying—especially when you hear neighbors and friends complain that they've already put away $15,000 for their kids' tuition and they're convinced that it still probably won't cover the bills.

Relax. You still have time to put together a solid portfolio that will go a long way toward paying for college. Invested intelligently, even $200 a month will grow to almost $30,000 8 years from now. But this is the time to carefully assess your investing strategy. Whether you're just starting to put money away or you've been saving all along, this can be a tricky time for tuition saving. With 5 to 9 years to go until college, you've got enough years to really feel the effects of compounding. On the other hand, school isn't so far off that you can afford to risk actually *losing* money.

For now, you'll want to keep 25 percent of your assets in top-returning funds to make the most of the years you have left. Then you'll need to shift a total of 50 percent of your portfolio to the Medium-Volatility funds described above. Finally, for the safety that comes from extra diversification, you'll want to move 25 percent of your savings to our Low-Volatility funds.

All three of our Low-Volatility funds temper the risk of their large company stock holdings with investments in Treasury securities or convertible bonds, which are less volatile than stocks. Some of these funds also turn to cash investments when the market is particularly choppy. The mix of asset classes makes these funds far less risky than straight stock funds.

14–16 Years Old

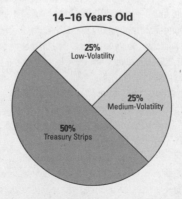

With only a few years until that first tuition bill, preserving your hard-earned stash is key. You want to know that most of your nest egg is completely safe so you can clear your head for other worries, like SAT scores and college applications. On the other hand, you still want to get as much growth as you can. That's why at this stage you should keep the 50 percent chunk of your portfolio in Medium-Volatility and Low-Volatility funds intact. But it's also time to move 50 percent of your assets into 100 percent guaranteed U.S. Treasury strips.

Treasury strips, sometimes known as zero coupon bonds, are simply the interest-bearing coupons of 30-year Treasury bonds, which you buy at a discount to their face value, usually $1,000. Strips offer all of the government-guaranteed safety of regular Treasury bonds with a slightly higher return. Recently, if you bought $5,000 worth of strips, you would have paid $4,260 for 5 strips that repaid you $5,000 in 3 years. That's a 5.8 percent return, almost a percentage point higher than the average taxable money market fund. (You can buy strips from a discount broker, usually with a minimum of $5,000 and a commission of less than 1 percent.)

The best time to move this money is during your child's sophomore year in high school. The goal is to set aside enough in strips now to cover the first 2 years' worth of tuition payments for college. By buying strips with 3 and 4-year maturities, you'll guarantee safety but beat the return of a money market fund. Meanwhile, the rest of your portfolio can take advantage of the 4 to 6 years you have before the later tuition bills come due.

One caveat: Timing is critical if you are applying for financial aid. When you apply for aid (usually in the fall of your child's senior year of high school) you'll most likely have to submit the tax return from the previous calendar year. If your child will enroll in the 1999–2000 school year, for example, you'll have to show your 1998 returns. You don't want any of the capital gains from the college savings that you've recently reallocated to show up as income on those tax returns. Say, for instance, you move $20,000 from a mutual fund to Treasury strips. The gain on that 20 grand will show up as investment income on your tax return. Colleges will count that as part of your yearly income, in addition to including it in your assets. Income is weighted far more heavily than assets when calculating financial aid. So instead, try to liquidate your investments before the January of your child's junior year in high school or after your child's junior year in college.

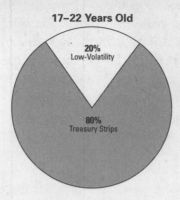

The pressure to save for college doesn't stop the day your child goes off to school. There are still 3 more years (at least) ahead to pay for, and you need an investment strategy that maximizes your returns without sacrificing the safety of your savings. Although most tuition-planning advice suggests moving everything to cash at this point, we still prefer Treasury strips as a way to garner superior returns while also guarding your savings.

Thus, you'll want to move almost all of your mutual fund assets to Treasury strips that mature in the last 2 years your child will be in college. But because you still have several years to go until your child graduates, we also suggest that you keep 20 percent of your portfolio in Low-Volatility funds to increase your chances of getting some last-minute returns. That can make all the difference as college costs continue to increase, albeit more slowly than in previous years.

Say your child starts 4 years of public school next year. By the time he or she graduates, you will have paid an extra $3,000 in rate hikes alone. But say you have $50,000 saved. If the $10,000 you allocate to Low-Volatility funds earns just 8 percent each year over the next 3 years, you could earn $2,300 before taxes on that investment—which will go a long way toward making up for the increase in schooling costs.

Step Three: Making the Most of Financial Aid

When you're knee-deep in financial aid applications, desperately trying to figure out how you're going to pay for your child's college

The real world: Three kids, one budget

E dwin and Karen McConkey always felt blessed to have three children. Until the college tuition bills started rolling in. From the time their eldest son, Dale, headed off to college in 1983 until 1995, when youngest child Wendy graduated, they have faced more than $130,000 in costs.

Quite a burden, even considering Ed's position as an engineer at a Virginia government contractor. Taking care of three kids had always eaten up everything he earned. When college time came, he didn't have a dime set aside to deal with the new expense.

So how have the McConkeys managed? Paying for each child has been as different as the children themselves. When Dale was accepted into Eckard College in April 1983—which had a $40,000 four-year tab—Ed began by borrowing $15,000 against an annuity he owned. Dale also managed to win a $16,000 merit-based academic scholarship from Eckard. But that still left them $9,000 short.

During that spring Ed and Karen talked deep into the night on many occasions, trying to figure out how to come up with the money and how they would handle the next two children when it was their turn. The prospect proved too overwhelming, and inevitably they ended up going to bed irritable and worried, with no plan in place. They did apply for financial aid at Eckard, but even with Ed's salary running at $60,000 a year, the school turned them down.

Then, at Dale's high school graduation ceremony, Ed's father offered them a glimmer of hope. In previous weeks, Ed had been grousing about his tuition problems to his sisters. That day Ed's father—a farmer who was often short of cash himself—handed over a check for $10,000, to help defray expenses for all three of the kids. Before the day was over, Ed and Karen had decided to put it all toward Dale's college bill.

Three years later, Stephen was accepted into Virginia Commonwealth University—and the $10,000 gift was already gone. The worrying began anew. There was no equity left in the annuity to borrow against, and no huge academic scholarship. Ed and Karen could try getting a loan, but Ed was worried about mortgaging their retirement years. The kids might have to support them later, and he certainly didn't want that.

Karen stepped into the breach. She had been a stay-at-home mom for 20 years but now volunteered to go to work. Ed resisted—perhaps they could squeeze the tuition costs out of his income. Besides, he didn't want Wendy to be unsupervised after school. But Karen insisted. And over the next four years—dishing out food in a school cafeteria, cleaning other people's homes, even managing a neighborhood newspaper delivery service—she pulled in $24,000. Stephen's bill was paid.

And what about Wendy? Ed got a big raise just before she started college, and that might well have done the trick. Then Ed's father passed away. His only real asset was his farm, but when it was sold, Ed's share came to $100,000. It was more than enough.

The ABCs of prepaid tuition plans

Tuition prepayment plans, where parents can pay in today's dollars the price of college 18 years away, sound great in principle. But are they really such a fantastic deal? Here's a closer look at four types of prepaid college plans.

The Contract Plan

This is the most popular of the prepaid tuition plans. You pay the price of today's tuition to cover your child's future matriculation at a public school in your state. You choose a contract that is worth, say, 2 years' tuition at a community college. You can pay in a lump sum, or over time with interest. In Florida, which has the largest program in the country, participants pay 5 percent to 7.5 percent interest compounded annually.

Sounds like an okay deal at first. But the contract plan makes sense only if you are willing to wager two things will happen. One: Your child will want to go to a public college in your state. Two: That tuition there will rise faster than your own investment portfolio might.

Those are long-shot bets. Who can guess where a 5-year-old might someday go to college? If your child decides to go to an out-of-state school, you may get back just a 5 percent annual return, or even less. You are probably better off building your own investment portfolio and not limiting Junior's college choices.

But, as your child gets older and you want to move your portfolio from equities into cash anyway, these plans start to make a little more sense. Compare the return your state plan guarantees to the return on a Treasury strip. If the state pays more, and your kid is likely to go to a state school, then it may be worth buying into the plan. These plans are taxed as income at the student's rate, and Treasury strips are taxed as income to whoever owns them. Unfortunately, most plans guarantee you less than even the 5.80 percent you can get on a three-year zero coupon Treasury bond.

The Unit Plan

Rather than buy a contract for a set number of years of tuition at a particular type of school, unit plans allow participants to prepay any amount of college tuition.

Ohio's Prepaid Tuition Program is a good example. The state sells units worth 1 percent of the average tuition at Ohio's 13 four-year public universities. In the 1997/1998 academic year, a unit cost just $40.44. The good thing about the Ohio plan is that you can spend your units at any college in the country. Your return will be whatever the rate of tuition inflation has been in Ohio. Moreover, the units can be transferred to any family member. Think of this investment as a AAA-rated zero coupon bond that will return the rate of Ohio's tuition inflation. Distributions will be taxed as income to the child.

If you have the money to pay for college today and don't want to take any risks in the stock or bond markets, this plan will buy you peace of mind and your child an education.

The Massachusetts Plan

Here too, you pay today's price to go to college tomorrow. But the program has a twist. The distributions you get from it are tax-free. How's that? You buy state general-obligation bonds, and these bonds have a return that's fixed in a way that ensures your costs will be covered. (This is a little hard to follow, but here's how it works: The return is equal to the rate of inflation, plus the difference between the rate of inflation and the average annual tuition increase of participating colleges, up to 2 percent over the inflation rate. If tuition rises faster than that, the schools in the Massachusetts College Savings Program eat the difference.)

So far, 83 of the state's 91 public and private colleges have joined the plan. Harvard and MIT are not in. Unlike other plans, this one is open to nonresidents of Massachusetts. If your child decides not to go to a college in the program, you get back your principal plus the consumer price index, tax-free. But then, that's no big bonus. You could earn a lot more investing elsewhere. Still, if you have the money to pay for college today and don't want to take any market risk, this program may be right for you.

The Savings Plan

This one is the least attractive of all. Kentucky's savings plan, for example, guarantees a 4 percent minimum rate of return, but it doesn't promise to cover the cost of future tuition. Plus, unless the law changes, your child will pay income tax on distributions from the fund. If your child doesn't go to college, you pay a small penalty of $25 or 2 percent of assets, whichever is less.

Think of this plan as a conservative bond fund with a guaranteed minimum rate of return. It would be a good deal if interest rates fell below 4 percent. But how likely is that? Besides, you can guarantee yourself a higher yield than 4 percent with no interest rate risk by buying Treasury strips (zero coupon bonds). You can buy strips from a discount broker, usually with a minimum of $5,000 and a commission of less than 1 percent.

Say your child is going to school 18 years from now; you can buy strips that mature in 2015 with a coupon of 6.46 percent. You get the appreciation at maturity and pay income tax on it. If your child is older, you can still buy strips which mature in, say, four years that pay 5.86 percent.

If you want to find out more about your state's program, the College Savings Plans Network *(www.collegesavings.org)* provides links to most state plans.

education, it's easy to forget one thing: The laborious process offers as many opportunities as it does headaches.

Take the case of Jennifer Hanlin. She used one of the most successful negotiating strategies to win more financial aid—leveraging one school's package against another's. A couple of years ago Hanlin was accepted to study architecture at Harvard and Yale; Harvard was her first choice. But her dream school came up with only $1,000 in aid, versus $3,000 from Yale. Rather than settling for her second choice, Hanlin called Harvard, telling the aid officer that she had a better offer from Yale (though she didn't tell them how much it was for). She ended her conversation by simply stating that she couldn't attend Harvard with only $1,000 in assistance. Harvard called back an hour later—with an $11,000 total aid package.

How much money do you need? Colleges use two numbers to answer that question: their annual costs and your expected "family contribution." They reach the latter number by plugging the information you give them into a federal formula that takes into account parents' ages, family size, number of children in college, total assets, and income. The more family members attending college and the closer parents are to retirement, the more generous the government will be.

Sound simple? Don't believe it for a minute. This path is strewn with potential land mines. Take the issue of divorce and remarriage, for instance. The federal government requires that schools include a stepparent's income when calculating family contribution—even if the stepparent has no legal obligation to support the child, no plans to help pay his or her way through school, or even if the stepparent has college age children of his or her own to pay for. "A working stepparent contributes to the general standard of living in the household," explains Christopher Campbell of the National Association of Student Financial Aid Administrators (NASFAA). "That's a resource single parents just don't have."

Private colleges and universities have their own formulas and may figure in your home equity and the amount you expect to contribute to retirement accounts while your child is in school, as well as a student's expected income and assets. (Most private colleges expect students to contribute at least $900 a year to their own education.)

To calculate your need, schools simply subtract your family contribution from the total cost of attending college—not just tuition but also books, room and board, transportation, and living expenses. The difference is defined as your need.

But don't expect your school to automatically cough up that cash. How much you're awarded depends in part on how many other applicants need money, how desirable your son or daughter is as a student, and the finite pool of government and institutional money the school has available to award. William Heffernan of Ocala, Florida, learned the last point the hard way. When his ex-

---

A tax-free saving strategy

Paying a mere 5 percent or so in interest a year, Series EE Savings Bonds aren't exactly the greatest investments for college savers. But they do have some tax advantages you should be aware of.

For instance, you may be able to redeem them tax-free if you use the proceeds to pay for college.

Naturally there are a lot of restrictions on this tax break. Chief among them: The savings bonds in question must have been issued *after* 1989 in the name of someone who was at least 24 years old at the time. (Bonds bought in your child's name are ineligible, as are any old pre-1990 bonds issued in your name.) Also, the tax-free deal is whittled away if you earn too much. For 1998 redemptions, the tax break started getting phased out when joint filers' modified adjusted gross income topped $78,350, and it was wiped out once you go over $108,350.

Happily, the 1997 tax law added two potentially helpful options if you expect your adjusted gross to be too high by the time your child reaches college age.

- You can redeem qualified savings bonds tax-free if you turn around and contribute the proceeds to a qualified state tuition program, like the ones described on page 244. The tax benefits offered by these programs are *not* subject to any income-based phaseout rules.
- You can also redeem qualified bonds tax-free if the proceeds are contributed to an Education IRA set up for your dependent child. To set up an Education IRA and make the maximum $500 contribution each year, joint filers can't have an adjusted gross income of more than $150,000.

To make tax-free savings bond redemptions under these rules, you'll need to file Form 8815 (Exclusion of Interest from Series EE U.S. Savings Bonds Issued After 1989) with your 1040 for the year of redemption. You also use Form 8815 to calculate the exact amount of accrued interest that you can exclude under the income-based phaseout rule.

Making the most of the latest tax changes

The politicians who passed the Taxpayer Relief Act of 1997 are still congratulating themselves for helping America's families. And give them some credit. The law can help you save for college, pay for it while the kids are there, and even pay off their loans when school is done.

Here's what you need to know to make the most of it.

Ever-more-flexible IRAs

The '97 tax bill created a new kind of account called an Education IRA. It hasn't anything to do with retirement—the "R" in IRA—but who's quibbling? The important thing is that you can contribute up to $500 a year per child until he or she hits age 18. Unlike a regular IRA, you use after-tax dollars, but the plus side is, you never pay taxes on the earnings as long as the money is used for college expenses. Joint filers with incomes up to $160,000 are eligible.

It's a nice little deal, but just keep in mind that it's no panacea. The main problem: At this point you can invest only $500 a year for each child. Even if you start at year one, make the maximum investment for each of the next 17 birthdays, and earn 8 percent a year, you will have only $18,725—or about one-tenth of the projected cost of private college in 2014. Also, by cashing in an Education IRA, you become ineligible for any of the new tuition tax credits for that child in that year (more on this in a moment). Yet another downside: You can't make a contribution to an Education IRA in the same year you're making a prepayment to a state tuition program, like the ones we described on page 244. If you do, you have to withdraw the IRA money immediately or face a 6 percent penalty on your contribution.

While it was creating the education IRA, Congress also added a third tax-deferred account called a Roth IRA and changed the rules on the standard IRA account. Now you can withdraw money to pay for college from regular IRAs as well as from the new Roth IRAs without paying the 10 percent penalty that usually prevents people under the age of 59$\frac{1}{2}$ from touching those accounts. But be careful. For regular IRAs, any money you withdraw will be taxed as income. For Roth IRAs, you will have to pay taxes on your gain, if you are younger than 59$\frac{1}{2}$.

Tax Credits

Not only does the new tax law help you save for college but it also gives you a nice gift while your kids are attending school. This comes in the form of two tax credits, known as the Hope scholarship and the Lifetime Learning credit. The more generous Hope credit amounts to 100 percent of the first $1,000 of annual tuition plus 50 percent of the next $1,000, in the first 2 years of college. The Lifetime Learning credit is mainly intended to help defray college costs after the first 2 years, when the Hope credit is gone. The amount equals 20 percent of annual tuition up to $5,000, for a maximum of $1,000 per family, no matter how many students there are. Both credits are phased out for adjusted gross incomes between $80,000 and $100,000 for joint filers, and between $40,000 and $50,000 for singles. ("Phased out" is a term developed by Congress to describe the illusion created by appearing to give you a tax break with one hand while simultaneously removing it with the other.) Remember, you can't take these tax credits in any year that you withdraw money from an Education IRA.

Student Loan Interest Deduction

If you have to borrow some money to pay for college (and who, exactly, doesn't?), you can also benefit under the new law. Congress has created a new "above the line" deduction for interest on education loans.

There are some real limitations, though. The write-off is capped at $1,000 for 1998, $1,500 for 1999, $2,000 for 2000, and $2,500 for 2001. You can take the write-off for only 5 years from the time you start making loan payments. Finally, the deductions are phased out for adjusted gross incomes between $60,000 and $75,000 for joint filers and between $40,000 and $55,000 for singles.

---

wife filed the federal financial aid form for his daughter's freshman year at Auburn University 3 months late, the girl received only $1,000 in Pell grants—government-sponsored gifts for low-income students—even though, by Heffernan's calculations, she should have been eligible for some $4,000 in aid. Why the discrepancy? Auburn had already given away the bulk of its campus-based aid by the time it heard from Heffernan's daughter.

Mastering the Paperwork

There is no one financial aid form. That, of course, would be too easy. First, most people looking for aid will have to fill out the Free Application for Federal Student Aid (FAFSA), the standardized national form for U.S. government grants, work-study jobs, state grants, and student loans, such as Perkins (for low-income students) and Stafford. Your numbers will be run through a central computer to calculate your family contribution and need, which then will be forwarded to the schools on your list. You'll get a copy as well.

About 800 private colleges—from Harvard to Missouri's Rockhurst College—will also ask you to fill out the CSS/Financial Aid Profile Form, or Profile, administered by the College Board (305-829-9793), which charges a $5 registration fee, plus $15 for each

Your money's worth

Your mission: To save half of what your newborn will need for private college tuition, room, and board 18 years from now. (You're optimistically assuming financial aid—or loans—will cover the rest.) Your savings goal: $150,830. Now, how on earth will you get there?

Worth it: You really ought to be investing in the stock market, with mutual funds. Sure, stock funds are a lot riskier than CDs. But with college a full 18 years off, you can afford to be aggressive. Going back over the last 18 years, the *average* stock mutual fund returned 15.35% a year, according to the fund researchers at Morningstar Inc. At that rate, you could put aside monthly contributions of only $135 dollars a month and you'd hit the magical $150,830 figure in 18 years.

Not worth it: The College Savings Bank in New Jersey, like several other financial institutions, is offering what it calls a CollegeSure CD. This certificate of deposit guarantees that its rate of return will match the cost of college education, because the return is indexed to the average cost of college. (Currently, college costs are rising at an estimated 6.4 percent a year.) Sounds great, all right. But you'll have to save $375 a month—every month!—to hit that $150,830 doing it this way. Thus, while they sound safe and secure, CollegeSure CDs may simply be *too* safe to give you the kind of return you need.

copy it sends out to schools. In addition to the Profile's core questions, there'll be sections tailored to meet the criteria of the schools to which your child is applying. This is where the private schools will get information on your home equity, retirement contributions, and the like. Finally, some private schools—especially the elite universities—have their own financial aid applications, which they may ask you to fill out in lieu of (or in addition to) the Profile.

Divorced parents may face one more form: Some schools require that noncustodial parents fill out the Divorced/Separated Parent's Statement, available from the College Board. Private schools often assume that a noncustodial parent will be helping to pay for college. Of course, that's not always the case. If a noncustodial parent's divorce decree specifies that he or she won't be contributing, now is the time to let the school's financial aid officer know. Or, for custodial parents who can't depend on their ex-spouse's help—if an ex-husband has a record of not making child-support payments, say—make sure the school's financial aid officer knows of the situation. In either case, this additional information should go straight to the school—do not attach it to the FAFSA or Profile.

To make sure you know which forms to fill out for each school, call and ask each college to send you its complete financial aid application. You'll only have to fill out the FAFSA and Profile once, but if any of your child's choices requires its own form, you'll have it on hand.

Whatever you do, remain patient. Don't throw up your hands midway through the process because you think you'll never qualify for aid anyway. Even if you're right and you do have too much in income or assets to receive any grants, chances are you're going to need to do some borrowing to pay tuition bills. If you don't fill out the FAFSA, you can't qualify for any of the federal student-loan programs.

Don't hand everything over to a financial aid or education counselor. There's nothing these pricey consultants (between $500 and $1,500 a session) can do that you can't with the help of this book, your high school guidance office, your local library, and your college's financial aid office. Most of these consultants have no certification and no special training. Worse, they may give you dangerously misleading advice.

"I had a parent call me a few years ago and tell me that an aid counselor had told her to use all of her savings to pay off the mortgage," says Anna Sinnet, director of financial aid at DePauw University. "The thinking? Because the federal government doesn't count home equity in the expected family contribution, the adviser figured the family could hide its assets and, with less money in the bank, qualify for more aid."

There's only one problem: DePauw is a private university—and private schools can count home equity when awarding their own grants. "The high home equity might disqualify them from receiving our aid," says Sinnet. "And they wouldn't be able to get at the money they would need to pay tuition bills."

Because a paid adviser—or anyone else who helps prepare your application—must also sign the forms, your application may get extra scrutiny. "The high-cost schools often ask for more financial information when they see an outsider's name on the form," says Jeffrey Zahn, financial aid director at St. Norbert College in Wisconsin. "They want to make sure people aren't hiding assets or using any other so-called tricks."

Finally, don't rule out schools just because of their price tag. Today private colleges and universities can actually be cheaper than state schools, when aid is taken into account. And increasingly, schools—yes, even good schools—are offering students incentives to enroll, with many openly advertising the dollars they've got available. It's called merit aid, and it's handed out regardless of your family's income. (If colleges were car dealers, we'd call this process by its real name: discounting.)

Camille Fredrickson is one parent who has taken advantage of the new college economics. The Fredricksons weren't poor enough to expect substantial need-based aid for their eldest son, Keith—or rich enough to foot the bill themselves. (Camille runs a human resources consulting business; her husband, Eric, is a cabinetmaker. Together they make in the low six figures.) So the mother of three thought the options were clear when Keith started to think about where to apply for the fall of 1995: "State school or struggle." Keith's first-choice schools, New York University and Bard College, both cost more than $25,000 a year for tuition, room, and board. So the family spent spring vacation visiting Rutgers, the New Jersey public university, figuring that's where he'd end up. But when they got home, a letter from Bard was waiting. Not only had Bard accepted Keith, but the liberal arts college was also offering him $11,000 a year in "merit aid." Combined with the $14,000, 4-year scholarship he'd won from Eric's union, that meant Bard would cost the Fredricksons about $11,000 a year—less than Rutgers.

Such deals are not uncommon these days. At the University of Rochester, in northern New York, any student with a combined SAT score of 1350 or better is guaranteed a 4-year, $5,000 to $10,000 annual scholarship. At DePauw, a 3.5 grade point average and 1000 on the SAT earns you $4,000 off the school's $22,666 in annual tuition and fees. If your GPA is 3.75 and your SAT is 1400, $9,000 goes back into your pocket. The admissions office will even give you the formula to figure out how much you can take off the top. (It's GPA × 400 + verbal and math scores on the SAT-1.) And at Kenyon College, in Ohio, top students can compete for one of the school's 8 to 12 annual Honor and Science Scholarships (winners get either a full or half ride to the $26,840-a-year school) or, failing that, for a $6,000 annual Distinguished Academic Scholarship—the school gave out 90 of those last year. And *all* this money is awarded regardless of family income.

When You Get Your Aid—and It's Not Enough

You've done your part and, presumably, your child has done his, so in the spring the acceptance letters will start arriving. A few days after you get the good news, just when the fact that the next 4 years are going to cost at least $40,000 sinks in, the package from the financial aid office should arrive, laying out its offer. Most likely, this will include a combination of aid types: One or more of the federally guaranteed loans, a work-study job, and nonrepayable grants or scholarships from the government or from the school's own resources. Chances are, one or more of the schools won't have offered you enough. Or the package from one school will vary wildly from the other offers. Or something will have changed in your financial picture that's going to make it tougher to pay the college bills. Remember, this is not a take-it-or-leave-it situation. Whatever the specifics of your particular case, chances are good that you can get more aid.

Start by applying for local scholarships or alumni grants at your school. That's what Kendall Stagg, a sophomore business management major at the $12,000-a-year University of Nevada, eventually discovered. Stagg's stepfather makes too much money for Stagg to qualify for need-based grants, but the family doesn't have much extra cash: His mother is herself a medical student, and his two sisters are also in college. "Everything I saved was pretty much wiped out over the first year," says Stagg. "So I've really had to scrape together everything I can." To fill the $5,000 gap, Stagg first threw away $100 on a scholarship search firm. Not only didn't it find him any money but it also reneged on its "guaranteed refund," then went out of business. Stagg had better luck searching out private scholarships on his own, winning $3,000 in grants. The rest he pays out of his campus salary as a research supervisor.

Many high school guidance departments offer access to Fund Finder, the scholarship database put together by the College Board *(www.collegeboard.org)*. Or pick up a copy of *Free Money for Col-*

The going rate: The cost of getting in

Y ou want Junior to follow your footsteps into the old alma mater? Well, then you'd better start acting like a good alum. Here's how much it will set you back at four different schools.

	Harvard	University of Georgia	Boston College	Iowa State
Season tickets: football	$ 57.00	$ 138.00	$ 150.00	$ 132.00
Season tickets: men's basketball	50.00	140.00	177.00	330.00
Season tickets: women's basketball	37.00	50.00	40.00	60.00
Average alumni donation	49.00	160.00	100.00	50.00
Amount needed to be an "Elite" donor	1,000.00	1,000.00	2,500.00	1,500.00
A dozen logo golf balls	39.98	40.00	43.80	39.80
Children's T-shirt with college logo	12.50	12.00	8.95	10.95
University paperweight	125.00	19.95	29.95	11.00
Team toddler sock-booties	6.39	3.00	5.95	4.95
School pride wristwatch	190.00	162.00	89.95	42.95
Team hat	18.98	14.95	19.95	21.95
Year-long subscription to student newspaper	79.00	75.00	55.00	62.00
History of the university	37.50	29.95	12.95	17.95
Inscribed "Captain's Chair"	345.00	279.95	295.00	240.00
Key chain	24.00	9.71	17.95	5.95
Total	$2,071.35	$2,134.51	$3,546,45	$2,529.50

lege: A Guide to More Than 1,000 Grants and Scholarships for Undergraduate Study, a good compendium of scholarship information. Finally, your high school guidance office can give you the names of community and church groups that award academic and other types of scholarships. Students seem to have the most success when they concentrate their search in their own backyards, says Zahn of St. Norbert College.

Besides, what you really need to do is focus on getting the aid you need from the school your child wants to attend. As more schools compete for fewer students, negotiating a better deal has become more common. "Negotiation is rampant," admits Barry McCarty, financial aid director of Lafayette College in Easton, Pennsylvania. "I had families come into my office this past spring and lay out four different award letters. In some cases, it has worked."

We've already seen how smart kids like Jennifer Hanlin did it, but, as in any financial negotiation, some strategies work—and some backfire. To avoid having the situation blow up in your face, here are 4 ironclad rules to follow:

- **Bring new information to the table.** Is there something about your financial situation that's not apparent from your forms? Has a parent lost a job or taken a pay cut? Has a family member become ill? Financial aid officers can, and most often will, take your new circumstances into consideration. Almost every college in the Midwest, for example, increased awards for the children of farmers and businesspeople wiped out by the catastrophic 1993 floods.

  In the winter of 1993, Merryl Newler, an advertising executive in upstate New York, filed financial aid applications for her daughter Jordana with both Brandeis University and Bryant College. Around the time of the deadline, Newler lost her job. When she got the award letters in April, Newler found that neither school offered enough money under her new circumstances. She called both schools pleading her case and, happily, both reworked her package. Brandeis, her daughter's first choice, gave her $8,000 in grants. That, combined with the original package, took care of $24,000 of the first year's $29,900 tab.

- **Ask for a step-by-step explanation.** If you've suffered no extraordinary change in circumstances, ask the aid officer to review how he or she came up with your package. That way, as the two of you walk through the family contribution and your need, you can explain any discrepancies between the way the school figured your portion and the way you calculated it. Be sure to point out the specifics of your situation. The school may have overlooked the fact that the value of your family's home is less than the outstanding mortgage, for instance. Or an aid officer may have built cost-of-living increases into your salary that you know won't materialize.

  Some financial aid officers will take large consumer debts or IRS payments into account. Anna Sinnet, of DePauw, recalls one family that "had racked up $30,000 in consumer debt—6 department store credit cards, gas cards—just living on borrowed money." Although wary of rewarding people for living beyond their means, Sinnet didn't want to penalize the student who, after all, wasn't responsible for her parents' lifestyle. DePauw decreased the expected family contribution by $5,000.

- **Be nice.** If another school has offered you a better deal, tread lightly. You don't want to antagonize the person who controls the purse strings. "I didn't wear a white belt and white shoes to work when I was a financial aid officer," says NASFAA's Campbell, formerly aid director at Ashland University in Ohio. "I wasn't a used-car salesman and I resented people who treated me like one."

   The goal is to strike up a good working relationship that will pay off now—and in the future. Remember, college lasts (at least) 4 years, but financial aid doesn't. It's granted on a year-by-year basis, which means you'll have to go through the same tedious process each of the years your child is in school. And colleges have a well-known habit of offering freshmen the best packages, only to scale back later. A good rapport with your financial aid officer will help guard against those cutbacks or help you renegotiate if they do happen.

- **Know the competition.** This is especially true if you're trying to leverage one school's offer against another's. Financial aid officers note that some of the most competitive schools will automatically up their packages when they find out that an attractive student is threatening to go to a rival.

   To find out a school's biggest competitor, check in *The Princeton Review's Student Access Guide to the Best 309 Colleges.* (This strategy is most likely to work at the country's most selective schools.) Under each college heading there's a section listing where else the school's applicants most often apply. At Lehigh University, for instance, the big competitors are Cornell and the University of Pennsylvania. The guide also polls students at each college to find out which other schools they were most interested in when they chose a college.

   If the schools your child is applying to aren't included in the *Princeton Review* guide, check with your high school guidance office. Experienced counselors often have a sense of which schools in their area are battling for the most attractive students. Finally, when you're applying to schools, don't be afraid to ask admissions officers for the names of the schools they compete with most for students. They are by no means obligated to tell you, but some schools are quite open about it.

14

The Big Picture

A thousand dollars to join the hockey team. Two thousand for sleepaway summer camp. Twenty-five hundred for a new computer. They're like little time bombs going off in your savings account.

Clearly, you've got to put aside some money to pay for all this stuff. But where? It's certainly convenient, and safe, to put all your cash in a money-market account. It's all the more tempting after the stock market has gone through another one of its regular rocky spells. Try explaining that one to your kids: "Sorry, you can't have the piano lessons we promised this year—because the market tanked."

Yet we believe that being supercautious is the wrong course for most parents. By limiting yourself to the most conservative investments, you'll miss out on the kind of growth that, in all likelihood, you will *need* to help pay for your kids' expenses—not to mention your own.

And so you arrive at a familiar dilemma: You know it's important to invest your money wisely, but you haven't the time or energy (or perhaps even the inclination) to become a Wall Street whiz.

We've got a solution. It's called an asset allocation plan.

Whether you realize it or not, you are already allocating your assets by dividing what you own into various investment categories: real estate, cash, stocks and mutual funds, bonds and money-market funds. Put simply, asset allocation embodies the time-honored adage "Don't put all your eggs in one basket." But very few people, at any moment, can say with any certainty what percentage of their total assets is devoted to any particular investment. And even fewer have any idea how to approach the task of asset allocation.

We've created a program called SmartMoney One to meet these needs. Using the worksheet on page 262, which should take you no more than half an hour to complete, you can create a customized allocation based on the variables that really matter to you: your age, your family's size, income, net worth, risk tolerance, and expectations about the future. You won't need to worry about price/earnings ratios or yield curves or anything of the sort. The program will direct you to a handful of investments. You'll know it's time to adjust your holdings when you experience changes in your per-

The best funds for your asset allocation

Fund Name	Phone Number	Minimum Initial Investment	Average Annual Total Return*
Large-Cap Stock Funds			
Legg Mason Value Trust	800-577-8589	$ 1,000	27.3%
Vanguard Index 500	800-662-7447	$ 3,000	21.4%
Safeco Equity No-Load	800-624-5711	$ 1,000	20.0%
T. Rowe Price Dividend Growth	800-225-5132	$ 2,500	19.2%
Investment Company of America	800-421-4120	$ 250	17.6%
Fidelity Equity Income II	800-544-3902	$ 2,500	16.8%
T. Rowe Price Capital Appreciation	800-225-5132	$ 2,500	12.7%
Small-Cap Stock Funds			
Ariel Growth	800-292-7435	$ 1,000	15.6%
Baron Asset	800-992-2766	$ 2,000	15.3%
T. Rowe Price Small-Cap Stock	800-225-5132	$ 2,500	12.6%
Vanguard Small Cap Stock	800-662-7447	$ 3,000	10.9%
International Stock Funds			
Vanguard Index International Growth	800-662-7447	$ 3,000	10.1%
Hotchkis & Wiley International	800-346-7301	$10,000	10.0%
Bond Funds			
American Century Benham Target Maturity 2015	800-345-2021	$ 2,500	10.6%
Eaton Vance Short-Term Treasury	800-225-6265	$ 5,000	4.9%
Balanced Funds (stocks and bonds)			
American Balanced	800-421-4120	$ 500	13.6%
Hotchkis & Wiley Balanced	800-346-7301	$10,000	10.9%
Cash			
Managers Money Market	800-835-3879	$ 2,000	5.0%**
Strong Municipal Advantage	800-368-1030	$ 2,500	4.6%***

*For the five years ended October 30, 1998.
**30-day effective yield as of October 30, 1998.
***One-year return through October 30, 1998.
Data: Lipper Analytical Services

sonal circumstances or your outlook—and you can make those adjustments simply by revisiting the worksheet. (If you have Internet access, check out the electronic version of the worksheet at *www. smartmoney.com.*)

Why are we so high on asset allocation? For one thing, it's easy—something any harried parent will appreciate. More important, though, it forces you to diversify your investments. Study after study has shown that portfolios invested in different kinds of assets—large and small companies, both here and abroad, as well as different types of bonds—perform better and are less risky than portfolios that are heavily weighted toward one type of asset. This way you're not chasing one hot investment sector only to arrive just as the party ends. Instead, you will be there when it starts, ready to reap all of the gains.

Using the SmartMoney One Worksheet

The first questions on the worksheet focus on your family. That's because the number of children you have and their ages will help determine how aggressive you can be with your money. Someone

---

Your money's worth

You know you ought to open a brokerage account. And since you'll be making your own investment decisions, you can save a lot of money by choosing a discount broker. But which one?

Worth it: Waterhouse Securities (800-934-4410) isn't the cheapest discount brokerage around. But its commissions are still a fraction of what you'd pay at full-service firms like Merrill Lynch. Besides, it has an excellent website and an extremely wide product selection, including Treasury securities and, should you want to get even more adventuresome, futures. You like mutual funds? The firm, which nabbed the top ranking in *SmartMoney's* latest survey of discount brokers, offers more than 3,000 of them.

Not worth it: Datek, one of the many new Internet discount brokerages springing up lately, is certainly cheap. As of mid-1998, a stock trade at *www.datek.com* would cost you a mere $10. Yet the firm has a puny product lineup, a middling mutual fund program, and a reputation for less-than-stellar service. In *SmartMoney's* most recent discount broker survey, it finished dead last out of 21 contenders.

with 1 young child, for instance, should invest more aggressively than a parent with 3 teenagers on their way to college. A market downturn could make it hard—or impossible—to pay those fast-approaching tuition bills.

From there, the worksheet moves on to your financial situation. First we look at your savings, including the amount you are now (having read chapter 13) investing for college. The more money you have, and the more you're saving each year, the more risk you can take. The exception is when you have extremely high near-term spending needs. If a large expense will wipe out most of your savings within the next 5 years, the worksheet will suggest more conservative investments than it would for someone with the same amount of money saved up but no major upcoming expenses.

When we ask about your assets, we mean all your investments, including college funds and retirement accounts (but not your home). That's because our asset-allocation plan covers all your wealth, even money you won't use for expenses like tuition. By including that money, you will be able to diversify more easily, which will boost your performance and reduce risk. Adding your retirement money to your asset allocation will also tell you if you are setting aside too much in tax-deferred retirement accounts and too little for your more immediate expenses.

When we ask you to estimate your spending needs, you can use the current price of each item. That's because the worksheet accounts for inflation. And don't be surprised when we ask if your projected expenses are greater than your current savings. That's a common situation for parents, especially when dealing with college costs. Your money will grow between now and the date you will need to spend it, and if it doesn't grow enough, you may have to borrow to cover the costs. If you fall into this category, the worksheet will place you in more conservative assets, because you can't afford to take a short-term loss on your investments. But the important thing is that by following a good investing strategy, you will probably reduce your borrowing needs, so you will dig yourself out of the deficit more quickly.

Why do we ask about your federal tax rate? This helps refine your allocation among bonds and large- and small-company stocks. In general, the higher your tax bracket, the more you want to avoid the interest payments you get on bonds and the dividends

The SmartMoney One for parents

Part A

To fill out the SmartMoney One asset-allocation worksheet, you will first need to answer the following questions about your family, your financial situation, your spending needs, and your investment outlook. We suggest you highlight or circle the entire row (under columns A through D) of the response that best fits your situation. This way, it will be much easier to find the score that applies to you when you answer the questions on lines 2, 4, 11, and 15 in Part B, which is on the next page.

Note: You will not know the correct response to the last question (Interest-Rate Exposure) until you fill in line 7 of Part B.

	A	B	C	D
Number of Children				
How many kids do you have?				
One	0	N/A	N/A	N/A
Two	3	N/A	N/A	N/A
Three or more	6	N/A	N/A	N/A
Kid's Age				
How old is the oldest?				
Younger than five	−2	10	2	N/A
Between five and 10	4	10	0	N/A
11 or older	8	0	−4	N/A
Portfolio Size				
What is the value of your investment portfolio?				
Less than $40,000	4	0	0	0
Between $40,000 and $150,000	0	15	2	4
Between $150,000 and $250,000	−2	20	4	6
Greater than $250,000	−4	20	8	10
Yearly Savings				
How much do you save a year?				
Less than $4,000	7	N/A	0	0
Between $4,000 and $8,000	1	N/A	2	2
Between $8,000 and $15,000	−2	N/A	6	4
More than $15,000	−3	N/A	8	6
Short-Term Spending Needs				
How much of your current portfolio do you plan to spend in the next five years?				
0 to 25 percent	−2	20	6	N/A
26 to 70 percent	3	15	2	N/A
71 to 100 percent	8	5	−1	N/A
More than 100 percent	12	0	−4	N/A
Longer-Term Spending Needs				
What portion of your current portfolio do you plan to spend in the period five to 15 years from now?				
0 to 30 percent	−4	N/A	15	10
31 to 80 percent	0	N/A	5	4

	A	B	C	D
81 to 150 percent	4	N/A	0	0
More than 150 percent of what you've saved	6	N/A	−2	−2

Federal Tax Bracket

What is your marginal federal tax rate?

	A	B	C	D
15 percent	1	N/A	0	N/A
28 percent	−2	N/A	3	N/A
31 percent or greater	−3	N/A	10	N/A

Volatility Tolerance

How much volatility can you live with?

	A	B	C	D
As little as possible	4	5	−2	0
A moderate amount	−1	15	5	3
A lot	−4	20	14	6

Economic Outlook

What is your reading on the U.S. economy over the next 12 months?

	A	B	C	D
Weak	2	20	0	10
Average	−3	10	7	0
Strong	−6	0	10	−10

Interest-Rate Exposure

To make sure you are not overly exposed to interest-rate risk over the long term, you will adjust your small-cap foreign allocations for the size of your bond holdings. When you get to line 7 of Part B, note if the bond allocation is . . .

	A	B	C	D
Less than 20 percent	N/A	N/A	0	0
Between 20 and 40 percent	N/A	N/A	6	10
Greater than 40 percent	N/A	N/A	10	20

PART B

1. **Enter your age** _____
   (If you are younger than 25, enter 25; if you are older than 50, enter 50. If you are filling out the worksheet as a couple, average your ages.)

2. **Fixed Income: Choose the score in column A from Part A.**
   a. Number of Children .... _____
   b. Kid's Age... _____
   c. Portfolio Size... _____
   d. Yearly Savings .... _____
   e. Short-Term Spending Needs... _____
   f. Longer-Term Spending Needs... _____
   g. Federal Tax Bracket... _____
   h. Volatility Tolerance... _____
   i. Economic Outlook .... _____

3. **Add line 1 to the sum of lines 2a through 2i.**.............................. _____

4. **Bonds: Choose the score in column B from Part A.**
   a. Kid's Age... _____
   b. Portfolio Size.. _____
   c. Short-Term Spending Needs... _____
   d. Volatility Tolerance... _____
   e. Economic Outlook .... _____

5. **Add lines 4a through 4e.**.. _____

6. **Divide line 5 by 100.** .... _____

7. **Multiply line 3 by line 6.**
   This is your Bond allocation.. _____%

8. **Subtract line 7 from line 3.**
   This is your Cash allocation.. _____%

9. **Stocks: Subtract line 3 from 100.**... _____

10. **Small Caps: Subtract line 1 from 70.**.. _____

11. **Choose the score in column C from Part A.**
    a. Kid's Age.. _____
    b. Portfolio Size.. _____
    c. Yearly Savings... _____
    d. Short-Term Spending Needs... _____
    e. Longer-Term Spending Needs... _____
    f. Federal Tax Bracket... _____
    g. Volatility Tolerance.. _____
    h. Economic Outlook... _____
    i. Interest-Rate Exposure... _____

12. **Add line 10 to the sum of lines 11a through 11i.**........................... _____

13. **Divide line 12 by 100.**.. _____

14. **Multiply line 9 by line 13.**
    This is your Small-Cap allocation.. _____%

15. **Foreign Stocks: Enter 40.**... _____

16. **Choose the score in column D from Part A.**
    a. Portfolio Size.. _____
    b. Yearly Savings... _____
    c. Longer-Term Spending Needs... _____
    d. Volatility Tolerance.. _____
    e. Economic Outlook... _____
    f. Interest-Rate Exposure... _____

17. **Add line 15 to the sum of lines 16a through 16f.**
    (If the result is negative, enter zero.).. _____

18. **Divide line 17 by 200.**.. _____

19. **Multiply line 9 by line 18.**
    This is your Foreign-Stock allocation... _____%

20. **Add line 14 and line 19.**.. _____

21. **Subtract line 20 from line 9.**
    This is your Large-Cap allocation... _____%

22. **Your Investment Mix: Enter the total value of your portfolio**................$ _____

23. **Allocation Amounts:**
    a. **Multiply line 22 by the percent on line 7.**
       Bonds ....$ _____
    b. **Multiply line 22 by the percent on line 8.**
       Cash ....$ _____
    c. **Multiply line 22 by the percent on line 14.**
       Small-cap U.S. stocks..$ _____
    d. **Multiply line 22 by the percent on line 19.**
       Foreign stocks..$ _____
    e. **Multiply line 22 by the percent on line 21.**
       Large-cap U.S. stocks...$ _____

paid by most large companies, because they are taxed as income at rates up to 39.6 percent. By contrast, most of the gains from small-cap stocks come in the form of capital gains, which are taxed at 20 percent for assets held more than 12 months. So people in higher tax brackets will be steered more toward small-cap stocks.

The next two questions reveal your personal views. Your volatility tolerance is the emotional component to investing. Most people, especially those who have not lived through a market crash, should probably stick to the low and moderate answers, unless you are sure that you have an iron stomach.

Finally, your economic outlook affects all of the asset classes. We are not talking about the outlook for the next several months. Rather, we are more concerned with your opinion of where we are in the broader business cycle. If you think the current economic expansion will continue, our worksheet will have you invest more heavily in the stock market, because stocks rise with improved profits and rising national income. If you believe we are in the later stages of an economic cycle, the worksheet will put you more heavily in bonds, because as the economy slows, interest rates usually fall, meaning bond prices rise. A pessimistic outlook will also increase your exposure to foreign stocks, because if the U.S. economy slows down, others will probably speed up, so a bigger foreign allocation is more likely to pick up those gains.

In the worksheet's second section, Part B, we start with a standard allocation based on your age. (The longer you have to invest, the more you can afford to be in stocks.) Then we adjust it based on your answers in Part A. By the time you finish the worksheet, you'll have specific allocations for stocks, bonds, and cash.

Where to Invest

Investments are *not* something you have to track every day, with constant, frenzied calls between you and a stockbroker ("Buy! Sell!"). The fact is, you can build a simple, low-maintenance portfolio that you'll only need to check in on every year or so—or when your circumstances change, such as when you need to make a big, one-time expenditure.

This is exactly the kind of investment portfolio most young parents should create for themselves. It doesn't take a lot of time and

Make the most of your retirement savings

Next time you're standing around the watercooler complaining about your boss, swapping tales with your colleagues about how you're overworked and underpaid, trying to top one another with examples of how you're being exploited, keep this one thought in mind: Your employer is probably making you rich.

Got a 401(k) plan at the office? Does your employer match your contributions? Are you contributing the maximum amount you're allowed each month? Then all this should add up to a very comfortable retirement, one that you'd be hard-pressed to match if you were doing it all on your own and thus couldn't benefit from the extraordinary tax breaks that come with one of these company-sponsored retirement plans.

Look at it this way. If you had invested just $100 a month over the past 20 years in a standard 401(k) stock fund, taking into account the power of tax-free compounding and a typical 50 percent match from the employer, you would have ended up with $184,000 by now—$50,000 more than if you'd invested in a regular individual retirement account and much more than you could hope for if you'd invested with even the best money manager.

The key thing: that match. Where else can you find an investment that gives you the equivalent of a 25 percent, 50 percent, or, in some cases, 100 percent return on the first day?

Of course, it would be nice if we could contribute as much as we want to a 401(k) and have our company match part or even all of our contributions. But that's just not the real world. Some companies don't have a 401(k) plan, and others don't match your contributions.

So what do you do? To find out, the editors at *SmartMoney* recently took more than 100 different investing scenarios and tested them against market data covering the past 30 years.

Here's what the research showed.

Once you've maxed out on contributions in your retirement plan that earn a match from your employer, you should stick your next retirement savings dollar in one of the new Roth IRA accounts. (To be eligible, married couples must have less than $150,000 in adjusted gross income; if you're single, the number is $95,000.) The Roth IRA is a better option than putting it in the 401(k) without the match. It's true that you won't get a tax deduction for making a Roth investment, but you can eventually take it out *free of tax,* and that outweighs any immediate gain you'd get from a tax deduction now.

With the tax-deductible money in a 401(k), you'll pay taxes at your income tax rate when you take it out. That could lop a quarter to a third off your gains. Thus, keep putting your excess savings into the Roth until you've used up the $2,000 that you're allowed to contribute to it each year. Then, if you want to save even more than that, make whatever unmatched contributions you are allowed to in your 401(k).

If you can't open a Roth because you and your spouse make more than $150,000, the next best place for your savings after you've maxed out with your company plan—both the matched and unmatched portions—is a nondeductible IRA. Here also the annual limit is $2,000, but anyone can open one. After 20 years, the tax-deferred compounding on an average stock market investment will give you 5 to 15 percent more to spend during retirement than the same investment in a taxable account would.

When you've exhausted all these options, in most cases you should turn to a taxable investment, especially if you plan to put the money in stocks of any type: small-cap, mid-cap, large-cap, or foreign. The key to choosing taxable investments for your retirement savings is to keep your expenses down and get the most benefit from the 20 percent capital gains break. That means holding your stocks for at least 12 months—longer, if possible—and choosing mutual funds with a low annual turnover (the rate at which the fund manager buys and sells holdings). Since the law requires that gains from selling stocks be distributed to mutual fund investors, the higher the turnover rate, the greater the amount of your return each year that will be subject to taxation—and that amount may be taxed at higher rates.

Finally, where do variable annuities enter into all of this? Variable annuities are those retirement investments so beloved by financial advisers and insurance salesmen. Surely you've gotten one of those sales pitch phone calls by now. Forget them. Their exceptionally high expenses often counteract the fact that the money's growing tax-deferred.

energy, for one. And, importantly, it encourages you to buy investments and hold them for the long term, not trade in and out of them. (Studies have shown that active trading—sometimes known as market timing—rarely works as well as simply buying good investments and holding them through their ups and downs.)

Now chances are you've already got some money invested—such as a college fund, perhaps, or a little cash set aside for emergencies. We're not asking you to start all over. Instead, you should use those investments as the building blocks for your portfolio.

Here's an example. Let's say you've done the college tuition worksheet on page 232 and it tells you to save $200 a month, invested 75 percent in High-Volatility funds and 25 percent in Medium-Volatility funds. You selected Ariel Growth for the former and the Safeco Equity fund for the latter. Now you move on to this chapter's worksheet, on asset allocation. The result is that, overall, you should be 50 percent in large-cap stocks, 30 percent in small-cap stocks, 10 percent in bonds, and 10 percent in cash.

What now? You simply fit the funds you've already chosen for college into the asset allocation. Safeco Equity is a large-cap fund (see the table on page 259). So you count whatever money you've already got in there as part of your 50 percent allocation in large-

The importance of getting started early

B y getting a jump on your retirement savings now, when you've still got a number of years to go, you should be able to build a sizeable nest egg. How sizeable? Look at the table below. As you can see, starting early—and taking advantage of employer matching in a 401(k)—makes a big difference. With 40 years to go until you retire and a 50 percent employer match, for example, you can build a portfolio big enough to generate income of $85,000 a year by putting aside just under $3,000 a year. Wait 20 years to start and you'll need to be saving over $18,500 a year.

	Annual savings needed with . . .		
Desired Income in Retirement	. . . 20 years to retirement	. . . 30 years to retirement	. . . 40 years to retirement
$ 45,000	$ 9,897.32	$3,787.63	$1,560.87
$ 65,000	$14,296.12	$5,471.02	$2,254.58
$ 85,000	$18,694.93	$7,154.42	$2,948.30
$105,000	$23,093.74	$8,837.81	$3,642.02

Assumptions: You live 30 years in retirement, inflation averages 3% a year, and you earn 12% on your investments annually before retirement and 8% after.

The going rate: The cost of being an investor

T o make money, goes the old saying, you have to spend money. Here's what it costs to get on your way as an investment mogul in five cities.

	Bloomington, Ind.	Laramie, Wyo.	Ventura, Calif.	Ann Arbor, Mich.	Nashville, Tenn.
College savings account minimum balance	$ 25.00	$ 200.00	$ 500.00	$ 300.00	$1,000.00
Paperback copy of *One Up on Wall St.*	$ 13.95	$ 12.55	$ 13.95	$ 13.95	$ 12.95
Session with a financial consultant	$ 75/hr	$ 125/hr	$ 150/hr	$ 75/hr	$ 125/hr
Compaq computer for tracking investments	$2,550.00	$2,949.00	$3,123.00	$2,540.00	$2,799.00
Summer investment course at local college	$ 326.40	$ 273.00	$ 312.00	$1,044.00	$ 144.00
12 oz. Maalox	$ 5.85	$ 4.69	$ 7.42	$ 4.39	$ 5.89
Prescription-strength sleep inducer	$ 41.69	$ 40.69	$ 29.99	$ 29.99	$ 35.40
Massage for half hour	$ 35.00	$ 25.00	$ 40.00	$ 30.00	$ 40.00
Celebratory cigar	$ 5.50	$ 2.50	$ 4.15	$ 6.99	$ 5.99
French Blue "power shirt"	$ 35.00	$ 29.00	$ 35.00	$ 38.00	$ 43.00
Total	$3,113.39	$3,661.43	$4,215.51	$4,082.32	$4,211.23

cap stocks. Ariel Growth is small stocks, so whatever you've got in there fits into your 30 percent small-cap allocation.

Note: Two of the funds we selected for college savers are "balanced" funds, which are made up of both large-cap stocks and bonds. If you own either of these two, American Balanced or Hotchkis & Wiley Balanced, think of half the money as part of your bond allocation and half as large stocks.

If you'd like more information about which stocks and bonds to buy, be sure to check out *SmartMoney* magazine, which reports on the latest investment ideas every month, and its website, *www.smartmoney.com,* updated daily. In the meantime, here's how we suggest you get started.

STOCKS

The easiest way to invest in the stock market is to buy mutual funds. But there are thousands of such funds on the market, each one vying for your attention with promises of world-beating gains. Which ones should you buy? The funds we cited as good choices for college saving, on page 235, are certainly a good place to start.

Of those funds, the following would fit the large-cap stock portion of your asset allocation: **Legg Mason Value Trust,** and **T. Rowe Price Dividend Growth.** Looking for small caps? Try **Ariel Growth** or **Baron Asset.**

Another good way to fill the large- and small-cap portion of your portfolio is to buy index funds—that is, funds that mimic an index such as the Standard & Poor's 500 (big stocks) or the Russell 2000 (small ones). In an index fund, you will never suffer the indignity of underperforming the market average to which the fund is keyed. You'll never outperform, either, of course, but our main goal here is getting you into stocks, both big and small. In both categories we like funds from Vanguard. For large caps, there's the **Vanguard Index 500 Portfolio,** and for small stocks it's **Vanguard Index Small Cap Stock.**

Unfortunately, there aren't any great international index fund choices available, in our view. Thus you ought to consider actively managed, well-diversified international funds such as **Vanguard International Growth** and **Hotchkis & Wiley International.**

BONDS

On the fixed-income side, we've again kept it simple, dividing the category into no-fuss short- and long-term Treasury bonds. Our choice for the short term is the **Eaton Vance Short-Term Treasury** fund. Thanks to an elaborate quantitative system that finds the highest-yielding Treasury for a given maturity, Eaton Vance's 4.7 percent 5-year average annual return, through mid-1998, was well above average for short-term Treasury funds.

For a long-term choice, we like **American Century's Benham Target Maturity 2015,** which invests primarily in zero coupon bonds maturing around that year. This fund represents an easier way to invest in Treasurys than buying bonds directly from the government or Treasury strips from a broker. If you hold on to this fund until it expires in 2015, you're likely to get back 100 percent of your principal—just like an actual bond.

CASH

In the cash allocation, you'll need to make a choice between the tax-exempt **Strong Municipal Advantage Money Market** or the taxable **Managers Money Market** fund. To do so, look back and see how much of your assets are in retirement funds. If it's more than 70 percent, you probably don't need to invest your cash in a tax-exempt fund.

Ten Things Your Mutual Fund Won't Tell You

1 *There's something rank about our rankings.*

No question about it, the mutual fund industry is a numbers game—and the one number that counts is "No. 1." Luckily (for the fund companies, anyway), there are so many ways to slice the performance pie that every fund and its sister can boast a top-tier ranking of some kind. The question is, What do those numbers really tell you about a fund's prospects? Not a whole lot.

Take Oppenheimer Main Street Income & Growth. Back in 1997, it had returned an average of 24.8 percent over the past 5 years, placing it squarely at the top of its peer group. Impressive, sure—but that record gave nary a hint of the fund's troubles. Over the previous 3 years, in fact, only 16 percent of its fund peers did worse. By then, the fund manager who had been in charge during its best days was long gone.

2 *Warning: This fund will self-destruct in 30 seconds.*

A switch in fund managers is one thing, but more frightening for shareholders is when a fund's performance suddenly comes undone due to a current manager's aggressive miscues.

The trouble is, even a stellar 5- or 10-year track record can sometimes mask such precipitous falls. Witness Crabbe Huson Special, whose returns over the 5 years through June 1997 ranked it in the top third of all aggressive-growth funds, according to Morningstar, the Chicago fund-rating company. But over the previous 3 years you'll find Special in another special position: the bottom 10 percent.

What went wrong? Back in 1995, portfolio manager Jim Crabbe began betting that certain technology stocks were ripe for a fall. He was wrong, and as a result, the fund slumped. "To be honest, we executed quite poorly," says Crabbe. "That move cost my shareholders quite a bit of money."

3 *Our real expenses? Read the fine print.*

When you own a fund, it will charge you for the manager's compensation, marketing bills, and administrative overhead. These costs are laid out in the fund's prospectus. But not on the list are charges that can eat as much as a percentage point or two of performance each year: the brokerage commissions your fund pays when its manager buys and sells securities.

That's not to say that funds don't disclose these costs. They are clearly buried—er, printed—in their Statement of Additional Information. Not familiar with this document? That's because fund companies won't send it to you unless you call up and ask for it.

4 *What you see ain't what you'll get.*

OK, here's a pop quiz: Alliance Quasar A compounded at 21.1 percent a year from mid-1992 through mid-1997, versus 19.0 percent for John Hancock Emerging Growth B. Assuming you had invested $10,000 in each fund, which portfolio made you more money? Answer: Hancock. Although it didn't increase in value as rapidly as Alliance, it better shielded shareholders' gains from the IRS.

Look for funds with low turnover rates, which is a measure of how often the fund managers trade their shares. The less a fund trades, the less likely it is to generate a big tax bill for you.

5 *You think our return was bad? Wait till you get your tax bill.*

Even worse is getting a tax bill when your fund has lost money. That's right, lost money.

Take the examples of Govett Smaller Companies, Perkins Opportunity, and Smith Barney Special Equities B. In 1996, a year in which the Standard & Poor's 500 stock index rose 22 percent, these funds all saw their share prices decline. As if that weren't bad enough, each fund also hit shareholders with a taxable capital gains distribution. What happened? In each case, the manager was selling stocks he'd owned from years before, causing him to earn capital gains. When those gains are passed on to you in the form of cash or new shares in the fund, you owe tax on them.

6 *We're No. 1 . . . in more ways than you think.*

Mutual funds are quick to market their leading performance figures. But when it comes to their ranking in another key statistical measurement, most chart toppers tend to be, well, a bit modest. The category? Standard deviation—otherwise known as risk. Take, for example, Firsthand Technology Value. It returned an incredible 43.5 percent a year for the 3 years ending April 30, 1998. But as it happens, the fund also blows away most other funds in standard deviation, which measures the range of a fund's returns.

The higher the standard deviation, the greater the volatility. As for Technology Value, it rings up a 3-year deviation of 42.7, or about 3 times that of the S&P 500.

In bull markets, you expect funds with high standard deviations to gravitate toward the top of the performance charts. But volatility works both ways: When the market plunges, these funds get hit hard. And, no surprise, in May of 1998 (when the S&P 500 lost 1.72 percent of its value) Technology Value tumbled by 13.3 percent.

7 *Our record was made in ideal conditions. Your purchase was not.*

Few funds topped Van Kampen American Capital Growth's stunning performance in 1996. Then again, few funds enjoyed this portfolio's advantages. You see, Growth was an "incubator" fund. And as the name suggests, these funds start out in a highly nurturing environment.

For starters, their tiny size (typically, fund companies seed these portfolios with less than $1 million) allows their managers to concentrate assets in a few winning names—something large-fund managers can't do. They're also closed to the public, so the lack of shareholder redemptions means they can stay fully invested in stocks; by contrast, most regular funds keep 5 to 10 percent cash on hand to meet redemptions—a potential dead weight in rising markets.

Growth, which was started by Van Kampen in December 1995 with $300,000, made the most of these advantages. But then, once it opened to the public, it went into a slump.

8 *Our "cheap" shares may not be.*

As distasteful as the idea of paying a sales fee (or "load") is, some-times there's no getting around it, especially if you want to employ the talents of star managers, such as the duo who run AIM Value. Just make sure you don't purchase the wrong share class. The one that intuitively looks the cheapest can cost you more in the end.

AIM, for example, offers its Value fund in two share classes, Class A and Class B. Class A features a hefty front-end load—5.5 percent. Class B does not. So Class B is the better choice, right? Not necessarily, because it has higher annual expenses. Hold your shares longer than 7 years (assuming a 9 percent annual return) and you'll end up paying more with Class B than you would with A's hefty load.

9 *Now you see it . . . now you don't.*

Think you own the top-yielding money-market fund? You may want to look again. Money funds often waive some or all of their expenses in order to boost their yield. Because yields vary so little from fund to fund, expense waivers can mean the difference be-tween a superior and a so-so yield. "Money funds are the only funds that can practically guarantee a No. 1 ranking by waiving expenses," says Peter Crane, managing editor of IBC's *Money Fund Report*. And in this trillion-dollar industry, Crane adds, the No. 1 fund "brings in lots of cash."

Of course, the ranking drops when the fund reinstitutes its ex-penses. Although it smacks of "bait and switch," this practice is legal and quite common. More than half of all money funds waive at least some of their expenses, in fact.

10 *Our bond holdings aren't as safe as you think.*

Conventional wisdom says that the best gauge of a bond fund's sensitivity to interest rates is the "duration" of its holdings—a mea-sure of the bonds' cash flows through maturity. For every percent-age-point move in interest rates, the rule of thumb goes, a bond fund's net asset value will move inversely by the amount of its du-ration. What many investors don't realize is that duration can be a poor way to compare the interest-rate risk of municipal bond funds, which are prized for their tax-exempt income.

Consider the performance of the following two national muni bond funds in the first quarter of 1997, when interest rates were rising. Van Kampen American Capital Tax-Free High Income A, which had a duration of 7.3 years, gained 0.47 percent. First Investors Insured Tax-Exempt A had a lower duration—7.2 years—but lost 0.54 percent.

Why? First Investors had 100 percent of its assets in munis with the highest possible credit rating, AAA. Meanwhile, Van Kampen's AAA-rated bonds were just 24 percent of assets. The lesson: In the world of muni bond funds, always check a fund's duration and the quality of its holdings.

Part 8

TAXING MATTERS

There are actually people whose tax returns are so simple that the IRS now lets them call up and file by phone, using the Touch-Tone keypad to punch in their income. No instruction booklets. No paperwork. Just a simple, toll-free call to Uncle Sam, and the refund is on its way.

You, unfortunately, are not one of those people.

At least not anymore. Because now you're a parent, and parenthood brings with it a whole load of changes that render your tax return more complicated than ever before.

Just what you needed to hear, right? Well, it's not all bad news. Children bring opportunities for *saving* money at tax time as well. And we're here to help, with advice on hiring a good accountant, avoiding the "marriage penalty," audit-proofing your return, and making sure you get every last family credit and deduction you're entitled to.

15

Demystifying Your Tax Return

"My little tax deduction." Don't you just cringe when you hear people describe their children that way?

Still, they have a point. Children actually do represent a pretty valuable way to trim what you owe on April 15, assuming you can figure out how to make the most of it. Even the dreaded "Kiddie Tax," levied on investment income for kids under age 14, is something most parents can beat. It just takes a little advance planning—and a basic understanding of how the system works.

In the pages that follow you'll find answers to parents' most pressing questions about doing your taxes.

How Do I Hire a Good Accountant?

If ever there was a time to ditch the drudgery of tax work, this is it. The IRS estimates that it takes nearly 10 hours to complete Form 1040 by hand. You're a parent now. You've got 10 hours to spare?

While it's tempting to turn to that CPA your sister has been dating, you can—and should—do more shopping around.

Consider Gregory Sullivan. Most of the time he does taxes and financial planning. Now and then, though, the McLean, Virginia, accountant has to mop up for other people's mistakes. And that can be costly: One recent client wound up owing $19,000 in penalties and extra taxes because of his previous accountant's shoddy work. Sullivan had to file a revised return and bargain with the IRS to lower the penalties.

So first, cast a wide net. Ask for recommendations not only from friends and family but, more important, from people who know or share your financial situation. You don't necessarily need a certified public accountant, by the way. CPAs are trained in all manners of accountancy, including auditing companies' finances, while enrolled agents are almost exclusively tax focused. Both are authorized to represent you in front of the IRS. Then, once you have a handful of candidates, don't just interview them—put them to the test. "When people call me, all they usually ask is, 'What do you charge?' " says David J. Silverman, a New York tax preparer. "They really should know more about me than that."

Here are nine questions you should ask to determine whether a tax adviser deserves your money.

1. *I think I might be subject to the alternative minimum tax this year. Can you explain it?*
While most professionals are required to attend a certain number of training programs every year, there's no guarantee they're actually paying attention. This is one quick way to see if your candidate is up to date on the new tax law. The correct answer: The AMT is a special tax that is designed to snare people whose shrewd use of loopholes leaves them paying little or no taxes. You are especially vulnerable if you have lots of deductions and real estate depreciation, or if you have exercised incentive stock options. If an adviser hems and haws or grabs for the tax code to explain it, cross him off your list.

2. *I spend a lot but don't keep very good records. What can I get away with?*
This is a question that will help you judge whether you're interviewing a conservative tax adviser or someone who's a bit more freewheeling. Assuming you want to hire a straight-shooter, the correct answer is "You've got a problem."

3. *What happens if I'm audited?*
The only answer you want to hear: "I'll represent you and do the talking." A tax adviser who won't stand behind his or her work is not one you want to bother with.

4. *How often do your clients get audited?*
Keith Fevurly, vice president of education at the College for Financial Planning in Denver, says that an accountant who has few audits suggests good, detail-oriented record-keeping. True, thousands of randomly selected taxpayers are audited each year. But if your candidate has an unusually high level of audits (more than 2 percent of his clients), that may suggest there are deeper problems.

5. *If your clients do get audited, how much do they usually pay in fines or additional tax?*
The correct answer: "They usually don't pay, because we have all the documents to back up our calculations. If they do have to pay, I'll try to negotiate lower penalties."

6. *Who pays if you screw up?*
By law, the taxpayer is responsible for any errors, but a good adviser will pick up the tab for penalties or interest due to his or her mistakes. Ask before hiring anyone, and it's perfectly ordinary to get it in writing.

7. *Who's actually doing my taxes?*
Don't be alarmed if it's a staff member. That happens a lot at big-

---

Let a PC be your CPA

Unless you've got a really complicated return, with a tangle of self-employment taxes and rental properties and income earned in more than one state, chances are a software program will do your taxes just fine.

You'll have to buy a new copy of the program each year, to keep up with our nation's ever-changing tax laws, but look at it this way: They cost a lot less than going to an accountant.

The editors of *SmartMoney* magazine recently tested the two best-selling programs, and when it came to filling out your tax return and explaining the tax laws, both Intuit's **TurboTax** (with MacInTax for Macintosh users, both $49.95) and **Kiplinger TaxCut** ($39.95) by Block Financial were more than equal to the task. Confused about the tax laws on home sales or capital gains? Wondering whether you qualify for the child care credit? Both programs will give you the information you need. The difference is in how the information is presented. And this is where TurboTax stands out.

With TurboTax, when you want to know about, say, the new lifetime learning credit, you simply click on the common tax questions icon, hit Search, and type in your query. The answer comes back immediately. Again and again, TurboTax gives you clear guidance on the best tax moves for you. (Kiplinger TaxCut, in contrast, will take you in circles trying to "help" you figure out whether you should itemize your deductions.)

One of the added benefits of using software is tax planning. Here again, TurboTax beats the competition. You can project your taxes using dozens of different scenarios, and the program will compute your tax bill and make planning recommendations based on your own situation. With Kiplinger TaxCut, you fill out a tax form (there's no Q&A format in this section), and your tax bill is announced. Case closed—no planning advice.

ger firms. A CPA will interview you, and a staffer will plug in the numbers. If that's so, be sure to ask:

8. *If I have a question about my taxes, whom do I call?*
Wrong answer: "My staff will handle it."

9. *Will you calculate my taxes by computer or by hand?*
Manual calculations are a thing of the past. A good computer program makes it easy to create different tax scenarios and can catch errors that even the best accountants might miss.

Keep in mind that the level of service you get depends partly on what you are willing to pay. Though it varies by region, enrolled agents usually charge around $75 to $90 an hour, while CPAs get upward of $125, and some specialized tax attorneys rake in $250 an hour. Some firms charge by the number of forms they prepare. Always ask for an estimate of how much your return will cost, and get it in writing.

If the price seems too steep, you can always negotiate. You can also cut your costs by getting your paperwork in order before visiting the adviser's office. There's no need to have the meter running while a professional digs through your shoebox of old receipts.

Whose returns get examined

	Percent Audited in Fiscal 1996
*Forms 1040, 1040A, 1040EZ**	
Income of $25,000 to less than $50,000	0.95
$50,000 to less than $100,000	1.16
$100,000 and over	2.85
Schedule C (Sole Proprietorships)	
With gross receipts under $25,000	4.21
$25,000 to under $100,000	2.85
$100,000 and over	4.09
Estate-Tax Returns	
Gross estates of less than $1 million	7.85
$1 million to less than $5 million	21.42
$5 million and over	49.33

*Total personal income before deductions, losses, and other adjustments.

A clever trick you can pull with savings bonds

The beauty of U.S. Savings Bonds—apart from any patriotic stirrings you may get from them—is that the interest they spin off goes untaxed until you cash them in. At that point, though, the hammer comes down and the IRS gets its share.

However, there is a sneaky way to entirely cut or even eliminate the tax bill on savings bonds. Here's the deal:

You can *choose* to include each year's savings bond interest in your kid's income for that year, even though the bonds haven't been redeemed. This makes great sense if the child's annual unearned income—including the savings bond interest—will be below $700. Why? Because the first $700 of any child's income is completely untaxed. (That's the 1999 number. It's adjusted for inflation every year.) Even if making the election pushes an under-14-year-old's unearned income over $700, the excess is taxed at only 15 percent, as long as total unearned income stays below the $1,400 Kiddie Tax trigger point.

For example, say you've started buying Series EE bonds in your 6-year-old daughter's name with the idea that she will eventually redeem them to pay for college expenses. Your daughter has no unearned income from other sources. And the annual interest from the bonds is averaging, say, $400.

If you file a 1040 for your daughter and make the election to report the interest accruals annually, there will be no current federal income taxes because the income will always be completely sheltered by your daughter's $700 in tax-free earnings. When she eventually redeems the bonds (to pay for college or for any other reason), there will be only the final year's worth of accrued interest to worry about, and that amount should be pretty small and thus largely sheltered from tax.

To use this strategy, file a Form 1040 for the child and include the following statement on a separate sheet attached to the return (which will probably show zero tax due):

"Taxpayer hereby elects pursuant to IRC Section 454 to currently recognize as income the annual increment in the redemption price of U.S. Savings Bonds described in Reg. 1.454-1(a)(1). This election applies to such Savings Bonds owned on January 1 of [enter the year] and such Savings Bonds acquired after that date."

Be aware, too, that tax advisers can often keep operating legally even after they've gotten in trouble with the authorities. The American Institute of Certified Public Accountants (201-938-3100) and the National Association of Enrolled Agents (800-424-4339) can also tell you if a member is in good standing. But they won't tell you about any complaints or any investigations in progress. That's why it is crucial to speak to other clients. If a tax adviser won't name names, run for the door.

What Are the Special Tax Breaks I Get as a Parent?

BRILLIANT DEDUCTION

For every dependent child in your brood, you get what's known as an exemption, and it's worth several thousand dollars. (It is $2,750 for 1999, and it goes up every year, adjusted for inflation.) In other words, you can exempt that much of your earnings before arriving at your taxable income—the amount the IRS uses to figure out how much you owe.

To claim a dependent exemption, you've got to report the kid's Social Security number on your return. Don't have a Social Security number for your newborn yet? Call 800-772-1213 and ask for a copy of Form SS-5. Don't worry—it's one of the easier ones to fill out.

One thing to be aware of: Your deduction is phased out—that is, reduced—if you make too much money. The more you make, the less you can deduct. For 1999 income, for example, the IRS starts chipping away the exemption when married couples' adjusted gross income passes $189,950. (Adjusted gross income is the amount you make, minus certain adjustments such as a deductible contribution to an individual retirement account.)

CREDIT WHERE IT'S DUE

If you have a dependent child under age 17, and your adjusted gross income isn't too high, you'll qualify for a new tax credit that went into effect in the 1998 tax year. It's worth $500 a child for 1999 and thereafter. One nice thing about a credit: Unlike a deduction or exemption, which merely reduce the income you'll be taxed on, a credit directly reduces the taxes you'll owe, dollar for dollar.

Naturally, there's a phaseout on this one, too. Make more than $110,000 in AGI as a married couple, and the credit starts disappearing—fast.

CREDIT FOR CHILD CARE

Here's a deal for working parents. If you pay someone to take care of your under-13-year-old kids so you and your spouse can

The real world: Employing your children for fun and profit

Bill Bischoff is a self-described "village idiot" when it comes to computers. But taxes—that's another matter. Which is why the Colorado Springs, Colorado, CPA recently hired his two teenage sons to work on his office computer system over the summer. Not only did the boys install new software, remove some old programs, and generally clean up their dad's computer-related messes but they also produced a nice tax break for Bischoff—and each made several-thousand-dollar contributions to his college fund.

Do you have a small business, even if it's just a little sideline? If so, you really ought to consider doing what Bischoff did. "This break is one of the big advantages of being self-employed," he says. "Every chance I get, I encourage my clients to do it."

When you hire your own under-age-18 children, a number of good things happen:

- Unlike with regular employees, you don't owe Social Security or Medicare taxes on the money you pay your under-18 kids. So you avoid the employer half of these taxes (7.65 percent), and there's no need to withhold the employee half from your child's paycheck, either. Also, you won't owe the 0.8 percent federal employment tax on your kid's wages.
- You can deduct your kid's salary from your business income, which lowers both your income tax and your self-employment tax. This also reduces your adjusted gross income, which has other therapeutic side effects (namely, it will help you avoid the "phaseout" rules that reduce deductions and credits when your income exceeds certain limits).
- Your child shouldn't owe much tax, if any, on the money. That's because he can shelter up to $4,300 of income (in 1999; it'll be adjusted for inflation in later years) with his standard deduction. Any wages above $4,300 will be taxed at only 15 percent, up to $25,750. And don't worry about the Kiddie Tax. That's only on unearned income, like interest and dividends, not on wages.

One caveat: Unfortunately, you can't just assign any task to your child and then pay her lavishly for it. The wages have to be reasonable in relation to the work your kid did.

Now, it's true the rules are somewhat different if you're actually running a *corporation* (as opposed to a sole proprietorship, like Bischoff, or a husband-wife partnership). In that case, you would have to pay the Social Security and Medicare taxes on the kid's wages, and you'd owe federal unemployment tax as well. But even still, you could write off the wages as a business expense, as well as your share of those so-called payroll taxes. That would lower your income tax. And if you kept the kid's salary below $4,300, he would still owe no income tax—because of his standard deduction. Thus, says Bischoff, unless your company isn't making a profit, your income tax savings easily offset what you'd owe in payroll taxes.

work, you may qualify for it. Ahem. *If* you pay your child care provider legally.

Your child care provider has to be legal because you have to give the IRS her name and Social Security number. Fail to include it and the IRS will disallow the credit.

This gets a little complicated, so bear with us. The amount of credit you get is a *percentage* of your child care expenses, up to $2,400 for 1 kid and $4,800 for 2 or more kids. What's the percentage? It depends on how much you earn. If you earn anything above $28,000 a year, the most you can take is 20 percent of $2,400 (or 20 percent of $4,800 with 2 or more kids). In dollar terms, that means your credit ranges from $480 to $960. The paperwork you need: Form 2441.

Does your company offer a flexible spending account—one of those deals that lets you cover child care expenses with pretax dollars? If it does, you're almost always better off using it than taking the credit (see "How to lower the costs of child care" on page 48 for more information).

What's the "Marriage Penalty"— And Is There Anything I Can Do About It?

The marriage penalty is a tax code quirk that, since 1969, has imposed an extra levy on millions of dual-earner American couples.

Let's say you earned $100,000 in 1998 and took the standard deduction (that is, you didn't itemize). Your federal tax would have been $23,708. But if you and your spouse both earned $100,000 and filed jointly, your tax would not be just double $23,708: It would be $51,361. That's a marriage penalty of $3,945. (The good news is that the same quirk gives a marriage *bonus* to single-income couples or spouses with widely disparate incomes.)

What can you do about it if you've been stung by the marriage penalty? Well, you could get a divorce. Living together as unmarrieds, you would both pay taxes at the individual rate. But you may not have to go that far. Sometimes married couples come out ahead if they file separate returns. This is most likely going to work for you when one spouse has unusually high medical expenses, or if you had big casualty losses or lots of miscellaneous itemized deductions.

Unfortunately, there's only one way to find out which method is best: You have to crunch the numbers. Do 3 returns—1 married filing jointly, 2 married filing separately—and see which gives you the lowest total tax due.

(Incidentally, legislators like to make noise about repealing the marriage penalty every so often. Don't hold your breath. The fact is, the government generates billions of dollars from it, so this is one tax quirk that probably won't disappear in your lifetime.)

What's the Kiddie Tax—and What Can I Do About It?

The Kiddie Tax was dreamed up by Congress to make sure cagey people didn't shift all their investment income into their kids' names, and thus pay tax at the lower kids' rate.

Think about it. Wouldn't it be nice if you could give your income-producing investments to your baby daughter? She'd owe just 15 percent tax on it, compared with the 28 or 31 or even 39.6 percent you'll owe.

The way Congress clamped down on this was to make kids pay tax at *your* rate until they're 14 years old. After that they pay at their own rates, which is 15 percent for income and 10 percent for capital gains.

Your money's worth

The last thing you need, come midnight of April 14th, is a calculator that goes on the blink. Here's what to buy:

Worth it: Texas Instruments Heavy-Duty Printing Calculator ($59.99 at Staples). This workhorse calculator comes with a 12-digit fluorescent display. It prints out hard copies at a rate of 3 lines per second, so you can check your math, and it's sturdy enough to withstand angry stabs with the pencil when the math isn't to your liking.

Not worth it: T1-30X solar calculator ($12.99 at Staples). You're online, in the middle of paying a bill, and you need to do some quick math to double-check the bank. You try to turn on your calculator and nothing happens. You wave it in front of a lamp, head over to the window, finally get the thing working—and your computer automatically logs off. Need we say more?

So that means the Kiddie Tax spoils everything, right?

Wrong.

What people often forget is that their kids' unearned income (that is, interest and dividends) has to hit a certain threshold before the Kiddie Tax goes into effect. In 1999, that threshold is $1,400. So until your kid owns enough investment assets to produce at least $1,400 of annual income, the Kiddie Tax is nothing but a theoretical concern. (FYI, in mid-1998, you would have needed about $24,500 in 30-year Treasury bonds to produce income of $1,400 a year.)

So how do you beat the Kiddie Tax? Simple. You keep your kid's income under that threshold. Among the ways you can do so:

Buy and hold. Rather than trading in and out of the investments in your kid's name, make this the account where you buy securities and really hang onto them. Ideally you'll hold them until after the child has turned 14. Then those long-term capital gains profits you've reaped will be taxed at the kids' rate, which is a low 10 percent (compared with 20 percent for you).

Stick to low-dividend growth stocks and funds. Lots of investors love dividends—those quarterly payouts from the company's profits. But since you're trying to minimize income, you're better off buying

---

The going rate: The cost of doing your own taxes

S o you think it's a no-brainer: You do the taxes and avoid paying an accountant. But if you add up the following costs, you may find plenty of justification in handing off that grocery bag full of receipts to someone else.

	Chicago	Cleveland	Des Moines	Minneapolis	Philadelphia
Quicken TurboTax Deluxe	$ 59.99	$ 49.99	$ 34.99	$ 49.95	$ 49.99
Pack of #2 pencils	1.49	0.99	0.99	1.89	0.99
Large gum eraser	0.58	0.39	0.50	0.50	0.45
Bifocals	79.00	98.00	128.00	187.00	108.00
Tums (150 tablet)	4.99	2.99	3.99	4.39	5.29
At-a-Glance (daily) calendar	7.29	9.39	9.39	9.99	9.99
Jack Daniel's whiskey (a fifth)	16.99	17.15	12.62	7.29	15.49
Advil (100 tablet)	10.39	9.55	6.29	8.29	10.39
One-way flight to Grand Cayman	474.00	561.00	646.00	608.00	476.00
Total	654.72	749.45	842.77	877.30	676.59

companies that invest their profits back into the business. Microsoft is a good example. It's not just a low-dividend stock. It's a *no*-dividend stock. You prefer to invest in funds? Of the "11 great mutual funds for college savers" we described in chapter 13, Ariel Growth and Baron Asset qualify as low-dividend funds.

Invest in Series EE U.S. Savings Bonds. We wouldn't overdo it on these bonds—they pay only 5 percent or so in interest, which is not exactly stellar. But they do have an important tax advantage: The interest on them is deferred until they're cashed in. Thus, if you buy them in your kid's name and don't cash them in until after the child is 14, *voila*—no Kiddie Tax is due. You'll only owe tax at your child's income tax rate, which, again, is a puny 15 percent.

Now That I'm a Parent, Do I Need to File Another Return for My Kid?

Probably not. You only need to file a return for your kid if he or she earns income from investments or as a child model, say. And even then, instead of going through the hassle of filing a separate return for your child, chances are you can include his or her income on your return. The form you need is 8814, and it gets attached to your 1040.

This option is available if:

- your child is under 14 at year-end and has only interest and dividend income;
- the child's gross income—from investments—is more than $700 and less than $7,000 (these are 1999 numbers and will be adjusted for inflation in the future); and
- you haven't made any estimated tax or tax-withholding payments in the child's name and Social Security number.

The upside of going this route is simplicity—1 return instead of 2 or more, depending on how many kids you have. The first $1,400 of each child's interest and dividend income (again, '99 numbers) is still taxed at favorable rates, the same as it would be with separate returns. Any unearned income beyond that threshold is still taxed at your rate, just as it would be with a separate return for the child under the Kiddie Tax rules.

However, there are a couple of potential downsides. For one, putting the kids' income on your return will increase your adjusted gross income, which could cause you to lose out on various deductions, credits, and other tax breaks that get phased out when your AGI is too high. (Among them: You can't contribute to an Education IRA with adjusted gross income of more than $160,000.) Also, it's worth finding out whether your state has an equivalent to the Kiddie Tax. If it doesn't—and many of them don't—you may be better off filing a separate return for your child and taking advantage of the state's lower rates for kids. (Unfortunately, you have to do both returns the same way; you can't put your child on your federal return and leave her *off* the state one.)

I'm Terrified of Being Audited. Should I Be?

Getting audited by the Internal Revenue Service really isn't the end of the world, as columnist Dave Barry once calmly observed. "All that happens is, you take your financial records to the IRS office and they put you into a tank filled with giant, stinging leeches. Many taxpayers are pleasantly surprised to find that they die within hours."

Talk to a few people who've really been through the process and you'll realize Barry wasn't exaggerating all that much. If it wants to, the IRS can seriously mess up your life, in ways that often seem arbitrary and bizarre.

The chance that you'll actually suffer an audit, however, is quite remote. Fewer than 2 percent of all the individual income tax returns filed in each of the past several years were audited, IRS reports show.

How does the IRS decide to audit someone? A lot of it depends on the secret IRS computer program that scans every return and then assigns it a score indicating the likelihood of questionable items. Despite the IRS's penchant for secrecy, some entries the computer searches for are fairly obvious, former IRS officials say. Among these are itemized deductions that represent an unusually large percentage of the taxpayer's income. Other ways of singling out returns are less sophisticated, such as the agency's "related examinations." These are what you get, for example, for doing business with someone whose return is audited. There are also "chance" audits, triggered largely by, well, chance. Perhaps an agent saw something about you in your local newspaper or on television that piqued his curiosity.

Here are some of the other items that tend to raise examiners' eyebrows:

- Filing Schedule C. If you own your own business, deal in large amounts of cash, and file Schedule C, your chances of being audited rise sharply.
- Taking a home-office deduction. The rules here are so complex and limiting that IRS agents figure they have a good chance of squeezing more revenue out of many taxpayers who claim a home office.
- Writing off large amounts of travel and entertainment expenses.
- Racking up large losses in a business each year for many years.
- Taking large casualty-loss deductions. Very few people qualify for such deductions. Thus, says a former IRS official, those filers who take them tend to stand out and get asked questions, even if they are innocent.
- Being careless or lying. One easy way to get asked tough questions is to not report income you received that was reported to the IRS by whoever paid you. That's why it is so important to make sure whatever you write down matches exactly whatever is on an "information return" such as the W-2 form you receive from your employer.
- Living better than you seem able to afford. Even the IRS's ancient computers are smart enough to figure out that a Beverly Hills address is tough to maintain on Burger King wages.
- Filing an estate-tax return. These returns draw unusually heavy scrutiny, reflecting the large amounts of money typically involved.

Worried that you might be lined up in the IRS's crosshairs? Lately, some accountants have been touting "audit insurance." The deal: For a surcharge ranging from 10 to 15 percent of the fee you already pay to have your taxes prepared, your accountant also agrees to represent you in the event of any type of IRS inquiry about your return, for no additional fees.

It might not be a bad deal if you've got a really complex return. Jim Weikart, a partner at New York's Weikart Tax Associates, recalls one case in which a client's audit lasted close to two weeks and "would have run him about $14,000 in my fees alone. If he hadn't had insurance, I would have advised him to settle earlier. It wouldn't have been worth the money we'd save in taxes after my fees."

But most taxpayers probably ought to stay away. "Simple returns generally don't have big problems," observes Michael Mares, head of the tax division of the American Institute of Certified Public Accountants. "If you're paying $50 a year and you have about a 1 percent chance of an audit, the odds may not be worth it."

Ten Things Your Tax Preparer Won't Tell You

1 *I love it when you get audited.*

The pain of enduring an audit has no redeeming side, right? Well, it does if you're an accountant. That's because audits typically mean money in the bank for accountants. How much? Depending on the breadth of the IRS's inquiry, you could easily spend three times more on an audit than you did getting your tax return prepared, because of the many hours of work involved.

Perversely, it can often be your accountant's own mistakes in preparing your return that trigger an audit. But that doesn't prevent some tax preparers from guiltlessly enjoying the extra cash. "We call this the screw-up rule," says one New York accountant who, for obvious reasons, requested anonymity. "The more we screw up, the more we earn."

2 *I take risks with your return that I would never take with my own.*

Want a big tax refund? Some accountants make it sound easy. All they need to do is scrape up some deductions, and, bam, you're in the black. But what the refund kings won't tell you is that they often push a little too far, liberally interpreting the gray areas of the tax code and routinely taking risks that most taxpayers would shy away from if they fully understood the potential downside.

A study by Peggy Hite, an accounting professor at Indiana University, reveals just how conservative most taxpayers are: In a survey of taxpayers' sentiments, Professor Hite's subjects responded that, on average, they would be willing to take a chance with a gray area on their tax return if they are about 70 percent certain that their interpretation of the law is correct. Yet tax preparers have carte blanche to be far more aggressive: According to IRS rules, tax preparers must be a mere 33 percent sure that their positions will stand up under scrutiny. Only if they gamble beyond that point will accountants personally risk IRS penalties.

What's the financial risk to a preparer who is overaggressive? A flat IRS fine of only $250.

3 *My CPA license? It's just a marketing gimmick.*

Most CPAs are proud of their hard-earned initials, and many can probably get away with charging you more once they've earned them. But the fact is that a CPA isn't necessarily qualified to handle your personal tax matters. That's because acquiring the coveted credentials actually requires very little specialized knowledge of taxation.

CPA training revolves around public accountancy—the reviewing and certifying of financial statements for businesses. While that can be a complicated, sophisticated endeavor, it doesn't demand a full-scale knowledge of the tax code. As it turns out, less than 25 percent of the grueling exam accountants must pass to earn a CPA's license is focused on tax.

A more pertinent title for a tax specialist may be enrolled agent. To qualify, individuals must pass a test given by the IRS that focuses entirely on tax matters. Another impressive credential: a master's degree in taxation. To claim one, you generally must complete a two-year program that covers a broad range of tax topics, from trusts and estates and the taxation of real estate to questions of international taxation.

Even these credentials, though, don't mean much if the accountant doesn't have a good deal of practical experience. In the end, you're probably better off with someone who spends the bulk of his time preparing returns (even if he is a CPA) rather than an accountant who only turns to tax preparation around April 15 as a way to bring in extra cash.

4 *I love lousy records.*

Most accountants charge by the hour. So if you walk into your accountant's office with a shopping bag full of disorganized records and rely on him or her to put them in order, you are going to spend a lot more money than you should. Accountants will charge you their regular rates, say $100 an hour, to do work that you could easily do yourself. If the idea of organizing your own records is too loathsome for you to contemplate, at least turn your records over to a bookkeeper, who will charge much more reasonable rates, probably no more than $20 an hour.

5 *I'm accountable to no one.*

Despite the baffling complexity of our tax system, our government has said that just about anyone can make a living doing other people's taxes. Aside from a few states where state regulators require tax preparers to be licensed and registered, the rest of the country allows absolutely anyone to hang out a shingle and prepare tax returns. And while the IRS has set up ethical guidelines for the tax preparers who have credentials—CPAs, enrolled agents, and attorneys—all others are free to define their own standards.

6 *If you don't check over my work, you're crazy.*

Your accountant isn't likely to make a habit of turning down work. But truth be told, as April 15 nears he probably has way too much of it. And that means mistakes will be made—particularly during the last four weeks of the season, when the pressure mounts on accountants to finish literally hundreds of returns. "You wouldn't want a doctor probing at your appendix if he hadn't slept all night," says Doug Stives, a CPA in Red Bank, New Jersey. "On March 15, the accountant's mind is tired and drifting."

7 *I'm not the one doing your work.*

While going to a big, well-known accounting firm with a solid reputation may give you peace of mind, it rarely makes sense for individual taxpayers. Even though big firms may have more wide-ranging expertise within their ranks, the most experienced people on the staff spend little time doing personal tax work. Rather, they focus on the more profitable clients with more complicated problems—businesses and high-net-worth individuals—and leave the preparing of individual returns to their subordinates.

8 *You don't need me.*

If your tax is reasonably simple—your income is from wages, interest, and dividends, and you have basic itemized deductions—you probably don't need an accountant. Why? Because for around $50 you can get a computer program such as TaxCut or TurboTax, which will do all the necessary work and calculations for you. In fact, even if you do use an accountant, he or she may well be relying on the same type of software to prepare your return.

If you're convinced that your situation requires the added expertise of a professional, you can still save money by using a computer program to get your records in order before your trip to the accountant, so the session is more efficient and focused.

9 *I'm not saving you money.*

Some tax preparers will talk a lot about refunds because it is a quick and tangible way to prove their worth to a client. But when it comes to your overall tax liability, adjustments made at filing time generally have a limited impact. The best way to keep your tax tab to a minimum is to think ahead when you make financial moves during other parts of the year.

Unfortunately, though, attention to year-round tax planning by accountants is often woefully inadequate. "Many accountants say, 'Here's your return, I'll see you next year,' " says Gary Schatsky, a New York financial planner. "But if you don't get planning, you are just paying for someone with secretarial and bookkeeping skills and perhaps a little additional expertise."

10 *Don't buy anything from me—other than advice.*

You may be lucky enough to find an accountant whose financial advice you trust, but that doesn't mean you should listen. If your accountant is recommending that you put your money into vehicles that pay him a commission, you may be better off looking elsewhere for suggestions.

One-stop shopping for tax advice, investment vehicles, and insurance products has a host of pitfalls—so much so that some in the accounting business consider it an unethical way to practice.

The first part of the problem is potential bias. Say, for example, your accountant tells you that the remedy for your tax problems can be found in a certain municipal bond fund. How much can you trust that advice knowing he stands to profit from the sale? The other part of the problem is expertise. Keeping up with our complicated tax system is a full-time job. So is understanding how to invest in mutual funds, insurance, and real estate. You should be skeptical of anyone who claims to be able to handle all of these things at once.

Part 9

ESTATE PLANNING BASICS

It's the night before your first vacation away from that precious little bundle of joy. You're tossing your bathing suits and tennis rackets into a suitcase like a couple of spring-break-crazed college sophomores when suddenly you stop and stare at each other: What if the plane goes down? Who will take care of the baby? Where will he live? How will he afford to attend college?

Take comfort: You're not alone in your negligence. Some 70 percent of American adults don't have wills. Why not? Blame inertia. People know they're going to die eventually, but nobody plans to die next week. So they put off thinking about it.

Which means they also fail to confront an essential reality of child-rearing: Your responsibilities as a parent never end. Not even when you're gone.

The decisions you make today can have unimagined repercussions down the road. Will your heirs get everything they deserve? Or will Uncle Sam? Will you unwittingly unleash a bitter family feud—with your kids stuck in the middle?

This chapter will walk you through the basics of getting your affairs in order. As a parent, there's no excuse for procrastinating—it's time to bite the bullet. Because if you don't, somebody else will make these critical decisions for you. And you won't be around to make sure they're the right ones.

16

Where There's a Will

Right now, the term "estate planning" may sound almost comical, better suited to elderly dowagers than to the parents of toddlers. Scrambling to make ends meet, struggling to pay off bills, you've got more pressing concerns.

Or do you?

Think about it this way: If you insist on putting off estate planning, you're jeopardizing your family's future.

No, we're not talking about the *tax* aspects of estate planning, though they're important, too, particularly as you get older and start to accumulate more assets. We mean the more basic side of estate planning: What happens to your family if you die unexpectedly?

You simply can't overestimate the importance of this process, says Nancy Z. Niedt, a New York City attorney specializing in estate planning. "It's total panic" when a spouse dies without having done the proper planning. In one case, it took Niedt a whole year to unravel a client's finances after his wife died unexpectedly. "The husband was totally devastated," she says. "The delays [in resolving her estate] were very hard for him." By contrast, when someone leaves clear instructions, "It's like clockwork," she says. "There's not a lot of stress involved."

So we've assembled this simple, 5-step program to get you on the road to a well-planned estate. You probably won't be able to manage every step solo; most people will want to hire a lawyer for parts of it. But you will realize how important it is to get started.

Step 1: Organize your assets and calculate your estate's value.

Back in chapter 1, we asked you to tally up all your assets and subtract your liabilities to arrive at a net worth. This, however large or humble it may be, is your estate.

The real world: Who will take care of the kids?

For Denise Phillips-Winter of Plano, Texas, choosing a guardian for her young son Jay was easy. The hard part was telling her mother—who'd volunteered to do the job herself—that it wouldn't be her.

Indeed, Denise couldn't bring herself to break the news to her mom for weeks after the decision had been made. Every now and then she'd get up the nerve and be ready to blurt it out, but then at the last second she'd back away.

Finally, though, Denise couldn't hold it in any longer.

"Mom, we need to talk," she began, explaining that she and her husband, Dave, had settled on his parents—Gene and Elaine—as guardians. Denise could see the hurt in her mother's eyes.

"Why did you choose Gene and Elaine?" asked her mother, Janet.

Though Janet began trying to make a case for herself, Denise remained firm. She felt strongly that her father, in particular, was not up to raising any more children. "We made this decision and I'm sticking with it," she said.

"I feel like you're punishing me," Janet said, near tears.

The conversation was quickly dropped, but Denise felt bad about it for days afterward. Even now, she concedes, the subject is "touchy" between Denise and her mother.

Truth be told, Denise and Dave scarcely gave a thought to naming *anyone* but Dave's parents as guardians. "All of our brothers and sisters were out," Denise recalls. "Some were struggling to get their feet on the ground financially, and others didn't even have families yet." Dave's parents had financial security (Gene was the president of three banks at the time), and more importantly, they were strong, healthy, moral parents with religious values that matched Dave's and Denise's, she says. "I just looked at Dave and saw how prepared for the world he was, and that was a direct comment on how together his family was," Denise recalls. "I was the opposite, and I wanted Jay raised the way Dave and I would have raised him."

That decision took on a whole new resonance just weeks after their will was finally drawn up, when Dave was struck and killed by a drunken driver. Suddenly, Denise's will wasn't just some abstract idea that existed only in her lawyer's office. It was real life. "People underestimate what happens if you don't have a will," Denise says. "They think that everything will somehow get taken care of. It won't."

Denise shudders to think what would have happened had she been in the car with Dave. "I was supposed to be with him, but at the last minute, our baby-sitter got sick, so I stayed home," she says. "I'm one of the lucky ones."

Denise's experience has made others realize the importance of a will. She asks everyone she knows to write one, and says that her family all drafted wills after Dave was killed. "I've become a will advocate," she laughs. "I tell everyone I can to get one—now." Denise's sister-in-law and her husband, both lawyers, didn't have wills until they talked with Denise. "I just can't believe the people who don't have anything to protect them. You never think anything will happen to you, but it can and it does."

Denise and her current husband Mike didn't waste any time drawing up their will.

"Mike knew what I had gone through. Everything is wonderful in my life now, but you never know when something else will happen. Waiting wasn't an option this time."

Even after Dave's death, Denise remains close to his parents, Gene and Elaine. They talk on the phone four or more times a week; and, although Denise is remarried and has two stepchildren, the families vacation together. "It's a tribute to why Dave and I chose them as guardians and not anyone else," says Denise, 36. "I want my children to be around them because they're good, kind people."

And what does Denise's mother think of her now? If she felt bitter about not being chosen guardian at first, it has vanished with time. "Denise is the woman I most admire in the world," says her mother. "I have to respect any decision she makes."

To avoid any surprises once you're gone, take a few minutes now and type up a list of everything in that estate—along with where it's located. Leave copies of this list in your file cabinet, with your lawyer, and in your safe-deposit box.

While you're typing, this is a good time to start thinking about who would get which of your possessions if you died (if there could ever be a "good" time for that kind of contemplation). Though most young parents elect to distribute their assets as a lump sum, letting the heirs sort out who gets what, some parents feel strongly about leaving specific pieces of jewelry or antiques to certain children.

Why is it important to know your estate's *value?* This is where the tax part of estate planning comes in. When you die, your heirs will not owe a penny of tax on the first $650,000 you leave behind. This includes the value of all your possessions as well as investments and equity in real estate. (This figure will begin rising in 2000 and will cap at $1 million in 2006.) But anything beyond that number gets nailed: For every dollar above $650,000 the IRS will take at least 37 cents. At $2 million, this "marginal tax rate" hits 49 percent. And everything over $3 million gets taxed at 55 percent.

Sure, you don't have hundreds of thousands in assets now. But as you'll see in Step 2, it's worth getting a handle on how much you actually own. For even if you don't have more than $650,000 in assets today, there are a few simple maneuvers you can do now that will drastically reduce your heirs' tax bill, should you reach that magical $650,000 figure before you die.

What you need to know about probate

I t's expensive, time-consuming, and universally dreaded. So why does every will have to go through probate?

Simply put, probate exists to make sure your beneficiaries get what they're entitled to, after payment of debts and taxes. It identifies your rightful heirs and gets the legal title of your property out of your name and into theirs.

Probate causes headaches principally because it's an archaic system requiring a lengthy series of formal steps. Lawyers must be consulted, notices must be sent, judges must pass approval.

Here's how probate works: After you die, your executor files papers related to your estate in the local probate court. This proves the validity of your will and provides a list of your assets and your debts, along with who is to inherit what. The next step is for your executor to officially notify relatives and creditors of your death. Then your executor must find, secure, and manage your assets during the probate period, which usually takes from nine months to a year.

Why does it take so long? Probate takes several months just in required notice periods. Depending on your state, your executor may have to file a 20-day notice to begin, a 90-day notice to creditors, and a 20-day notice to finish. If your net worth is over $650,000, probate may easily take a couple of years, including IRS approval and resolution of any disputed claims, such as doctor's bills. If you own property in several states, your estate may be subjected to multiple probate proceedings.

Why is it so costly? The probate court is authorized to pay both the executor and the executor's attorney for their services—in equal amounts. While in many cases the executor is a relative or friend who will refuse payment, compensation must be provided upon request. Fees are determined by each state. In California, for example, maximum executor's commissions and attorney's fees are calculated by a percentage of gross probate estate value. (This excludes assets that avoid probate, such as assets held jointly, assets in a living trust, and life insurance or retirement plan assets payable to a beneficiary other than the estate.) A California lawyer can charge 4 percent of the first $15,000; 3 percent of the next $85,000; 2 percent of the next $900,000; 1 percent of the next $9,000,000; and 0.5 percent of the next $15,000,000. This means that on an estate valued at $500,000, the fees would add up to $22,300—even if the net value of the estate is worth a lot less after reduction for mortgages and other debts (and even if all the lawyer did was process a huge stack of paperwork).

Step 2: Write a will.

Everyone, regardless of his or her assets, needs a will. If you don't bother to create one, your heirs will be handed the universal one written by your state. In most cases, this means your spouse will get one-third, and your children, two-thirds. That's hardly a practical arrangement, since minor children won't have access to your assets until they're grown and your spouse won't be able to use those assets, either, because they'll be in the kids' names.

The most important thing at this point is to get something down on paper. "Many couples come in and start the process and never finish," says Niedt. "They get caught up in some part of it that they can't resolve. I tell them, 'You can change your mind next week, but you have to put something down.' Unless you complete and sign your will it means nothing."

No matter your circumstances, your will must:

- Name an executor (this person has to figure out where all your personal property is and then deal with it appropriately—paying bills and taxes, selling assets, settling debts, managing investments).

What's covered by your will—and what's not

You've done a will, so everything you own is accounted for. Right?

Wrong. Certain assets aren't covered by a will. These include things you own that are governed by contracts (like the proceeds of your life insurance policy or your retirement account) and things you own jointly (like a summer house you bought with another couple).

The moral is, you've got to be sure all your contractual assets name the proper beneficiaries. For example, let's say your will says that your individual retirement account be divided between your two young children. That's fine—unless, when you opened the IRA, you named only your oldest child as the beneficiary. In that case, he'll get the money, and his sibling will be cut out of his share.

In the case of property owned jointly by a married couple, assets pass automatically to the survivor, despite any claims made by a will. Half of the property's value is subject to estate taxes. If property is owned jointly by an unmarried couple—or by, say, friends—it receives slightly different treatment. While the survivor gets the assets, no matter what the will says, the full value is taxed unless the financial contribution of the survivor can be proven.

Is a living trust for you?

Living trusts—legal documents that purportedly take the place of a will—are hot. Or as hot as estate planning devices can get. "I strongly recommend them to people who have any particular means and wherewithal," says Stuart E. Bloch of the Florida firm Bloch & Minerley. "I just signed up a couple last week, both under the age of 30, with one child, who are trying to have another."

Here's the deal: When you establish a living trust, you put all your personal property into the trust. After you die, everything in it is distributed to the trust's beneficiaries—such as your spouse or your kids. One of the advantages of doing it that way is that your assets move to your heirs without having to go through probate—the process by which the state examines your will and declares it valid. That's a big plus for people in states like California and Florida, where probate can drag on for months, or for people with homes in more than one state, which would require ancillary probate. Also, unlike probate, a living trust is private—a plus if you don't want outsiders to know who got what.

So should you get one? Probably not. At $1,500 to $4,000, they're much more expensive to set up than wills. And to make them effective, all your assets—your house, your brokerage accounts, everything—must be transferred into the trust. As a new parent, you're likely to do a great deal of acquiring over the next few years. To put all of your assets in a trust, you'll be swimming in paperwork. Besides, since you have young children, you'll need to execute a will to spell out your wishes for their care, anyway: You can't use a living trust to name a personal guardian for your kids.

- Name a guardian, and a back-up guardian, for your minor children (this is the person who'll be in charge of raising your kids in your absence).

In addition, your will should:

- Establish at least two trusts, and name trustees. (This sounds more daunting than it really is. More on the subject in a moment.)
- Spell out—in absolutely clear terms—how you want your property distributed. (This will help prevent your estate from being drained by legal bills.)

You can draw up a simple will in a single afternoon using a software package such as Nolo Press's *Willmaker*, which retails for around $45. You can also buy legal forms, such as *How to Prepare Your Own Last Will & Testament*, for less than $30 at your local office supply store. Most people feel more comfortable hiring a lawyer, which should cost between $500 and $1,500, depending on where you live.

Now, about those trusts. When you set up a trust, you are creating a legal entity—much like a corporation—that you can transfer property to. This can have tax advantages, and, as you'll see, it will help make sure your kid's inheritance doesn't get squandered.

A basic will for young parents should establish both a **minor's testamentary trust,** which is sometimes called a trust for the benefit of the children, and a **bypass,** or unified credit trust.

The first one puts someone responsible, a trustee chosen by you, in charge of your child's finances until he reaches an age you deem fit, such as 22 or 25 or whenever you think he'll be ready. (Otherwise he'll get access to it all when he reaches the so-called age of majority, which is 18 in most states.)

The second trust is basically a tax dodge, and here is how it works. Let's say your spouse dies before you do. If your family's will includes a bypass trust, your spouse's assets will flow into the trust on his death. In other words, your spouse's assets "bypass" you and go directly to your kids (though held in trust until you die). Why would you want to do that? Because of that $650,000 estate tax threshold. Remember? That's the deal where your kids can inherit $650,000 from a parent before owing any tax on the money. Without the bypass trust, *you* would inherit all your spouse's assets—not your kids. But you would only be able to pass on a maximum of $650,000 tax free when you die. Now, with the trust, the kids get your spouse's assets tax free, up to $650,000, plus up to *another* $650,000 tax free when you die.

Where to put your will?

Don't count on your safe-deposit box. In many states, a safe-deposit box is sealed upon the death of the renter—delaying the probate process and incurring additional costs. Leave the original copy of your will with your lawyer. Keep one copy in your home files and another, just in case, in your safe-deposit box.

The beauty of a bypass trust is that while the money in it is earmarked for your kids, the surviving spouse can collect the income off the money. As for the principal, the trust can be about as flexible as you want. Worried that your spouse might need to tap into the principal to pay for a medical emergency? You can set it up so money can be taken out for that.

Whenever Niedt drafts a will, she writes in the bypass trust as an option. "I set it up so the surviving spouse has nine months after the death to decide whether to pass a certain amount into the by-

---

Should my kids have a trust fund?

We'll venture that giving your money away might not be a top priority right now. But there can be real advantages to giving your kids some of your spare cash, and they're worth knowing about.

What kind of advantages? Tax savings, mainly. Every year, the law permits you to give an unlimited number of people up to $10,000 each (beginning in 1999, this figure will be indexed for inflation). If your spouse joins in making the gift you can double that to $20,000—without any tax liability. Many parents (and grandparents) use these $10,000 gifts to reduce their taxable estates and to shift the income to their kids (or grandkids), who are likely to be taxed at a lower rate.

The downside to giving your children money, as we discussed in chapter 13, is that it may hinder their chances of getting financial aid for college (see "Whose name should you save the money in?" on page 230). But if you're not likely to qualify for financial aid—if you have $200,000 or more in assets, say, and you earn $100,000 or more a year—then go right ahead. You certainly won't get any complaints from your kids.

But where to put it? Most parents simply open custodial accounts for their kids. Under the Uniform Gifts to Minors Act (UGMA) or the Uniform Transfers to Minors Act (UTMA)—only one applies in your state—you can set up custodial accounts for your children and make the maximum $10,000 contribution each year. It's easy: Just about any financial institution or mutual fund company will be happy to set one up free of charge, and there's a minimum of paperwork to be filled out. The custodian (you or your spouse, usually) makes all decisions on how the money is spent and invested until the minor child reaches maturity (either 18 or 21, depending on your state).

Worried that your kid will then splurge it all on something other than college? You might decide to open a more formal trust fund. The simplest type of trust fund is the 2503(c) Minors Trust. The difference between it and a custodial account: You can select the age at which your child gets the money, whether it's 21 or 61. If you want, you can even set it up so he or she gets the money in increments—25 percent at 21 years old, say, the rest at 30 years old. A lawyer will charge you around $1,500 to set one up.

pass trust," she says. "If the spouse feels like she can't afford to give up that money, she can always elect not to."

One other reasonably common trust for young parents: The so-called QTIP (qualified terminable interest property). Here, the surviving spouse gets income from the money but has no choice in who gets the principal when he or she dies (normally it goes to their kids). Thus, a QTIP prevents your spouse from remarrying and letting his or her new spouse spend the money. "I do these for people in second marriages all the time," says Niedt.

Who Will Take Care of Your Children—and Their Money—When You're Gone?

For most parents of young children, the hardest part of estate planning is naming guardians. Small wonder. Basically, you're asking somebody else to take your place as parents. Who could possibly love your child as much as you do? Who could possibly take such good care?

"This becomes the No. 1 stumbling block to completing the [estate] plan," says Niedt. "One spouse says, 'I want my sister,' and the husband says, 'You've got to be kidding.' They're sitting there in my office, fighting. I have to send them home!"

Part of the problem, says New York attorney Anne Farber, is that parents often get hung up on finding "the perfect solution." The fact is, that's probably not possible. The best you can hope for is a situation in which your children get a reasonable facsimile of your home environment. Expecting a carbon copy is simply unrealistic.

Got a couple of potential guardian candidates? Tell them you're doing some estate planning and were wondering whether they might be willing to be guardians. Then check their reaction to this news. The way they respond—"We'd be honored!" or "Um, can we get back to you on that?"—may speak volumes about whether they'd be right for the job.

Choosing a trustee, the person who's responsible for your children's assets until they reach an age you decide it's appropriate to distribute them, is another potentially sticky point. You can have the child's guardian be the trustee, or if you're uncomfortable with

how the guardian handles his own finances, it's perfectly reasonable to select another friend or relative. A lot of people do it this
way, both to spread the responsibility around and to have a system
of checks and balances in place for their child's future. "We picked
my wife's cousin and her husband to be guardians for our son—
and got my parents to be trustees," says one Virginia-based writer.
"The point is that neither couple would handle the boy *and* his
money, so he would have both sides of the family watching over
him."

Doing it this way also helps ensure that neither side of the family feels "left out." But in many families, that's simply not possible.
"My husband and I both come from large families, and there was
no way there wouldn't be hurt feelings if we chose one family member over another," says Peggy McGuiness, the mother of two
young sons in Darien, Connecticut. "We finally ended up choosing
one of my friends as guardian and one of his friends as trustee."

One other option: You can hire a professional trustee from a
bank or brokerage firm. That will run you around $2,500 a year
on a $500,000 estate, though. Niedt, for one, advises against it.
"Outsiders tend to be very conservative and very reluctant to give
distributions" when kids need the money, she says.

Finally, you need to choose an executor—the person who sorts
out your estate in the weeks and months after you're gone. Your
executor will get help from a lawyer, so he doesn't have to be an
accounting genius. But he has to be smart and dependable, and he
has to be sympathetic to your family's needs and wishes. Most parents ask a relative or family friend to handle the role. Just understand that you're asking a lot of someone. Even with a simple
estate, your executor can plan on dealing with all the paperwork
for 18 to 24 months—though not full-time, of course. It's not unusual to compensate someone for being your executor, even if it's
a friend or relative. The rate is usually based on a percentage of the
assets involved. Ballpark figure: An executor could charge around
$35,000 to handle an estate of $1 million.

Can You Be Sure Your Money Is Spent the Way You Want?

It's your money, so you can leave it to your heirs with all kinds of
strings attached—if you insist. Worried that Junior will decide to

skip college if you're not around to hector him about it? You can set up your will so that all or part of his inheritance will go to his sister if he doesn't use it for tuition. Or, if he doesn't have any siblings, you can have the money flow to the charity of your choice.

What *doesn't* work is when you choose conditions that can be challenged as discriminatory. Specifying that Junior must marry someone of a certain faith, for example, would probably not hold up in court. Likewise a will that set up unreasonable economic limitations—such as one that ties up your money for generations, leaving your kids penniless.

Either way, Farber thinks the whole idea of trying to be so controlling is rotten. If you want your kid's inheritance to be spent on tuition, tell that to the trustee—in a letter that goes along with the will. "I would say, 'I give $200,000 to trustees for the benefit of my child. It is my strong desire that it be used for tuition,' " she says. "This way, it's ultimately up to the trustee to decide if the money will be used for something other than tuition, but you've put in your vote about how you'd like it to be used."

Your money's worth

How safe is your safe? With all those documents inside, you can't afford to get a safe that is anything but.

Worth it: OK, so the Worldwide Safe (#UL1511, Worldwide Safe & Vault Co, 22 × 16.5 × 18.5, $365, 800-932-2278) isn't cheap. But the UL1511 has been approved by the Underwriters Laboratory for two hours of fire resistance, has a handle that is designed to shear off in the event of a forced attack, and a spring-loaded relocking system in case someone chops off the combination lock (only a locksmith can reopen it). A steel plate provides further protection against drilling. Also important: It can be bolted to the floor and weighs 215 pounds, both of which mean that any burglar hoping for a fast exit will end up with your television instead.

Not worth it: With the Sentry 1330 (Sentry Fire Safe, 22 × 17.25 × 18.5, $199.99, 800-828-1438), you'll save money. This is why: This safe only has a UL fireproof rating of one hour as opposed to two. It weighs almost 100 pounds less than the safe above and doesn't come with hardware to bolt the safe down to the floor. Which means that a (strong) thief can simply carry the thing off.

Treating children differently "never works well," Farber adds. "Any bad feelings that may exist among siblings will just be exacerbated. It's very traumatic for people to lose parents, and this is not a time to differentiate. It may damage sibling relationships beyond repair."

Step 3: Sign a durable power of attorney, a health care proxy, and a living will.

Along with a will, you'll need these three short legal documents. First, a durable power of attorney states that if you are disabled, incapacitated, or out of the country, you have granted authority to another person to manage your financial affairs on your behalf. A health care proxy selects someone to make medical decisions for you if you're incapacitated. And a living will is where you lay out what you want to happen if you're severely hurt: Should your family put you on life support or not?

Ordinarily you give this power to your spouse, with a trusted friend or family member as an alternate. You can modify or revoke the power of attorney at any time, but it's called durable because it

---

The going rate: The cost of dying

You think you shell out a lot for groceries and the phone bill each month. Wait till you see what your heirs will fork over when you die. Here's what it costs to be properly laid to rest in four cities around the country.

	Dayton, Ohio	Las Vegas, Nev.	Orlando, Fla.	Portland, Ore.
Cremation	$ 695.00	$ 860.00	$ 910.00	$ 350.00
Marble urn	318.00	295.00	200.00	150.00
Funeral	1,995.00	2,130.00	2,500.00	2,600.00
Steel casket	1,095.00	1,695.00	1,450.00	1,395.00
Guest book	20.00	15.00	25.00	10.00
Grave marker	373.00	1,071.00	500.00	1,320.00
Flower limo	135.00	75.00	100.00	75.00
Death notice	90.00	0.00	105.00	60.00
Hearse	247.00	175.00	195.00	210.00
Cemetery plot	470.00	500.00	850.00	1,295.00
Motorcycle escort	55.00	N/A.00	0.00	260.00
Lone bagpiper	75.00	150.00	100.00	150.00
Total	$5,568.00	$6,966.00	$6,935.00	$7,875.00

remains in force if you become disabled or incapacitated. "I had a guy who had a stroke on the street, and he hadn't given a power of attorney," says Niedt. "The hospital was calling and we couldn't get access to any of his accounts. So we had to call a social worker, have a court appoint a guardian, have the guardian investigated to see whether he was truly competent. . . . It went on for months. If he'd had a power of attorney, we could have taken care of everything that day."

Your lawyer can draft all these items for you when writing up your will, usually for little or no extra charge. Or, if you're a determined do-it-yourselfer, the forms are available at most office supply stores.

Step 4: Establish funeral and burial plans.

Even parents who've done their homework and drafted airtight estate plans often haven't considered the grimmest part of their mortality: funeral and burial plans. If you have specific wishes about how you want your remains handled, don't just leave a letter in a desk and assume your family will find it before it's too late. Leave a copy with your lawyer, to be handed to your executor and/ or your spouse and children, and leave copies with select members of your family.

One glimmer of good news in all of this: Funeral and burial costs, along with expenses of administering an estate, such as appraisal fees, executor's commissions, and attorney's fees, can be deducted from estate taxes.

Step 5: File it—but don't forget it.

Planning your estate isn't a one-time thing. Once your will is complete, you should revisit it every 3 years or so, or on a major life change, such as the birth of another baby, an adoption, a divorce, or an inheritance. "As you grow older, your opinions change about things," notes M. Anne O'Connell, a trust and estate lawyer in New York. People often switch guardians, for example. "You see relationships that your children have developed with family members and feel like your children may be more comfortable with someone who wasn't the original choice," O'Connell says.

The only legal way to make even the smallest change in your will is by executing what's known as a codicil, which is like an amendment. You should never cross out a provision and ink in a new one. All changes must be signed, dated, and witnessed appropriately.

You'll also want to keep on top of your beneficiary choices for assets such as your life insurance policies, retirement plans, and bank and brokerage accounts. If you have another child, say, and want to add her as a beneficiary, call and request the paperwork. It's simple; you shouldn't need a lawyer's help to fill it out.

Ten Things Your Lawyer Won't Tell You

1 *My meter's running even when your case is the last thing on my mind.*

Imagine you had a job where you put in 8 to 10 hours a day, but you got paid for 12 or 16 or even 20 hours.

This is the way it works for a lot of lawyers, thanks to a neat little trick called double-billing. When your attorney is waiting in court for a handful of cases to be called, or when he's traveling for one case but catching up on some reading for another case, he'll often charge both clients for that same time.

How to avoid becoming a pawn in your lawyer's billing shenanigans? Ask about double-billing when you first talk fees. Like most aspects of any legal agreement—including the hourly rate or, if your lawyer is working on contingency, the percentage of your award he receives—this one is often negotiable.

2 *My bills come with more padding than a Posturepedic.*

You think you've gotten a good deal because you negotiated the fee—until you learn your bill has been padded with all kinds of exorbitant costs: $1 per photocopy, $4.25 for the first page of a fax and $1.25 thereafter, hefty tabs for word processing, secretarial time, meals, and cabs. The list goes on and on.

It's called profiting on costs, and lawyers do it in varying degrees. Even though the American Bar Association has issued an opinion that lawyers should charge only "actual costs," there's lots of wiggle room in that phrase. Does the cost of a photocopy include just the paper? Or part of the salary of the machine operator, or maintenance fees for the copier? The ABA doesn't say.

To make sure you're not getting taken, speak up at the outset. Insist upon paying only actual costs and ask exactly what those actual costs are.

3 *I'm on the bar's "most wanted" list.*

Want to know whether your attorney's been the subject of misconduct complaints by other clients? While lawyers may proclaim the virtues of an open legal system, they've managed to keep their own dirty records a secret.

Most states will start publicly disclosing complaints about lawyers at about the time the state's grievance committee decides to issue charges against the attorney. But that can take months, if not years. Sometimes a case never becomes public; rather, it ends with a mere "private reprimand" or "admonition," known only to the lawyer and possibly the complaining client.

So where does this leave you? Ask your state bar's grievance committee for the records it can reveal about your attorney. After that, about all you can do is ask your lawyer himself.

4   *That computer on my desk? I've never turned it on.*

In many legal matters, time is money. So the more technologically efficient your lawyer, the smaller your bill. Lawyers, however, have been slow to join the high-tech revolution. "If you're getting paid by the hour, computers help you make less money," contends Sidney N. Herman, managing partner of Chicago's Bartlit Beck Herman Palenchar & Scott. His firm takes a contrarian approach: flat-fee billing and high-tech offices.

Scan your lawyer's desk. Do you see a laptop, or a manual typewriter? If there's a PC, ask your lawyer what she uses it for. Can she communicate with you via e-mail, for instance, rather than by letters on embossed parchment prepared by a secretary? Says Herman, whose firm uses no printed memoranda internally, only e-mail: "Why should you pay for them to make a letter pretty on nice stationery?"

5   *I'm not bulletproof—though I act that way.*

If your attorney messes up—even by mere carelessness—a legal malpractice suit may be your only chance at recovery. Suing lawyers, in fact, is a tack that more and more disappointed clients are taking these days. "In the old days, as it were, clients were more inclined to just swallow it," says Joe Acton, publisher of the *Lawyers' Liability Review*.

But a malpractice suit could be worthless if your attorney doesn't have malpractice insurance. And many of them do not. To find out if your lawyer is insured, you'd better ask. "Every firm, no matter how good, makes some kind of mistakes," says Kirk Hall, CEO of the Oregon State Bar Professional Liability Fund.

6 *I'm not the legal eagle my ads portray me to be.*

"Admitted to the Texas Supreme Court" brags some Texas lawyers' Yellow Pages ads. Big deal—so is every other lawyer licensed to practice law in Texas. Enticed by those TV ads featuring a gray-haired fellow promoting a firm's services? The real attorney behind the 800 number—not the TV commercial actor—may be an inexperienced youngster fresh out of law school.

With the U.S. Supreme Court having affirmed their rights to advertise, lawyers have taken their case to the airwaves and the phone books. But there's usually no screening process when it comes to advertising.

In the past several years a handful of states, including Florida, Texas, Nevada, and New Mexico, have attempted to assert more control over lawyer advertising, such as imposing extensive disclosure rules or requiring that all ads be submitted to review boards. One brochure that recently didn't make it past the Texas bar came from a lawyer who listed recent jury verdicts in the county. The only problem: They weren't his cases.

7 *Take my referral with a big grain of salt.*

If you're having trouble getting the name of a good lawyer from friends or acquaintances, you might consider one of the many referral services popping up these days. But proceed with caution. Referral services aren't always reliable. Some, in fact, have been revealed as mere money-making schemes for lawyers. Concerned that consumers could be misled about whose interests referral services had in mind, the ABA has passed a set of standards for referral services.

A basic tenet: The attorney must have some experience in the practice area for which he receives referrals. Before relying on a referral service, ask if it has been approved as meeting ABA standards. If the one you're considering is not ABA-approved, ask what criteria the service imposes before putting lawyers on its roster.

Two important ones: that attorneys have basic experience and legal malpractice insurance. Above all, don't ever pay for a service; it's the attorney getting the referral who should pay.

8 *I'm not really a partner . . .*

Your attorney's name is right there on the letterhead in the "partners" column, so he must be a full-fledged partner, right? Wrong. In the past several years, growing law firms have found themselves crushed by the number of associates coming up for partner at the same time as the market for legal work has been tightening. Rather than choose between granting these lawyers full-partner status and kicking them out altogether, the firm keeps them on as "junior" or "nonequity" partners. The outside world knows them only as a "partner," so they seem respectable, but they don't have a full stake in the profits or perhaps even a vote in the governance of the firm.

If the true meaning of the title "partner" matters to you, just ask your lawyer if he's junior or nonequity, and if so, why.

9 *. . . but I'm still overqualified.*

You wouldn't ask Lee Iacocca to repair your transmission. He would charge too much, and besides, he might not be the best person for the job. But if you're used to dealing with big-time lawyers in your workplace, you may be tempted to hire one to handle your will.

Lawyers who charge $300 an hour and up offer some significant comforts, among them impeccable credentials and offices with comfortable chairs and great views. For sophisticated financial deals and high-stakes corporate litigation, such lawyers are usually preferable. But the dirty secret is that most legal work is quite routine once you get the hang of it. It has little to do with legal theory or constitutional analysis, and much to do with knowing which form to fill out and which county clerk will process it more quickly.

Generally, the best test of likely competence is how often a lawyer has completed the particular task and how recently.

10 *In fact, you may not even need me.*

A mountain of resources is making it easier than ever for Americans to tackle the challenge of lawyering on their own. Nolo Press, the leader in self-help law books, has hundreds of titles, ranging from *Patent it Yourself* to *Win Your Personal Injury Claim* to *Plan Your Estate*. There's no shortage of software programs, either. And new online outposts seem to be popping up every day.

What's driving the surge in legal self-help? Money, for one. You can prepare a will yourself for next to nothing, compared with fees of $500 and up to hire a professional. But while we wouldn't recommend doing that, if you're on a tight budget it can make sense to hire a lawyer as a consultant and to do most of the work yourself. In other words, you can draft the document, using a standard form as a guide, and then present it to your lawyer for fine-tuning. The point, suggests Professor Stephen Gillers, who specializes in lawyer-client relations at New York University law school, is that sometimes "you can hire one-tenth of a lawyer instead of ten-tenths."

Part 10

BLENDED FAMILIES

Walk into a bookstore or roam around on the Internet and you will find plenty of information for stepfamilies. How to manage expectations. How to resolve disputes between stepsiblings. Even "how you and your blended family deal with your pet." But you will find almost *nothing* about how stepfamilies should manage their money. And if anything can turn an already complicated arrangement into a tense one, it's money.

Fifty percent of all families are blended, which means that most Americans have finances that spill over into the lives of several people, some of them unrelated. In this chapter, we'll outline what parents should do to make sure that things go as smoothly as possible when it comes to child support, tuition, estate planning, taxes, and more.

Then you can get back to sparring over more important things, like whose couch should go in the living room.

17

Step By Step

"My family is what I like to call 'pureed,'" says Stacey McCarthy of Kansas City, Missouri. "I've been married three times. I have two children from my first marriage, one from the second, and am expecting my second child with my third husband. They all live under our roof."

Sound like an unusual set-up? Well, not really. According to recent figures from the Stepfamily Association of America and the Census Bureau, about 75 percent of people who get divorced eventually remarry. The percentage of these second marriages that fail? An astounding 60 percent.

There are many reasons why second marriages don't work out. It's clear, though, that the financial stresses in a combined family are a big part of it. In a blended family, each parent arrives with an already established financial style, not to mention children from previous marriages and ex-spouses who often need financial support. In fact, money is the second largest cause of blended family break-ups, according to the New York–based Stepfamily Foundation. (No. 1 is relationships with stepchildren.) As one stepmother told us, "It is not an adventure for the faint of heart."

In light of all this, it's critical to plan out a financial strategy ahead of time. True, it may not be all that appealing to sit down and discuss the nuts and bolts of electric bills and college tuition when you'd rather be planning your honeymoon, but it's nothing compared to what will happen later if you don't do it. "I can have the most savvy business people, and they will not want to deal with this one, though they would deal with it in a business," says Jeanette Lofas, founder of the Stepfamily Foundation. Couples who come in for counseling often tell her it's unromantic to reduce a relationship to a financial partnership so early on, even for the sake

The real world: A good relationship turns bad

We've all read those ugly stories about divorced celebrities slugging it out over child support. But surely that would never happen to you, right?

Guess again. Even the friendliest, least-contentious divorces can easily turn sour—especially when a new spouse enters the picture. If you think prenuptial agreements and separate accounts and trusts are just for "other couples," you are seriously mistaken.

Look at what happened to Sean Elder and his first wife, Bonnie.

For the first few years after their 1985 separation, everything seemed like it was going to work out great. They agreed to share custody of their 2-year-old son, Adam, splitting most child-related expenses down the middle. Even when girlfriend Peggy Northrop moved in with Elder in 1987, everyone got along well, and there weren't any real financial issues as far as Adam was concerned. "No one had much money, and it was all very cordial," recalls Northrop, who eventually put Adam on her employer's health plan. "I was the extra parent and when things needed to get paid for, I chipped in. We didn't distinguish between my money and Sean's money. We just did what we needed to do."

Elder and Northrop got married when Adam was 7, and things continued to be amiable. In fact, the three adults were getting along so well that when Northrop and Elder adopted a little girl, Franny, they chose Bonnie as her godmother. Financially, the two children were treated the same, according to Northrop. "I had always kind of accepted that if Sean had a kid, he needed to be taken care of," she says. "It all seemed fair."

But then, in the mid-1990s, everything changed. Elder, a New York magazine editor and writer, had lost his job and started work on a screenplay, and the couple's finances became strained. Relying on the good relationship they'd always had with Bonnie, who lived in California, they asked her to accept less in child-support payments until Sean found work.

Her response wasn't exactly what they expected: Bonnie sued Elder and Northrop for even more child support than she'd originally been getting, under the premise that Northrop, also a magazine editor, was supporting Elder and thus should be supporting Bonnie, too. (Bonnie declined to comment on their dispute.)

Northrop, already under financial duress, had to shell out $6,000 to put a lawyer on retainer, she says. Even worse, however, was the damage done to the couple's relationship with Bonnie. "It was very acrimonious for me," Northrop recalls. "We had always had a good co-parent working relationship. I felt blindsided and betrayed. I haven't spoken to her since."

The lawsuit eventually resulted in a negotiation between Elder and Bonnie, which was just fine with Northrop, who wanted to stay out of the whole thing and didn't want to set a precedent for Bonnie having access to her money. Adam went on Bonnie's health insurance, while Elder found work and started paying his ex-wife $800 a month in child support, plus half of whatever costs the health insurance didn't cover.

About two years ago, in keeping with a long-standing plan, Adam moved to New York to attend middle school. Elder flew out to California to renegotiate the agreement with Bonnie. She agreed to pay $200 a month, plus a portion of the plane tickets, after-school costs, and other general expenses. Northrop and Elder would cover extras like braces, karate lessons, and allowance money. Because Bonnie was heavily in debt at the time of the mediation, Elder and Northrop agreed to let her wait until the new year to start paying child support. That was 2 years ago, and they've seen just one payment, they say. Elder is reluctant to fight back, to put it mildly. "Since she never lived up to the agreement we reached in mediation—a costly and emotionally exhausting process, closer to an autopsy than couples counseling—I thought, 'Why go through that again?'"

Now, the dispute hangs over just about every financial move they make. "What if, worst-case scenario, we have the same kind of problems?" Northrop says. "How do we protect ourselves when we know what she's capable of and what the law is capable of putting us through?"

For instance, Elder's will stipulates that one-third of his assets will go to Adam and two-thirds to Northrop. But if Northrop dies before Elder, all of her possessions will go to Franny. "My fear was that if Sean inherited everything from me and nothing was put in trust for Franny, Bonnie would make a claim against Sean for more child support . . . and that there would be nothing left for Franny."

As for college, Northrop now saves money for Franny in a trustee account. "I don't want [Bonnie] to be able to get ahold of our savings," she says. "I feel like I have to protect Franny against her. Even if she didn't have any grounds to sue, I know how much it would cost to defend it if she did." And Adam? "Sean has a small account for [him]," says Northrop. "I pay no attention to it. I used to, but I don't any more. The situation [with Bonnie] is not working and the idea of me saving money for Adam on top of that just riles me. The horrible thing about this is that I love Adam. I really do feel like he's my kid."

of their future. She has only one answer for these people: "Divorce is even less romantic."

In the following pages, we'll walk you through the major financial decisions your new family will face—and help you to figure out your best plan of action.

First Step: Draft a financial constitution.

Now is the time to lay all your financial cards on the table. What obligations do each of you have coming into the marriage—child support, car payments, credit card debt, college tuition, etc.—and what obligations will the two of you take on together once you've said your vows? The guiding principle: full disclosure. "What you have to look at is the financial needs of each spouse and each child," says Gary Schatsky, a fee-only financial adviser and attorney based in New York. "Then there has to be a very frank discussion." Anything you leave out now increases the potential for a major battle later on.

Some experts on blended families suggest you put these agreements in writing, using a prenuptial agreement. But you probably don't need an "official," lawyer-drafted prenup unless there are a lot of assets involved, or there are enormous financial inequities between you and your spouse-to-be. The fact is, sitting down across a table and writing up your own "fake" prenup will probably serve you just as well, not least because prenuptial agreements don't always hold up in court.

Here are the issues you'll want to cover:

HOUSEHOLD ACCOUNTING 101

The first decision you'll need to make as a couple is how your money will actually be divvied up. Will you pool everything together in joint bank accounts and credit cards, will you keep everything separate, or will you take the middle road and do a little bit of each?

Your money's worth

More may be merrier, but it certainly puts a strain on closet space. What's a blended family to do?

Worth it: Getting two kids' wardrobes to fit into one little closet is easy with Ply*Gem Manufacturing's Versatilities install-it-yourself closet organizers, available at stores such as Hechinger's, Home Quarters, and Builder's Square. You can mix and match shelves, drawers, hanging rods, and so on, to create a system that fits your needs—and easily exchange or add other parts later on. All you need is a screwdriver. What's more, Versatilities organizers can be assembled into a freestanding unit (no damage to the walls), and can be taken apart and made into any number of things, such as a cabinet or a desk. Organizing an 8-by-2 foot closet will run you about $180 in white melamine; in pine, it'll cost more like $250.

Not worth it: Invariably, a closet will go through makeovers as a family's needs change. So whatever you do, don't get a unit that'll be hard to readjust. Steel ventilated wire closet organizers like those from Lee Rowan ($150 for an 8-by-2-foot closet) may be cheaper at first, but it could turn out to be more costly than you think: The wall-mount system requires you to drill holes into your wall, so any change later will require you to patch up the holes, paint, and start all over again.

The route you choose will depend partly on the level of comfort, both financial and emotional, each of you has with the other person's previous debts and obligations. Many people who have had bad experiences pooling their money in a first marriage—and in some cases have even entered their new marriages burdened by credit card or loan debt incurred by a former spouse—choose to keep their money partially or entirely separate the second time around for peace of mind. Others like the fact that by keeping things separate, they aren't unwittingly donating money to their spouse's child support, alimony, or previous debt payments.

That's one of the motivating factors for Kelley and Les Collins of Roy, Utah. Kelley has a daughter from a previous relationship and Les has three kids from an earlier marriage. They've always kept separate accounts, and though they divide up their household bills equally, Les pays the child support out of his account. This way, Kelley doesn't feel like she's directly contributing to Les's child support payments, but she's free to buy gifts or extras for his kids at her own discretion. "It works well," she says. "Money can be such a tense point."

One Denver couple, who asked that we not use their last names, prefers the middle-of-the-road approach, depositing some money into joint accounts and keeping some separate. "We have one joint checking account and one joint credit card," says the wife, whose name is Terry. "We match funds each month to cover household expenses. Mike then has all his child support, alimony, etc., to pay, plus his car, insurances, gas, and so forth out of the remainder of his check. After I match my share of the funds for the month, the remainder of my money is to do with what I please." As with the Collinses, this helps Terry avoid direct involvement with payments to Mike's ex-wife. "I do not provide him with any financial assistance when it comes to his child support or alimony payments," she says. "They are not my responsibility—I didn't have the kids and I didn't marry the woman . . . Money is a touchy subject in our family and very rarely can we discuss it without getting into an argument." They do, however, use funds from their joint account to feed and entertain her four stepkids when they visit.

Stacey McCarthy and her husband prefer the third approach: They lump all their finances together, including the child support payments Stacey receives from each of her two previous husbands.

Although she receives much more support from one of the men than the other, all of the money goes into the family budget, and they dole it out as they see fit. "We just add it to the budget and don't make a big thing of it," she says. "We buy the children the things they need and don't let the money rule who gets the biggest piece of the pie." Be warned, though, that while this method of accounting may work within your blended family, it doesn't always agree with the people paying the child support. If you choose to pool all of your money, you might be asked at any moment to give proof of where child support payments are going, and you'd better have it.

ALIMONY AND CHILD SUPPORT

If you're marrying someone who's been through a divorce, there's a good chance he'll be paying alimony to his ex-wife and child support to his kids. And guess what: It's almost guaranteed that he'll get hit up for more.

The laws governing alimony and child support are different in every state, but you should know that some *do* take the new spouse's income into consideration. Even if your state doesn't expect you to contribute directly to your spouse's alimony or child support (which they rarely do), it may figure your spouse now has extra disposable income because he lives with you and thus benefits from your money. In short, he may have to raise his payments, and there's not much you can do about it, even if you keep your money separate. If this is a concern to you, we suggest you visit *www. divorcenet.com,* a website with helpful listings of where you can go for more information about the laws in each state. Another place generally worth contacting: Your local Child Support Services office, usually reachable through the state Department of Health.

You may take some solace in the fact that you won't be responsible for paying alimony or child support if your spouse defaults on his payments or loses his job suddenly. As the new spouse, you have no financial obligation to a husband's ex-spouse or their kids, even if your funds are co-mingled with your husband's. As long as he can prove that his income has been very low or nonexistent, the court can't touch yours. (Only under extraordinary circumstances, such as your spouse remaining voluntarily under- or unemployed, will you be called upon.) If you and your new spouse find yourselves in this situation, the smartest thing to do is go to court as soon as possible and seek a downward modification or suspension of the payments. If you wait, he'll still be liable for all the payments he missed before the modification.

There are two basic ways that people arrange for child support: Either a lump sum is paid out every month, or the parents agree that each will cover certain specific expenses. Most states require a minimum payment each month, so often the two methods are combined. For instance, Susan Wilkins-Hubley's ex-husband pays (what she considers) a modest sum in child support every month, and then they work out the rest of the expenses. "Considering the low support being paid for my son, his father is happy to buy the big ticket items or go halves," says Wilkins-Hubley, the founder of an online community called the Second Wives Club. "I think this is a much better arrangement than sending gobs of money every month not knowing where it ends up."

Indeed, while handing over one monthly payment may be the easiest way to deal with money after an ugly divorce, you'll have to trust that the money is going where it should, and many times parents end up feeling it's not. In the Collinses's case, for instance, Les pays child support to his ex-wife and yet it still seems to him like he's picking up a lot of the children's other expenses as well. Says Kelley Collins: "I think we really get the shaft when it comes to covering their expenses." Terry and Mike have much the same complaint. Mike's kids "are dressed raggedly and are filthy every time we see them," says Terry. "It is very frustrating to know that [his ex] gets such a huge amount of money each month, but is not actually raising these children properly."

One aspect of alimony and child support you may not be prepared for: the legal bills. Parents of blended families are often handing over vast sums of money to lawyers, either to negotiate with an irate ex-spouse or just to protect themselves from his or her unreasonable demands. Unless you have the ideal relationship with your ex-spouse (and even if you do, there's no way to guarantee it will stay that way), you're bound to run into trouble at some point. Terry and Mike's attorney bills run between $500 and $1,000 a month, "depending on what mood the ex-wife is in," says

Terry. Sadly, the money used to pay lawyers often ends up being more than the sum being requested in the first place. As one New York lawyer wrote in a letter to an angry ex-spouse's lawyer, "It is a shame that funds which might have been used to pay for school will be used for attorney's fees instead."

With all these expenses, there may come a point when you and your new spouse realize you'll never be able to buy that summer house you'd always dreamed of, or send your kids to private school, or even buy extra groceries. This is a situation that almost every blended family has to face. The fact is, the new family or spouse often loses out in favor of the old, and there's no easy way to get around it. Terry's husband Mike is currently paying $2,500 a month in child support and alimony, plus about $50 a month in extra costs for his kids, who live with their mother. In her view, "the second wife does not benefit the way people normally do in a marriage."

Parents who don't have custody of their children often feel guilty about it and thus give in to their ex's financial demands more easily than their new spouses think they should. "We argue about this a lot," says Kelley Collins. "It's difficult for me to understand why Les humors [his ex-wife] so much. But he tells me he'd rather pay extras than chance it in court. We have already agreed to certain limits on clothes and shoes, but all the others get ugly."

How do parents settle this conflict? As one stepmother told us: "Not very well. This is the most troubling aspect of our marriage. My husband often can't say no to the ex's demands to pay for this and that beyond child support. Sometimes he just pays for kids' activities without ever asking for the ex for her share to avoid conflict with her. This creates conflict with me. We try to compromise, and for a while we had a set amount each month designated for his kids only. It worked well until the kids got heavily involved in sports, for which the ex-spouse refuses to pay. This still isn't resolved to my satisfaction."

About all you can do is be willing to compromise, and remember that child support isn't forever. That's what Kelley Collins does: "We live on a restrictive budget, but we are smart . . . and child support will be decreased in 6 years and gone in 8. I am certain that we will be well off some day, and I hope the money will prove to be less important."

HEALTH INSURANCE

This issue is kind of a wild card. While many health insurers don't make a big fuss about covering stepchildren—Les Collins, for example, has his children and Kelley's daughter on his insurance plan, and the couple pays everybody's premiums—but it's not always quite that easy. Some plans insist that the child live with you full-time. With others, the child has to be in your home more than half the year. Still others will cover stepchildren as long as they live in the same *state* as you. Depending on how complicated your blended family is, you might wind up in a handful of plans scattered all over the country. One stepmother gave us this scenario: "I carry and pay for the insurance on my son, while his father picks up copayments and non-covered expenses. I carry insurance for my husband's five-year-old and three-year-old. But my husband has a daughter who lives with his ex-wife. She is remarried, and *her* husband provides the daughter's insurance."

If you have trouble finding an insurer that will cover some or all of your stepkids, there is help. Many states now have programs specifically designed to insure kids who are ineligible for their parents' coverage, or whose parents don't have coverage themselves. In New York, for example, the Child Health Plus program is affiliated with various major insurance carriers, such as HIP and Empire Blue Cross Blue Shield, and offers complete out-patient coverage to children ages 19 and under. The premiums are based on your family size and income, and generally cost less than an individual policy.

HOME EQUITY

Homes are so much more than just four walls and a roof. Apart from all the emotional significance they hold, they're also the biggest investments most of us ever make. So when families merge and one spouse moves into a house that the other spouse has already partially paid for, or owns outright, what happens then?

In many cases, nothing. "His house became my house, and it was never a question," one stepmother reports. "We were very much like a nuclear family in that respect." But you may not feel like being quite that . . . generous. Don't worry: That's not anything to be ashamed of. Terry and Mike, the Colorado couple, live in a townhouse that Terry bought on her own, which has 20 years left on the mortgage. She wasn't prepared to give up all that equity to her new spouse, so they worked out a deal. "My husband makes no extra payments on it, although he does split all household expenses with me 50-50, including the mortgage," she says. "We had a prenuptial put in place which retains my 100 percent ownership of the townhouse."

If you're having problems deciding how to handle the finances in this area, one solution is to wipe the slate clean. "We started over," says one stepmom. "I owned a townhouse and sold it so that we could be a single family."

PAYING FOR COLLEGE

Who's going to foot those big tuition bills is a "major problem" among blended families, says Lofas, of the Stepfamily Foundation. "I have seen long-term marriages start to unravel over it."

No wonder. College tuition, already a massive, once-in-a-lifetime expense, can be doubly hard on stepfamilies. For one, you'll probably have to make do with less financial aid than you're expecting. When deciding how much aid to offer a student, many colleges look at the salaries of both biological parents, even though there may be a snowball's chance in hell of the absent parent actually coughing up any money. That's especially true at private colleges, which are not bound by federal financial aid regulations when awarding their own grants and scholarships. "Colleges forget that divorce means conflict," says Kristine Leander, who put three daughters through college after a divorce. "If this man and I agreed about things like money, we'd still be married."

"We see this kind of thing happening all the time," says Harriet Gershman, an educational consultant in Evanston, Ill. "You see parents who have disappeared, parents who refuse to pay, parents who will only pay the equivalent of state school tuition. Colleges are completely out of step with reality when it comes to handling students from divorced families."

In addition, if one or both parents have remarried, private colleges often take the *stepparents'* finances into account when figuring financial aid, even though they're not legally responsible. "Kids could be in the position where a college is figuring four adults' finances into the equation when only one of those adults is legally responsible for the bills," says Ray Loewe, head of College Money, a New Jersey consulting firm.

What can you do about it? Loewe advises custodial parents (the ones whose home the kid stays in) to keep scrupulous records of the other parent's financial contributions throughout the child's life. A financial aid officer isn't going to take your word for it that your ex-spouse won't pay. But if you can show a history of nonpayment on obligations such as child support, private school tuition, and so on, or if you've had to go back to court to enforce your divorce agreement, a private school will often take these special circumstances into account.

Second Step: Take a Good Look at Your Will

Estate planning for the traditional family can be challenging. For a blended family, it's downright confounding. Some blended families merge well enough to mimic the traditional estate planning framework: When the parents die, their children and stepchildren will share all the assets equally, as biological children do in a non-blended family.

But the fact is, that approach doesn't work for everyone. Maybe you're concerned that your son won't be getting much of an inheritance from his biological dad, so you want to leave him a little something extra in your will. Or maybe your stepdaughter has no other biological siblings, so you know she's getting a bundle when her father dies—and thus doesn't need any of your money. It's perfectly reasonable to write a will that accounts for these types of concerns, observes Schatsky, the fee-only financial planner. "Often you find all the families considered as one, and equally often you find that each spouse will give a large portion of assets to children from a previous marriage and some portion to a communal pot [to be split up equally among all the children]."

Many people, of course, enter marriage with the assumption that their spouse's assets will become theirs upon that spouse's death. But, like in every other instance, "with blended families there are always compromises that have to be made," says Schatsky. "You don't often see people leaving 'all assets to my spouse.'"

The problem with doing it this way is the uncertainty. When your spouse dies, is she going to pass *anything* on to her stepkids, or will your kids be totally shut out? There's no way of knowing for sure. One popular way to get around that problem is to set up a so-called Q-tip trust. Your money goes into the trust on your death. Though your surviving spouse will have unfettered access to any interest the estate spins off, he or she won't be able to touch the principal. Then, after the surviving spouse dies, all the principal goes to your children. "Q-tip trusts often work rather well," Schatsky says. "They can be very effective from a number of different perspectives. It's not a very complicated addition to a will and is one of the simplest ways to leave money to children from a previous marriage." (For more on Q-tips, and other trusts, see Chapter 16.)

As long as you're reshaping your will, why not look at the beneficiaries of all your retirement benefits and savings, brokerage accounts, and insurance policies? Now that more people are involved, you may want to purchase extra life insurance to benefit your children or stepchildren. At the very least, you might want to change the beneficiaries of already-existing policies. Unless you're in an extraordinary situation, you probably don't want that $100,000 life insurance policy going to your ex-husband. Beneficiaries for retirement accounts are up to you, and stepchildren are eligible to receive your Social Security benefits as long as they depend on you for at least half of their financial support. If you divorce the children's biological parent, they're no longer eligible.

Third Step: Make the Most of the IRS's Generosity

WHO GETS TO TAKE THE KIDS AS AN EXEMPTION?

Twenty-seven hundred and fifty dollars. That's how much each dependent child was worth, at tax time, in 1999. And it goes up every year, adjusted for inflation.

The parent who keeps the children for more than half the year—the custodial parent—generally gets the write-off, regardless of how much child support the noncustodial parent may be obligated to pay. However, parents can work around this general rule by agreeing to share the exemptions any way they see fit: The non-custodial parent can take the exemption for one child while the custodial parent claims the other one. The noncustodial parent can take both. Or you can alternate, each taking both exemptions every other year.

If you're a noncustodial parent and want to claim the exemptions, you've got to file Form 8332 (Release of Claim to Exemption for Child of Divorced or Separated Parents) with your tax return. Your ex-spouse has to sign off on the original form, which should then be kept with your permanent tax records. (If you're going through a divorce and will be the noncustodial parent, be sure to get Form 8332 signed by your ex at the final meeting when you both sign all the other divorce-related documents.)

The right to the exemption is crucial if you are claiming the child tax credit, the child care credit, either of the education credits

---

The going rate: The cost of a weekend with the kids for a divorced dad

	Fresno, Calif.	Des Moines, Iowa	Durham, N.C.	Hartford, Conn.
Cleaning service (before)	$ 80.00	$ 55.00	$ 82.00	$ 75.00
Frosted Cheerios (2 boxes)	6.98	4.58	5.98	7.98
Whole milk (1 gallon)	2.89	2.45	2.89	2.69
Apple juice (half gallon)	1.99	1.50	1.79	2.39
28-oz. Skippy peanut butter and 32-oz. Smuckers jelly (1 jar each)	7.88	4.25	4.78	5.88
Wonder bread (family-size loaf)	2.39	1.29	1.15	1.89
Tickets to the nearest pro sports game (3)	42.00	45.00	126.00	135.00
Video rentals (2)	5.98	6.98	7.82	6.50
Orville Redenbacher microwaveable popcorn	2.65	3.99	3.19	3.99
Movie tickets (1 adult, 2 children)	15.75	14.75	15.50	18.25
Bowling (2 games, with 3 shoe rentals)	16.50	22.35	25.50	25.20
Tickets to the nearest amusement park (1 adult, 2 children)	94.00	58.28	65.97	63.97
Chicken McNuggets meal at McDonald's (3)	9.87	10.05	9.51	10.47
Short-stack pancake breakfast at diner (3)	9.87	11.67	9.75	11.97
Large pepperoni pizza (2, delivered)	21.52	24.02	17.00	22.50
Roller-skating (with 2 skate rentals)	21.00	12.00	15.00	16.00
Cleaning service (after)	80.00	55.00	82.00	75.00
Total	$421.27	$359.18	$473.83	$484.98

for your child's college expenses, or the tax-free break for U.S. Savings Bonds redeemed to pay your child's college expenses. Even if you are footing all the bills, these deals are off limits unless you can also claim the exemption for the child.

THE RIGHT WAY TO DEDUCT ALIMONY

If there is one good thing about paying alimony, it's that you can deduct it on your taxes. So it should be no surprise that some people try to turn every dollar they give to their spouse into alimony. The government has fought back by creating a set of tricky tax laws that you must successfully negotiate to get the alimony deduction. Do it wrong and you can unwittingly turn tax-deductible alimony into child support or part of your divorce property settlement, neither of which is deductible.

Probably the most common error is the failure to specify that payments will cease if your ex dies. If you mess that one up, you can't deduct the payments, even if they are described as alimony in your divorce papers. You might get a second chance, though. Some states require that payments end at death, so if yours is one of them, you can still deduct the alimony.

The second big error is setting up alimony payment arrangements that call for reduced payouts when the children reach a certain age, finish school, get married, or the like. Under some very complicated rules, this can result in some or all of your intended alimony being reclassified as nondeductible child support. To avoid this trap, don't overstate your alimony payments to increase your deduction. You could be sorry later.

The third most common problem is when alimony payments drop drastically after the first 2 years. The IRS wants to make sure the money is really alimony and not an attempt to get a deduction for assets you are splitting up as part of your divorce.

Don't expect your divorce attorney to lead you safely through the alimony minefield, unless he or she is also a seasoned tax practitioner—a rare combination. You are well-advised to hire a CPA or other tax pro with substantial experience in divorce cases to deal with this issue and other tricky divorce-related tax matters. (For more on the subject, see Ten Things Your Divorce Lawyer Won't Tell You on page 339.)

THE RIGHT WAY TO FILE YOUR RETURN

The question seems impossibly straightforward: Were you married last year or not? But in the IRS's eyes, nothing is ever that simple. What counts is your marital status at the end of the year. If you were unmarried on Dec. 31, the IRS considers you unmarried for the entire year. That means you have to file as a single person.

Bad news? Not at all. Singles usually have lower tax rates than do couples, a result of the infamous "marriage penalty," which we describe in detail on page 286. If you've got a child, you can get even lower rates by filing as a "head-of-household." Filing as a single taxpayer in the 1999 tax year, for instance, you would hit the 28 percent tax bracket with just $25,750 of income, but as a head-of-household, you wouldn't reach 28 percent until your income hits $34,450. Added bonus: The standard deduction for head-of-household filers is $6,350, versus just $4,300 for single filers.

To get head-of-household status, you need to maintain a home that is the principal residence for more than half the year for both you and a natural child, stepchild, or adopted child. In other words, you must live in the same household as the child for over 6 months. After a divorce, both ex-spouses can file head-of-household returns, but only if each has at least one of the kids.

You can actually file as head-of-household even when you're married. You just have to prove you're an "abandoned spouse."

These conditions have to be met in order for you to be able to make that claim:

- You and your spouse lived apart during the last 6 months of the year.
- Your child lived in your home with you for more than half the year.
- You paid over half the cost of maintaining that home.

A COUPLE OF BREAKS FOR UNWED COUPLES

Unmarried couples have some unique opportunities to shift their tax burdens around. If you own your home jointly, for instance, you can divide up the deductions a different way each year. So if one member of the family earns a lot more than the other, he or she can take the bulk of the deductions. But your mortgage company will use only one person's Social Security number when reporting the mortgage interest you paid. If the other person wants to deduct this interest, he or she must attach a statement to his or her tax return explaining it and naming the other person who's sharing the interest.

You also might want to think about buying a second home. Since you and your partner are not married, technically you could own as many as 4 homes (2 apiece) and still deduct all the mortgage interest and real estate taxes. Don't like the thought of owning all those homes? Well, consider this: The IRS's definition of "home" is something with a bathroom, a kitchen, and sleeping facilities. Thus, boats and motor homes often qualify for the deduction.

ADOPTION CREDITS

If you adopt a child under age 18, you may be able to take as much as $5,000 in tax credits to offset your adoption expenses (the credits are phased out for those in higher income brackets). For a child with special needs, the credit can be up to $6,000. The maximum credit is the same regardless of whether you're married or not, though married people generally have to file jointly to qualify. (After 2001, the credit is available only for adoptions of children with special needs.) If you qualify, claim the credit by filing Form 8839 (Qualified Adoption Expenses) with your 1040.

Some companies offer qualified adoption assistance programs as an employee benefit. Under these plans, you can get tax-free adoption expense reimbursements of up to $5,000, or $6,000 for a special-needs child. Complete Part III of Form 8839 to claim this benefit. The tax-free status of the payments is phased out for people with higher incomes, and again, married people generally have to file jointly to qualify.

Ten Things Your Divorce Lawyer Won't Tell You

1 *You don't need me.*

When you broach the notion of a do-it-yourself divorce to a lawyer, you're likely to get a standard response: They work fine, as long as you've been married less than 3 years and you have no assets, debts, or kids in common. In other words, not on your life.

Don't believe it. While you couldn't pull it off in a contested divorce, friendliness is not a requirement; plenty of people who hate each other successfully file pro se (without lawyers) each year. When the issues are uncomplicated, "there's no reason anyone with a home computer, a copy of the divorce statutes, and child support guidelines and a clear idea of the settlement they want can't successfully do it themselves," says Michael Dittberner, a divorce lawyer in Edina, Minnesota.

2 *You've hired the wrong lawyer.*

When it comes to your divorce, it's tempting to seek out the advice and legal services of a senior partner. But the truth is, most work can easily be done by one of the firm's associates. And the difference can cut your bill in half. Even if you do opt for one of the higher-paid partners, he or she won't be working on the case alone—some of the tasks will be shunted off to junior (and, again, less expensive) staffers.

3 *We call it "discovery." It's legalese for "ripoff."*

Discovery—the legal term for making sure everyone has all the information they need—is a time-consuming and expensive process. While it's true that some people hide assets (particularly in small businesses) that require forensic accountants to detect, discovery usually boils down to exchanging readily available documents: checking account statements, pay stubs, income tax returns, employee manuals. "A few hours of sitting down with your spouse and going over the assets and your debts will save you thousands in legal fees," says Michael Robbins, a divorce lawyer in Birmingham, Michigan. "Lawyers don't usually suggest it because 90 percent of the clients can't do that—it's just too hard to be rational when you're emotional."

4 *A 1040 is a tax form, right?*

Virtually every decision has tax ramifications, whether it's paying deductible alimony or nondeductible child support. But don't count on your lawyer to give you advice. "Before signing any settlement, it's important to sit down with your CPA and talk about all the tax consequences," advises Alicia D. Taylor, a lawyer and mediator in Newport Beach, California. "I don't give advice on tax issues—that's one of the biggest malpractice issues of this industry."

5 *If I mess up your pension, there's no fixing it.*

Pensions have become the most significant asset for many couples, says Marshal Willick, a Las Vegas divorce lawyer. Yet plenty of lawyers still don't fully understand them; complex pension valuations, which require calculating the present value of a future stream of cash, usually require an actuary. And dividing them often calls for what's known as a QDRO, or Qualified Domestic Relations Order, which lawyers say can be fiendishly intricate. What if your lawyer fouls it up? "Tough," says Willick. "You can't unring a bell, and there's no going back and changing that."

6 *I may charge you for "research" I shouldn't need to do.*

Divorce clients, often looking at their first major legal bills, are surprised at being charged for research time—especially when their lawyer is researching a routine issue. An experienced divorce attorney shouldn't need to do much research to value a professional partnership. Of course, if your assets include an exotic-animal petting zoo, research bills make sense. "But if lawyers are holding themselves out as experts in divorce law, they should have a considerable database," says Nancy Simpson, a New York attorney. "The client shouldn't be forced to pick up the charge for their education."

7 *If you don't see a PC on my desk, you'll be paying me more than you should.*

Even the simplest divorce requires a fair amount of paperwork—anywhere from 4 to 15 documents, depending on the state you live in, according to attorney Robin Leonard, editor of several of Nolo Press's divorce books. Often, most documents can easily be customized from legal software programs. Drafting a petition from scratch can take hours, while spitting out a ready-made version can take minutes. Make sure to ask about the firm's software library before forking over $125 an hour in fees.

8 *If I overcharge you, good luck getting your money back.*

Deirdre Foltz learned the hard way that the bill for a divorce can be far more expensive than you expect. In fact, she was so outraged by her lawyer's fees that she fired her and took her to arbitration, trying to shave $2,000 off a $9,000 bill. Foltz lost, and she's not alone: Winning an arbitration against a divorce lawyer is extremely difficult. "Divorce clients are often terribly unhappy with their lawyers because they didn't get the thing they wanted most—retribution," says one lawyer. "So they turn around and complain about fees. Judges know that, and even though they're supposed to be objective, it's only natural that they side with the lawyer." So even if they have been overcharged, "clients have an uphill battle. And they will lose."

9 *If you've got the money, I'd be happy to get us a court date.*

All told, only an estimated 5 percent of all divorces go to trial. Roughly half are custody fights. The other half are disputes over assets, most often related to family-owned businesses, says Gerald Nissenbaum, past president of the American Academy of Matrimonial Lawyers. These cases can be a bonanza for lawyers, generating fees of more than $100,000 from clients with deep pockets. But there's a big risk for lawyers in litigation as well: Once a trial begins, there's no escape—even if the billing time amounts to more than the client could ever afford to pay. That's why lawyers charge much higher retainers for such cases.

10   *The only one who'll win a custody fight is me.*

For most of the century, custody disputes were unofficially governed by what judges called the "tender years" doctrine—the pre-
sumption that children almost always are better off with their
mother. While that's definitely changing, women still win most of
the time. But there's no shortage of lawyers taking in fat retainers
of $5,000 to $10,000 from men who have little chance of winning
a custody battle. "I've won custody for a lot of fathers," says En-
rico J. Mirabelli, a divorce lawyer in Chicago, "but the mothers
were bad, bad people—they were neglectful, or abusive." That's
not to say that men should roll over and play dead: "I insist on
joint custody. I won't see the husband reduced from parent to visi-
tor," Mirabelli says. "I tell them, 'If you really want to fight, fine.
But if not, take that $20,000, put it in a college fund, and let's
make a deal right now.' "

Index